Quotations for All Occasions

Quotations
for All Occasions

compiled by

Tony Castle

Marshall Pickering

Marshall Morgan and Scott
Marshall Pickering
34–42 Cleveland Street, London, W1P 5FB. U.K.

First published in 1989 by Marshall Morgan and Scott Publications Ltd
Part of the Marshall Pickering Holdings Group

British Library CIP Data

Quotations for All Occasions.
  1. Bible – Texts
  I. Castle, Tony, *1938–*
  220.5′2

  ISBN 0–551–01894–1

Text set in Linotype Baskerville by Photoprint, Torquay, Devon.
Printed and bound in Great Britain at
The Camelot Press Ltd, Southampton

Introduction

Storytelling is back in fashion. I have not only heard it said, but have practical evidence in the experience of a recent day course, 'Storytelling in classroom RE'. My teacher colleagues in the English Department have also attended similar courses.

It is not only in educational circles that the value and role of 'story' have been rediscovered; the theologians have been talking more and more about each individual's faith journey or story. Given the perpetual daily interest in the gossip story which enlivens countless conversations and the tabloid pages of our daily newspapers, it is difficult to understand how the value of 'story' was ever lost sight of.

No Christian speaker or preacher, with the powerful example of Jesus of Nazareth, the world's most influential storyteller, can ever have doubted the teaching value of a good story. Every experienced preacher, speaker or (in school) assembly leader knows that you must start where people are before leading them to higher thoughts and deeper considerations; and for this purpose humour must never be neglected.

This book is offered as an aid to those who have the great privilege of proclaiming the Good News. It contains hundreds of stories and a sprinkling of humour. The stories, the humour and the quotations are drawn from many different traditions and times and it is my hope that you, the reader, may find sufficient material that you can use in your own particular circumstances to enliven your work for God.

I am grateful for the help of Jacquie Galley who spent so many hours at the typewriter.

Tony Castle
Christmas 1988

Dedicated

to

Melanie and Vanessa

Acknowledgments

The compiler and publishers would like to thank the following authors, publishers and copyright holders for their permission to reproduce material of which they hold the copyright:

Church Missionary Society for 'An Indian Contribution to the Spiritual Life of the West', a leaflet by Dr P.I. Ittyerah.

Sheed and Ward Ltd for an extract from *A Rocking Horse Catholic* by Caryll Houselander.

The Reverend John Medcalf for an extract from his letters from Nicaragua.

Associated Catholic Publications (The Universe newspaper) for extracts from *52 Talks for Young People* by Maurice Nassan and *Woodruff at Random* compiled and edited by Mary Craig.

A.D. Peters & Co. Ltd for an extract from *An Only Child* by Frank O'Connor.

William Collins, Publishers, for *Autobiography* by Yevtushenko.

The Tablet Publishing Co. Ltd for *Viewpoint* by William Clark.

Dimension Books Inc. of New Jersey, for an extract from *Invaded by God* by George A. Maloney.

Paul Frost for passages from an unpublished manuscript.

Contents

x   Contents

Contents

Adam and Eve

1

Oh, Adam was a gardener and God who made him sees
That half a proper gardener's work is done upon his knees.
So when your work is finished, you can wash your hands
and pray
For the glory of the Garden that it may not pass away!
And the glory of the Garden it shall never pass away!

Rudyard Kipling

2

It is from the Talmud and not from Genesis that we get our
traditional idea of Adam and Eve with a fig leaf apiece, as
though foliage had been rationed from the start: and from
the Talmud, too, comes the story that Eve made all the
animals eat some fruit too, so that they should all be
involved in the same catastrophic consequences, and only
the Phoenix had the sense to refuse and fly . . .

Douglas Woodruff

3

Pointing to an unappetising cigar-butt in an ash-tray, a
painter friend once said to me: 'That has, for me, all the
beauty in the world.' She placated my raised eyebrows by
explaining: 'Look at the subtle way the light plays on that
mottled grey ash, upon the earthiness of the tobacco leaf,
how it runs like spilt milk round the edge of the tray – it's a
visual symphony.' My eyes began to discover nuances of
colour and tone and form to which previously they had
been blind. For a moment, sight regained its primal

innocence, glimpsed a visual Garden of Eden in which everything was redeemed by the grace of light.

John Alexander

4

'Teacher was telling us all about Adam and Eve today,' said a little girl to her mother. 'She said they lived ever so happily in the Garden of Eden till the servant arrived!'

Anon.

5

A teacher asked her class of small children to make a crayon picture of the Old Testament story which they liked best. One small boy depicted a man in a top hat driving an old car. In the back seat were two passengers, both scantily dressed. 'It is a nice picture,' said the teacher, 'but what story does it tell?' The young artist seemed surprised at the question. 'Well,' he exclaimed, 'doesn't it say in the Bible that God drove Adam and Eve out of the Garden of Eden?'

Anon.

Adoration

6

All true prayer is worship – the ascription of worth to the Eternal. Without adoration, thanksgiving may become a miserliness, petition a selfish clamour, intercession a currying of special favours for our friends, and even contemplation may turn into a refined indulgence.

George Arthur Buttrick

7

What I cry out for, like every being, with my whole life and earthly passion, is something very different from an equal to cherish: it is a God to adore. To adore: that means to lose oneself in the unfathomable, to plunge into the inexhaustible, to find peace in the incorruptible, to be absorbed in immensity, to offer oneself to the fire and the transparency.

Teilhard de Chardin

Adversity

8

Three hundred years ago, a man condemned to the Tower of London carved these words on the stone wall of the prison:

It is not adversity that kills,
but the impatience with which we bear adversity.

Anon.

9

It is related of Sebald, who dwelt at Nuremberg, that one day in the dead of winter he came to the hut of a cartwright, where he was wont to stop in going his rounds among the poor, and that he found the man and his family nearly perishing with cold. There was no wood left in the house, and the bitter frost had penetrated the room, so that the icicles hung in long rows from the rafters. Sebald said to the man: 'Take these icicles and put them upon the hearth and use them for fuel.'

The man did so and the fire blazed up, and he and his family were saved. What a childlike, transparent legend is this, expression of the truth that the very ills which seem calculated to destroy us, the miseries and heartaches and pains, may, if we use them rightly, become the means of filling us with a new warmth.

Felix Adler

Advice

10
No gift is more precious than good advice.

Desiderius Erasmus

11
To profit from good advice requires more wisdom than to give it.

Churton Collins

12
Advice is seldom welcome; and those who want it the most always like it the least.

Lord Chesterfield

Ambition

13
All the wants which disturb human life, which make us uneasy to ourselves, quarrelsome with others, and unthankful to God, which weary us in vain labours and foolish anxieties, which carry us from project to project, from place to place in a poor pursuit of we don't know what, are the wants which neither God, nor nature, nor reason hath subjected us to, but are solely infused into us by pride, envy, ambition and covetousness.

William Law

14
Cardinal Wolsey, dying, charged Cromwell:
'I charge thee, Cromwell, fling away ambition. By that sin

fell the angels: how can man, then, the image of his Maker,
hope to gain by't?'

Shakespeare

15

The original Jack Horner, the story goes, was steward to
Richard Whiting, the last of the abbots of Glastonbury. In
the 1530s, the time of the Dissolution of the Monasteries, it
is said that the abbot, hoping to placate Henry VIII, sent
His Majesty an enormous Christmas pie containing the
deeds of twelve manors. Horner was entrusted to take the
pie to the King. On the way he managed to open the pie
and extract the deeds of the Manor of Mells in Somerset –
presumably the 'plum' referred to in the rhyme.

Anon.

Angels

16

The difference from a person and an angel is easy. Most of
an angel is in the inside and most of a person is on the
outside.

Fynn, 'Mr God this is Anna'

17

The devil often transforms himself into an angel to tempt
men, some for their instruction and some for their ruin.

Augustine of Hippo

18

A sick woman longed to go to church, but could not.
Listening to the bells she fell asleep. An angel spoke to her,

saying, 'Come with me, I will show you what the angels hear.'

Arrived at the church, which was full of people, they heard a babel of noise: business, pleasure, frocks, money, plans were all being discussed.

'The angels hear the thoughts, not the words,' said the Guide; 'now I will show you what God hears.'

Silence then reigned, which was broken only a few times. First there was an angel bringing a little child's simple prayer for pardon – she had been naughty, and was really sorry. Then another brought a hearty 'thank-you' from a mother whose son had just returned from France. A third brought words of adoration from the priest at the altar, and that was all – yet the whole congregation were saying words of worship.

Then the woman awoke. When, soon after, she was well again, and able to take her place in the congregation, the words of the first collect in the Holy Communion service had, in her ears, a new and deep meaning.

Maud Higham

19

The qualities of the devil and all fallen angels are good qualities; they are the very same which they received from their infinitely perfect Creator, the very same which are and must be in all heavenly angels; but they are a hellish, abominable malignity in them now, because they have, by their own self-motion, separated them from the light and love which should have kept them glorious angels.

William Law

Apostles

20

When Christ had finished his work on earth, it is said, and had returned to heaven, the angel Gabriel met him.

'Lord,' said Gabriel, 'is it permitted to ask what plans you have made for carrying on your work on earth?'

'I have chosen twelve men, and some women,' said Christ. 'They will pass my message on till it reaches the whole world.'

'But,' said the angel, 'supposing these few people fail you – what other plans have you made?'

Christ smiled, 'I have no other plan,' he said. 'I am counting on them.'

Anon.

21

Apostle Spoons

These were originally made in sets of thirteen, each handle bearing the figure of an apostle except the thirteenth, which held the figure of Christ. At one time it was customary to give a newly-baptised child one of the spoons bearing the figure of his patron saint.

Anon.

22

The Apostles' Symbol

The badges or symbols of the fourteen Apostles (i.e. the original twelve with Matthias and Paul) developed and shown in Christian art from the early Middle Ages, are as follows:

Andrew, an X-shaped cross because he was crucified on one.

Bartholomew, a knife, because he was flayed with a knife.

James the Great, a scallop shell, a pilgrim's staff or a gourd bottle, because he is the patron saint of pilgrims.

James the Less, a fuller's pole, because he is said to have been killed by a blow on the head with a pole, dealt him by Simeon the Fuller.

John, a cup with a winged serpent flying out of it, in allusion to the tradition about Aristodemos, priest of Diana, who challenged John to drink a cup of poison. John made the sign of a cross on the cup, Satan like a dragon flew from it, and John then drank the cup which was quite innocuous.
Judas Iscariot, a bag, because he acted as a treasurer for Jesus and the Apostles.
Jude, a club, because he was martyred with a club.
Matthew, a hatchet or halberd, because he was slain at Nadabar with a halberd.
Matthias, a battleaxe, because it is believed he was first stoned and then beheaded with a battleaxe.
Paul, a sword, because his head was cut off with a sword.
Peter, a bunch of keys, because Christ gave him 'the keys of the kingdom of heaven'.
Philip, a long staff surmounted with a cross, because he suffered death by being suspended by the neck from a tall pillar.
Simon, a saw, because according to tradition, he was sawn to death.
Thomas, a lance, because he was pierced to death through the body, at Meliapore.

Anon.

Arms

23

The money required to provide adequate food, water, education, health and housing for everyone in the world has been estimated as £17 billion a year. It is a huge sum of money – about as much as the world spends on arms every two weeks.

Anon.

24

A parable
Two families lived next door to one another, with a thin
dividing wall through which they could plainly hear the
family next door, without quite understanding the words.
Each family became convinced that the other was planning
to break through the wall, murder them all, and occupy
their house. So each built a battery of burglar alarms, and
more and more sophisticated booby-traps, that would
immediately enable them to kill their neighbours should
they ever attempt to break through. But so burdensome
was the cost of all this burglar-proofing that neither family
could any longer afford many of the things they needed,
and ruled out any help for their more distant relatives who
lived further south, who were dying of hunger, thirst and
disease in great numbers.

The Tablet

Atonement

25

Eternity is the great atonement of finitude. The earthly is
reconciled with the endless. All atonement is fundamentally
this; reconciliation of the finite and the infinite.

Leo Baeck

26

The word 'atonement' which occurs in the Bible again and
again, means literally at-one-ment. To be at one with God
is to be like God. Our real religious striving, then, should be
to become one with God, sharing with Him in our poor
human way, His qualities and His attributes. To do this we
must get the inner life, the heart right, and we shall then

become strong where we have been weak, wise where we have been foolish.

Booker T. Washington

Authority

27

One of the most solemn facts in all history – one of the most significant for anybody who cares to ponder over it – is the fact that Jesus Christ was not merely murdered by hooligans in a country road; He was condemned by everything that was most respectable in that day, everything that pretended to be most righteous – the religious leaders of the time, the authority of the Roman Government, and even the democracy itself which shouted to save Barabbas rather than Christ.

Herbert Butterfield

28

He who is firmly seated in authority soon learns to think security and not progress.

J.R. Lowell

29

If you accept the authority of Jesus in your life, then you accept the authority of his words.

Colin Urquhart

30

A Government surveyor one day brought his theodolite alone to a farm, called on the farmer and asked permission to set it up in a field nearby to take readings. Seeing the farmer's unwillingness to let him enter the field, he produced his papers and explained that he had Government authority for entering the field and could, on the same authority, go anywhere in the country to take necessary readings. Reluctantly the farmer opened the barred gate and allowed him to enter and set up his survey table, but went to the other end of the field and let in the fiercest of his bulls. The surveyor was greatly alarmed at seeing the bull approach, and the farmer from the other side of the gate shouted to him, 'Show him your credentials: show him your authority.' The surveyor had the authority to enter but had not the power to resist the bull.

Anon.

Baptism

31

About 1877 a class of Zulu boys were being prepared for baptism.

Among those who dropped in casually was a middle-aged man, Maqumusela, one of the King's soldiers, who, coming regularly, and staying long, at last asked for baptism with the rest.

But the King's word was that if any of his soldiers became Christians he would have him killed. This was put before Maqumusela, who, having gone away and thought and prayed, returned, and asked still to be baptised by the missionaries.

The King came to hear about it, and just before the baptism sent soldiers to put Maqumusela to death. He asked first for time to pray, and after prayers for himself, the missionaries, the King, the soldiers and Zululand, said to the soldiers who were sitting around, waiting, that he was ready. They were, however, so impressed that they could not perform their duty, but beckoned to another man near, who dispatched the first Zulu martyr.

Anon.

32

Louis IX of France used to sign his documents not, 'Louis IX, King' but 'Louis of Poissy'. Someone asked him why, and he answered: 'Poissy is the place where I was baptised. I think more of the place where I was baptised than of Rheims Cathedral where I was crowned. It is a greater thing to be a child of God than to be the ruler of a kingdom: this last I shall lose at death, but the other will be my passport to an everlasting glory.'

F.H. Drinkwater

33

Baptise as follows: After first explaining all these points, baptise in the name of the Father and of the Son and of the Holy Spirit, in running water. But if you have no running water, baptise in other water; and if you cannot in cold, then in warm. But if you have neither, pour water on the head three times in the name of the Father and of the Son and of the Holy Spirit.

Didache (2nd century document)

34

In the world-famous Roman armies, the decisive act of becoming a soldier was called the *sacramentum*, that is, the military oath. The Christian Church adopted this word for the decisive act of becoming a soldier of Christ; Baptism, and especially the vows taken at Baptism, were called the *sacramentum*. By becoming a Christian through the *sacramentum*, we cease to be civilians, and we become soldiers actively engaged in Christ's battle for the world.

Anon.

35

A holy man returned to his native village after making the long and arduous pilgrimage to the Ganges. He walked bearing aloft the brass bowl in which he had brought home some of the sacred water. A poor beggar man watching him, knelt and begged a drop of the water that all Hindus consider washes away sins. At first the holy man ignored him, but when he persisted, turned and cursed him. Then said the beggar, 'He has washed his body in the Ganges but his heart is not washed' – and his faith in his ancient religion was broken.

Anon.

Bereavement

36

It was the second anniversary of her husband's death. 'It is sad to think', said I to the old lady, 'that in all the fairy stories, the couples finish up by living happily ever after; but in real life they never do. In fact not only have they got to die, but the one of them who is left behind is usually left with a broken heart.'

'It's not like that,' said the old lady. So I had to ask her to explain.

'Well,' she said, 'when Harvey died it was terrible at first, and today I still miss him. But it wasn't the end of our story, or of our love. I love him now more than I ever did. I'm learning now to love him enough to let him go.'

Brian Green

Beatitudes

37

If the Sermon on the Mount is the précis of all Christian

doctrine, the eight beatitudes are the précis of the whole of
the Sermon on the Mount.

Jacques B. Bossuet

38

The more we live and try to practise the Sermon on the
Mount, the more shall we experience blessing.

Martin Lloyd-Jones

39

Our Lord tells us that the poor in spirit are the lucky ones.
To be so, we have to stop thinking simply in terms of money
and begin to look at the world through the eyes of the poor,
and to feel as they feel. It is not just occasionally missing a
meal or not being able to afford a packet of cigarettes which
will help us to do so, but every snub, every deprivation,
every time we suffer rejection, every occasion on which we
are ignored or contradicted. It is that experience of poverty
which will give us some share in the condition of the poor,
and spark the emotion which is needed for their defence.
And it is through that experience that we slowly come to
learn what is truly precious in ourselves and in the world
that lies about us.

John Harriott

40

Blessed are the simple, for they shall have much peace.

Thomas à Kempis

41

Poverty is not a question of having or not having money.
Poverty is not material. It is a beatitude. 'Blessed are the
poor in spirit.' It is a way of being, thinking and loving. It is

a gift of the Spirit. Poverty is detachment and freedom and, above all, truth. Go into almost any middle-class home, even a Christian one, and you will see the lack of this beatitude of poverty. The furniture, the drapes, the whole atmosphere are stereotyped, determined by fashion and luxury, not by necessity and truth.

This lack of liberty, or rather this slavery to fashion, is one of the idols which attracts a great number of Christians. How much money is sacrificed upon its altar! – without taking into account that so much good could otherwise be done with it. Being poor in spirit means, above all, being unrestrained by what is called fashion; it means freedom.

Carlo Carretto

Beauty

42

When we ask poets and artists to tell us what they have found in God, they answer with one voice, 'We have found him in beauty. Only it is a beauty that never was on land or sea, a beauty that in its transcendent excellence makes our best handiwork seem tawdry.'

William Adams Brown

43

If you get simple beauty and nought else, you get about the best thing God invents.

Robert Browning

44

What God has resolved concerning me I know not, but this at least I know: he has instilled into me a vehement love of the beautiful.

John Milton

45

Some thoughts always find us young, and keep us so. Such a thought is the love of the universal and eternal beauty.

Ralph Waldo Emerson

Bible

46

What you bring away from the Bible depends to some extent on what you carry to it.

Oliver Wendell Holmes

47
The Seven Wonders of the Word

1. The wonder of its formation – the way in which it grew is one of the mysteries of time.
2. The wonder of its unification – a library of sixty-six books, yet one book.
3. The wonder of its age – most ancient of all books.
4. The wonder of its sale – best seller of any book.
5. The wonder of its interest – only book in the world read by all classes.
6. The wonder of its language – written largely by uneducated men, yet the best from a literary standpoint.
7. The wonder of its preservation – the most hated of all books, yet it continues to exist. 'The word of our God shall stand for ever.'

Anon.

48

Lay hold on the Bible until the Bible lays hold on you.

William Houghton

49

An American soldier was taught a valuable lesson by a South Sea islander during World War II.

The friendly host, trying to assure the visitor that they had many things in common, brought a copy of the Bible out of his hut and said: 'This is my most prized possession.'

With obvious disdain the soldier replied, 'We've outgrown that sort of thing you know.'

The islander, who belonged to a tribe which had formerly practised cannibalism, was unimpressed by this lack of courtesy as well as faith.

He calmly remarked, 'It's a good thing we haven't outgrown it here. If we had, you would have been a meal as soon as we saw you.'

Anon.

50

It is reckoned that the first edition of the *Gutenberg Bible* consisted of 120 copies on paper and thirty on vellum. Of these forty-eight survive, twelve of them vellum copies, and of the twelve, three are in perfect condition. They are each valued at well over a million pounds.

The *Black Bible* won its place in history because the word 'not' was accidentally dropped from the seventh commandment, leaving it to read, 'Thou shalt commit adultery.' The offending printers, Richard Barker and Martin Lucas, who issued an edition of 1,000 copies in 1631, were fined £3,000.

A similar fine was imposed on printers in the same era for transcribing a famous verse of Psalm 14 thus: 'The fool hath said in his heart there is a God.' Naturally, their edition (all copies of which were suppressed) came to be known as the *Fool Bible*.

A negative was also omitted from the so-called *Unrighteous Bible*, printed at Cambridge in 1653. Here the 'not' slipped out of a verse in 1 Corinthians 6, so that it read 'Know ye not that the unrighteous shall inherit the Kingdom of God?'

The *Sin On Bible* was the first Bible printed in Ireland and dated 1716. In it, John 5.14 has the misprint 'Sin on more' instead of the obvious admonition.

Anon.

51

A young man heard with disgust that his wealthy old uncle had left him a Bible in his will. The will read thus: 'To my nephew I leave a copy of God's priceless word which I trust he will use daily and find within its pages real treasure.'

The beneficiary threw the Bible into an old trunk in the attic, disgusted and disappointed with his share in his uncle's bequests. Years later, at a time of depression, he turned to the good Book for comfort. Between its pages he found many thousands of pounds.

Anon.

52

Here is knowledge enough for me. Let me be a man of one Book.

John Wesley

53

The Bible is a window in this prison-world, through which we may look into eternity.

T. Dwight

54

A Sunday School teacher asked her young class how Noah spent his time in the ark. When there was no response, she asked, 'Do you suppose he did a lot of fishing?'

'What,' piped up a six-year-old, 'with only two worms?'

Anon.

55

After hearing the story of Lot's wife in catechism class and
how she looked back and turned into a pillar of salt, a little
boy put his hand up and said, 'Please, Miss, when my
Mum was driving, she looked back and turned into a pillar
box!'

Anon.

56

The minister, addressing a Sunday School class, had taken
for his theme the story of Elisha on his journey to Bethel –
how the youngsters had taunted the old prophet, and how
they were punished when two bears came out of the wild
and ate forty and two of them.

'And now, children,' concluded the pastor, wishing to
stress the moral point, 'what does this story show?'

'It shows', ventured one little girl timidly, 'how many
children two bears can hold!'

Anon.

57

In talking about the story of Jacob's dream, a Sunday
School teacher asked the class, 'Why did the angels use the
ladder when they had wings?' One bright pupil quickly
replied, 'Because they were moulting!'

Anon.

58

A lady was posting a gift of a Bible to a relative. The post
office clerk examined the heavy parcel and inquired if it
contained anything breakable. 'Nothing', the lady told him,
'but the Ten Commandments.'

Anon.

59

A Sunday School class had just been hearing about the parable of the prodigal son. 'Now,' said the Sunday School teacher, 'who was not glad to know of the prodigal's return?' 'Please, sir,' replied one boy, 'the fatted calf!'

Anon.

Birth

60

My mother groaned, my father wept:
Into the dangerous world I leapt,
Helpless, naked, piping loud,
Like a fiend hid in a cloud.

Struggling in my father's hands,
Striving against my swaddling bands,
Bound and weary, I thought best
To sulk upon my mother's breast.

William Blake

61

Everything that is born of God is truly no shadowy work, but a true life work. God will not bring forth a dead fruit, a lifeless and powerless work, but a living, new man must be born from the living God.

Johann Arndt

Bread of Life

62

It is told of Sadhu Sundar Singh that many years ago he was distributing gospels in the Central Provinces of India

and he came to some non-Christians on a train and offered
a man a copy of John's Gospel. The man took it, tore it into
pieces in anger and threw the pieces out of the window.
That seemed the end, but it so happened in the providence
of God, there was a man idly walking along the line that
very day, and he picked up, as he walked along, a little bit
of paper and looked at it, and the words on it in his own
language were 'the Bread of Life'. He did not know what it
meant; but he enquired among his friends and one of them
said: 'I can tell you; it is out of the Christian book. You
must not read it or you will be defiled.' The man thought
for a moment and then said: 'I want to read the book that
contains that beautiful phrase': and he bought a copy of the
New Testament. He was shown where the sentence
occurred – our Lord's words 'I am the Bread of Life'; and
as he studied the Gospel, the light flooded into his heart.
Later he became a preacher of the gospel, in the Central
Province of India. That little bit of paper, through God's
Spirit, was indeed the bread of life to him.

Anon.

63

Here is bread, which strengthens men's heart, and therefore called the staff of life.

Matthew Henry

64

Napoleon won his victories largely by concentrating his
forces with unexpected speed. But this meant forced
marches for his soldiers, living on the country, where
supplies soon ran out. Lack of food meant much illness and
many casualties. 'An army marches on its stomach' he said,
and offered a prize of 20,000 francs to anybody who would
invent some way of preserving food. A Parisian chef won
the prize with a plan for a process of bottling food

previously heated. Later in London this was improved on, by substituting tins for glass bottles (the beginning of the canning industry). The manufacturers kept the French name boeuf bouilli, so the English soldiers called it bully beef.

The Eucharist supplies Christ's army on the march to heaven with the food it needs.

F.H. Drinkwater

65

Bread for myself is a material matter: bread for other people is a spiritual matter.

Nikolai Berdyaev

66

I am God's wheat; I am grounded by the teeth of the wild beasts that I may end as the pure bread of Christ.

Ignatius of Antioch

67

Our Lord did not say, 'Come unto me all ye faultless': neither did he say, 'Be sure you tear yourselves to pieces first.' There are only three necessities of a good Communion – Faith, Hope and Charity. To rely utterly on God and be in charity with the world – this is the essential. What you happen to be feeling at the moment does not matter in the least.

Evelyn Underhill

Brevity

68

An Argument for Brevity:
Lord's Prayer: 56 words
Twenty-third Psalm: 118 words
Gettysburg Address: 226 words
Ten Commandments: 297 words
US Department of Agriculture order on the price of
cabbage: 15,629 words.

'Encounter' Magazine

Brotherhood

69

William Penn, the Quaker, was granted land in the New
World by King Charles II in return for a large sum of
money which the King owed him. It was called Sylvania
because of its forests and the King insisted on adding the
name Penn. The Charter of Pennsylvania empowered Penn
to make war on the Indian savages, but Penn refused to
build any forts nor to have cannon or soliders in his
province.

It was prophesied that all his settlements would soon be
destroyed. But Penn took no notice of these prophecies. He
set about founding his capital city which he named
Philadelphia, the City of Brotherly Love. He made friends
with the Indians and they arranged that all quarrels should
be settled by a meeting of six white men and six red men.
The Indians enjoyed equal citizenship with the white men
and an equal choice of land. When William Penn died they
mourned him as their friend. After Penn's death, while
every other colony in the New World was constantly
attacked by the Indians, Pennsylvania was perfectly free

from attack as long as they refused to arm themselves.
Many years later the Quakers were outvoted in the State
and the colony gave way to pressure on them from the other
States and began to spend money in building forts and to
train soldiers against possible aggression. They were
immediately attacked.

E.B. Emmott

70

Love we as Brothers
For we are all Christ's creatures, and by his coffer are we
    wealthy,
And brothers of one blood, beggars and nobles.
Christ's blood on Calvary, is the spring of Christendom,
And we became blood brethren there, recovered by one
    body,
As *quasi modo geniti*,[1] and gentle without exception,
None base or a beggar, but when sin cause it.
Qui facit peccatum, servus est peccati.[2]
In the Old Law, as Holywrit tells us,
Men were men's sons, mentioned always
As issue of Adam and of Eve, until the God-man was
    crucified,
And after his resurrection *Redemptor* was his title,
And we his brethren, bought through him, both rich and
    poor men.
Therefore love we as lief brothers, each laughing with the
    other,
And each give what he can spare as his goods are needed.
Let each man help the other, for we shall all go hence.

1. As though of one family.
2. Whosoever committeth sin is the servant of sin (John 8.34).

William Langland (14th century)

Charity

71

Benjamin Franklin, tactless in his youth became so diplomatic, so adroit at handling people that he was made American Ambassador to France. The secret of his success? 'I will speak ill of no man,' he said, 'and speak all the good I know of everybody.'

As Dr Johnson said: 'God Himself, sir, does not propose to judge man until the end of his days.' Why should you and I?

Dale Carnegie

72

Before you say a word about another ask yourself three questions: Is it true? Is it kind? Is it necessary?

Anon.

73

We have made the slogan 'Charity begins at home' a part of our religion – although it was invented by a Roman pagan and is directly contrary to the story of the Good Samaritan. Charity begins where the need is greatest and the crisis is most dangerous.

Frank C. Laubach

74

Why do you disturb yourself
About fair or stormy weather?
Squalls must sometimes whistle round,
Where people live together.

Some will smile and some will frown,
Why should you ever mind them,

Travel on as best you can,
And take people as you find them.

Pass a little grievance by
Don't appear to heed it.
Be as helpful as you can,
Kind to those who need it.

Never flatter, never try
Skilfully to mould them
To your own, particular view,
Take people as you find them.

They may think you very wrong
You may think they wonder,
Charity will whisper then,
'Better not to ponder'.

Actions wear a different look
When motives are assigned them.
Keep your eyes upon yourself,
And take people as you find them.

Anon.

Cheerfulness

75

At one time, at Whitsuntide, in the Midlands and the
North many parishes held Sunday School Festivals. The
church of St John's, Horbury Bridge, where one such
festival used to take place, was a mile up hill from the
village. The priest-in-charge, the Rev. S. Baring-Gould,
thought it would be a fine thing for the children to march
that mile enlivened by a stirring song and tune, so on the
Whitsunday of 1865 he sat down and in about fifteen
minutes 'Onward, Christian Soldiers' was written. It was
learnt the following day by the children, and on the
Tuesday sung as they marched up the hill.

It would be difficult to say to how many other marches
this fine song has given spirit and life since that Whit-
Tuesday of 1865.

Maud Higham

76
Our loving God wills that we eat, drink and be merry.

Martin Luther

77
God is the creator of laughter that is good.

Philo

78
Robert Louis Stevenson, the author of Treasure Island, was
hardly ever well, but every day, when he gathered his
household together for prayers away in their South Sea
island home, he prayed for himself and them, that they
might do their duty 'with laughter and kind faces', and
asking that 'cheerfulness might abound with industry', and
that all might go 'blithely on their business all the day'. It
was the custom in Vailima, after all work and meals were
finished, to sound the 'pu' or war conch from the verandah
as an invitation to prayer, and in response the Samoans –
men, women and children – trooped into the large hall by
all the open doors. Through the bush they came, many of
them from considerable distances; carrying lanterns, if the
evening were dark. A great lamp hung from the ceiling: the
Samoans in reverent attitudes made a wide semi-circle on
the floor, and Robert Louis Stevenson and his family were
at one end of the hall. Then 'family prayers' began, partly
in English and partly in Samoan, with the singing of hymns
in the native tongue set to ancient often warlike tunes.

Here is a part of the Vailima evening prayers which show
Stevenson's spirit:

'We come before Thee, O Lord, in the end of Thy day with thanksgiving . . . give us to awake with smiles, give us to labour smiling . . . as the sun lightens the world, so let our loving kindness make bright this house of our habitation.'

Maud Higham

Children

79

Children's Letters to God

Dear God, Remember when the snow was deep there was no school? Could we have it again please?

Guy

Dear God, It's very good the way each kid has one mother and one father. Did it take you long to think of that?

Glenn

Dear God, I think the Bible is very good. Did you write any other books?

Alice

Dear God, Please send me a pony. I never asked for anything before. You can look it up.

Bruce

Dear God, My teacher says the North Pole is not really at the top. Did you make any more mistakes?

Herbie

Dear God, I am adopted. Is that as good as being real?

Paul

Dear God, Are boys better than girls? I know you are one but try to be fair.

Sylvia

Compiled by Eric Marshall and Stuart Hample

80

Father Sergio Gutierrez, a Catholic priest, is better known by the *nom de guerre* he uses in the wrestling ring: Fray Tormenta.

Fray Tormenta is a professional wrestler who, like most good professionals is in it partly for kicks, but mainly for the money. And all the money he makes clobbering, and getting clobbered, in towns up and down Mexico goes into an orphanage he runs in the parish of Xometla, a small, dusty village just north of Mexico City.

Father Tormenta – which means storm in Spanish – is forty-two years old, a stocky smiling man who wears a golden mask over his face in the ring and thick glasses out of it. He has been picking abandoned children off the streets for seventeen years. Interviewed in his parish office – the walls are covered in posters of Bruce Lee, Sylvester Stallone and the Virgin of Guadelupe – he explains how the idea of such an unpriestly activity struck him fourteen years ago.

'I'd always enjoyed watching fights on television. One day, when I learnt of the fantastic sums boxers made, I thought fighting would be a good way of making money to look after the children. Imagine my surprise when after my first fight all they paid me was 200 pesos (about £20 at the time).'

Undaunted, he went on to fight two or three times a week, which has proved enough to keep the 2,500 children who have been through his hands so far clean and well-fed.

Father Tormenta says the majority of the mothers of the eighty-six children in his care, who range from one to seventeen, were prostitutes. Some, still alive, have been only too relieved to sign away care of the child to him. The latest arrival at the orphanage is five-year-old Anita. Father Tormenta's sister found her one night lying under a blanket on a street in Mexico City.

John Carlin

81

Mother walked into her son's bedroom and found the little boy tying a bandage round his finger. 'My poor boy!' she exclaimed. 'What have you done to your finger?'

'I hit it with a hammer, Mummy.'

'But I didn't hear you crying, darling.'

'No – I thought you were out!'

Anon.

Christ

82

Christ cannot live his life today in this world without our mouth, our eyes, without our going and coming, without our heart. When we love, it is Christ loving through us.

Leon Joseph Suenens

83

In his life Christ is an example,
    showing us how to live;
In his death he is a sacrifice,
    satisfying for our sins;
In his resurrection, a conqueror;
In his ascension, a king;
In his intercession, a high priest.

Martin Luther

84

Christ is all sufficient. For the

Artist – He is the altogether lovely (Song of Solomon 5.16)
Architect – He is the chief cornerstone (1 Peter 2.6)
Astronomer – He is the sun of righteousness (Malachi 4.2)
Baker – He is the living bread (John 6.51)
Banker – He is the unsearchable riches (Ephesians 3.8)
Builder – He is the sure foundation (Isaiah 28.16;
    1 Corinthians 3.11)
Carpenter – He is the door (John 10.9)
Editor – He is good tidings of great joy (Luke 2.10)
Electrician – He is the light of the world (John 8.12)
Farmer – He is sower and the Lord of the harvest
    (Matthew. 13.37; Luke 10.2)
Florist – He is the rose of Sharon and the lily of the valley
    (Song of Solomon 2.1)
Jeweller – He is the living precious stone (1 Peter 2.4)
Lawyer – He is the counsellor, lawgiver and advocate
    (Isaiah 9.6; 1 John 2.1)
Labourer – He is the giver of rest (Matthew 11.28)

Anon.

85

Jesus Christ is the centre of all, and the goal to which all
tends.

Blaise Pascal

Christ – Divinity

86

He that cried in the manger, that sucked the paps of a
woman, that hath exposed himself to poverty, and a world

of inconveniences, is the Son of the Living God, of the same
substance with his Father, begotten before all ages, before
the morning-stars; he is God eternal.

Jeremy Taylor

87

Christ is not valued at all unless he be valued above all.

Augustine of Hippo

88

Then I see the Saviour over me,
Spreading his beams of love, and dictating the words of this
    mild song . . .
I am not a God afar off, I am a brother and friend;
Within your bosom I reside, and you reside in me;
Lo! we are One; forgiving all Evil; Not seeking recom-
    pense . . .

William Blake

Christ – Humanity

89

It was at that time that a man appeared – if 'man' is the
right word – who had all the attributes of a man but seemed
to be something greater. His actions were superhuman, for
he worked such wonderful and amazing miracles that I for
one cannot regard him as a man; yet in view of his likeness
to ourselves I cannot regard him as an angel either.

Josephus

90

What was born of Mary, according to Scripture, was by
nature human; the Lord's body was a real one – real,

because it was the same as ours. This was because Mary was our sister, since we are all descended from Adam. This is the meaning of John's words: 'The Word became flesh' as can be seen from a similar passage in Paul: 'Christ became a curse for us.' The human body has been greatly enhanced through the fellowship and union of the Word with it.

Athanasius

91

According to the old legend, the mother pelican wounds herself in order that she may give her blood to feed her little ones. There is a beautiful lectern in Durham Cathedral which represents a pelican with outstretched wings. Great red drops are on her breast, and in her bill was one great jewel to represent a drop of blood, as she bends to feed the little brood which gathers round her. The lovely jewel has since been stolen and has not been replaced.

Another bird legend is that of the robin red-breast. It is said that when our Lord hung suffering upon the Cross, a little brown bird, filled with love and sorrow, came fluttering down to his aid. There was so little it could do, but it plucked just one thorn from that awful crown. And ever since the robin's breast has borne the mark of the Precious Blood.

Anon.

92

One night in 1741, a bent old man shuffled listlessly down a dark London street. George Frederick Handel was starting out on one of his aimless despondent wanderings. His mind was a battleground between hope and despair. For forty years he had written stately music for the kings and queens of England but now the court society had turned against him. Four years before, he had suffered a cerebral haemorrhage, which had paralysed his right side, making it impossible for him to walk or write. Slowly he had regained his strength and the ability both to walk and write. But now aged sixty, with England in the grip of a hard winter, he felt old and helplessly tired.

As he walked he passed a church, and welling up from within him came the cry, 'My God, my God, why have you forsaken me?' He returned to his shabby lodgings. On his desk was a bulky package. He opened it and his eyes fell on the words, 'He was despised and rejected of men.' Reaching for a pen he started to write. Notes filled page after page. He worked almost non-stop for twenty-four days, taking little rest and even less food. When the *Messiah* lay finished on his desk he collapsed on his bed and slept for seventeen hours This tremendous masterpiece, one of the greatest ever composed, is now a traditional part of both Christmas and Easter.

Paul Frost

93
Manchild

To think God learned to walk,
in Nazareth.
Later there'd be hard
walking to do,
with heavier falls.
And talking: in Nazareth
God played Adam's game –
naming things,
bringing out words:
and saw His own begetting
imaged, in the word's spring
from the intent regard.
A grave infant world
studied for Calvary,
studied for Gennesaret,

prepared to say thrice;
Simon Peter, lovest thou me?
Mary was never asked
if she loved God.

Robert Farren

94

Here is a man who was born in an obscure village, the child
of a peasant woman. He grew up in an obscure village. He
worked in a carpenter shop until He was thirty, and then
for three years He was an itinerant teacher. He never wrote
a book. He never held an office. He never owned a home.
He never had a family. He never went to college. He never
travelled more than two hundred miles from the place
where He was born. He had no credentials but Himself. He
had nothing to do with this world except the power of his
divine manhood. While still a young man, the tide of
popular opinion turned against him. His friends ran away.
One of them denied him. He was turned over to his
enemies. He went through the mockery of a trial. He was
nailed upon a cross between two thieves. His executioners
gambled for the only piece of property He had on earth
while He was dying – his coat. When He was dead He was
taken down and laid in a borrowed grave through the pity
of a friend.

Nineteen wide centuries have come and gone; today He
is the centrepiece of the human race and the Leader of the
column of progress.

I am far within the mark when I say that all the armies
that ever marched, and all the navies that ever were built,
and all the parliaments that ever sat, and all the kings that
ever reigned, put together, have not affected the life of man
upon this earth as powerfully as has that one solitary life.

James A. Francis

Christian

95

A Christian . . .
> is a mind through which Christ thinks.
> is a heart through which Christ lives.
> is a voice through which Christ speaks.
> is a hand through which Christ helps.

John Galsworthy

96

A Christian is the keyhole through which other folk see God.

Robert E. Gibson

97

On account of him there have come to be many christs in the world, even all who, like him, loved righteousness and hated iniquity.

Origen of Alexandria

98

The main business of a Christian soul is to go through the world turning its water into wine.

Andrew Long

99

'Are you a Christian, Uncle Lawrence?' 'No, my dear; if anything a Confucian, who, as you know, was simply an ethical philosopher. Most of our caste in this country, if they only knew it, are Confucian rather than Christian. Belief in ancestors, and tradition, respect for parents,

honesty, moderation of conduct, kind treatment of animals
and dependents, absence of self-obtrusion, and stoicism in
the face of pain and death.'

John Galsworthy

100

The Christian life is a journey.' Do not wait for great
strength before setting out, for immobility will weaken you
further. Do not wait to see very clearly before starting; one
has to walk towards the light.

Philippe Vernier

Christian Maturity

101

God develops spiritual power in our lives through pressure
of hard places.

Anon.

102

I walked a mile with Pleasure.
She chatted all the way,
But left me none the wiser
For all she had to say.
I walked a mile with Sorrow,
And ne'er a word said she;
But oh, the things I learned from her
When Sorrow walked with me!

Robert Hamilton

103

Sometimes great difficulties are permitted only in order to
strengthen character.

R.H. Benson

104

'Why are you so sad?' said the West Wind to the Birch
Tree.

'Alas I am so useless,' said the beautiful Birch, 'I cannot
bear fruit like the cherry and the apple. Why even the
potato is useful and the dumpy turnip. Now I shall be of no
use till I am cut down and made into furniture and sold as a
bedroom suite. If I could only bear cherries, or currants or
gooseberries.'

'Ha! Ha!' laughed the West Wind, 'I have just heard the
apple grumbling, the cherry wailing, the potato and the
turnip complaining. They all have their complaints. But I'll
tell you something about love and yourself.

'There's a man who comes out of the city. Nearly every
day he comes like one who is bearing a burden, till he
comes to the edge of the wood where he can see *you*. Then
he raises his eyes and they suddenly fill with sunlight. So he
goes back brightened and cheered because of who you are,
and not what you do.'

H. Bellyse Baildon

105

Mishaps are knives that either serve or cut us as we grasp
them by the blade or by the handle.

James Russell Lowell

106

Many would be willing to have afflictions provided that
they be not inconvenienced by them.

Francis of Sales

107

In the apple-bearing section of the state of Maine, my
friend saw an apple tree so loaded with fruit that, all

around, the laden branches were propped to keep them
from the ground. When he exclaimed about it, the owner of
the orchard said, 'Go, look at that tree's trunk near the
bottom.' Then my friend saw that the tree had been badly
wounded with a deep gash. 'That is something we have
learned about apple trees,' said the owner of the orchard.
'When the tree tends to run to wood and leaves and not to
fruit, we wound it, gash it, and almost always, no one
knows why, this is the result: it turns its energies to fruit.'
We must know wounded apple trees in the human orchard
of whom that is a parable.

Harry Emerson Fosdick

108

A woman deserves no credit for her beauty at sixteen but
beauty at sixty is her own soul's doing.

Anon.

Christian Unity

109

Speaking from the moon, the astronaut Frank Borman said,
'We are one hunk of ground, water, air, clouds, floating
around in space. From here it really is one world.'

Frank Borman

110

In Malaya, during the Second World War, a sympathetic
native was helping an escaping prisoner of war make his
way to the coast – and from there to freedom. The two were
stumbling through a virtually impenetrable jungle. There
was no sign of human life and not even the slightest trace of
a trail. Having grown weary and becoming somewhat

wary, the soldier turned to his guide and asked 'Are you sure this is the way?' The reply came in faltering English: 'There *is* no way . . . I am the way.'

Anon

111

Form altogether one choir, so that, with the symphony of your feelings and having taken the tone of God, you may sing with one voice to the Father through Jesus Christ, that He may listen to you and know you from your chant as the canticle of His only Son.

Ignatius of Antioch

112

On 3rd February 1943 a convoy of American ships was bringing reinforcements from St John's in Newfoundland to Greenland. In the darkness a German U-boat struck suddenly. The torpedo hit the SS Dorchester in a vulnerable spot at 3.55 a.m. and the 5,252 ton transport began to sink rapidly by the bow into the icy waters some 150 miles from Cape Farewell. There were fourteen lifeboats on board and all were quickly lowered. Only two however were used to good purpose – the rest capsized. In such waters a man would have a life expectation of three to five minutes.

On the ship were four US Army chaplains: John P. Washington, a Catholic priest, Clark V. Poling and George L. Fox, Protestant ministers; and Alexander D. Goode, a Jewish rabbi. Unmindful of their own safety all four helped the officers to control the confusion which reigned and they encouraged the men and prayed with them. When the life-jackets ran short, each of the chaplains took off his own and gave it to a man who had none. As the doomed ship sank the men in the water could see the four chaplains on the deck, 'linked arm in arm, their voices raised in prayer'.

Of the 904 men on board only 299 were saved; the chaplains were not among them. One of the survivors, a coast-guard officer, John J. Mahoney, owed his life to Chaplain Goode. The rabbi took off his gloves and gave them to him. The gloves kept his hands from freezing and miraculously enabled him to cling to a life-boat for eight hours, awaiting rescue, while thirty-eight of the forty men in the boat froze to death or were swept overboard.

'The Messenger'

113

Bonhoeffer's last message as he was taken out to execution was to Bell (the Bishop of Chichester) through a British prisoner . . . 'Tell him [he said] that for me this is the end but also the beginning – with him I believe in the principle of our Universal Christian brotherhood which rises above all national interests, and that our victory is certain.'

Wolf-Dieter Zimmermann and Ronald Gregor Smith

114

Three clergymen – an Anglican priest, an Irish Catholic priest and a Scots minister were attending a conference in Scotland for Church unity. At the conclusion they decided to go for a day's fishing in the nearby loch and having hired a boat, set off and anchored a little way from the shore. They were having good luck with the fishing when suddenly the line of the Scots minister was fouled and, having no other of that particular tackle available, he decided to go ashore to get some more. Going down on his knees in the bow of the boat, he prayed very earnestly and then, stepping over the side, walked across the surface of the water to the shore, returning in like manner.

A little later the Anglican priest had need to go ashore and he also knelt down and prayed and then stepped over the side of the boat and walked over the water, returning in due course.

Presently, it was found that their supplies were running short so the first two ministers looked at the Irish priest who said that he would go ashore to bring back replenishments. He also knelt and prayed and then stepped over the side of the boat as his companions had done previously. But he went right down in the water, and as the other two ministers watched him sink, one said to the other: 'Perhaps for the sake of Christian unity, we should have pointed out where the stepping stones were!'

Anon.

115

One Sunday in an Irish village, three Protestant women visited a Roman Catholic church. Recognising them and wishing to show respect, the priest whispered to his server, 'Three chairs for the Protestant ladies.'

The server jumped to his feet and shouted, 'Three cheers for the Protestant ladies.' The congregation rose, responded heartily and the service continued.

'The Sign'

Christmas

116

They all were looking for a king
  To slay their foes and lift them high;
Thou cam'st, a little baby thing
  That made a woman cry.

George MacDonald

117

The first Christmas card was believed to have been sent by W.C.T. Dobson R.A., in 1844. Sir Henry Cole and

J. C. Horsley produced the first commercial Christmas card in 1846, although it was condemned by temperance enthusiasts because members of the family group were cheerfully drinking wine. After Tucks, the art printers, took to printing them in the 1870s, they really came into vogue.

Anon.

118

When Jesus was born in Bethlehem there were other animals in that stable besides the humble ass which brought His mother to the inn. There was the contemptuous camel, with a lip, the steed of some desert ranger. There was a proud war horse stabled there by a passing warrior. There was a strong bullock who drew the wagon of a great merchant. In the quiet of that Christmas night the four beasts munched their provender in silence.

We have all heard how that at midnight on Christmas Eve all the beasts in the world gain for a few fleeting moments the power of human speech; now this miracle began on this very night in the stable at Bethlehem. The four beasts watched the carpenter Joseph, his wife Mary and the new-born child who lay in the manger.

'Humph,' said the contemptuous camel, with a sniff, 'quite an ordinary child.'

'A little peasant child,' said the proud horse with a snort, 'a common little kid.'

The great ox gave a grunt and said, 'A weak miserable little thing', and they all went on munching their hay and forgot about Joseph and Mary and the Babe in the manger.

Then outside the stable there was a sound of footsteps and men's voices, which could be faintly heard through the half-open stable door. The humble ass who had felt much too insignificant to join in the conversation of his betters (indeed he would have been severely snubbed had he dared to do anything so rash), turned his long ears to hear what the men were saying. Then for the first time that night he spoke. 'They are saying', said the ass, 'that a King is born this day.' There was a stir among the noble beasts at that news. 'Ah, He will need me', said the camel, 'to cross the trackless desert, for surely this King will be a great traveller, visiting all the cities of the world in His wisdom and magnificence.' 'He will need me', said the horse, 'to ride in triumph through the streets of the cities that He conquers, for He will be a mighty warrior.' 'No, it is I whom He will need', said the ox, 'for it is a bearer of great burdens to carry His merchandise, His gold and His silver, that He will want the most.'

So they quarrelled that night as to which of them the new-born King would need, and of the Baby in the manger they thought nothing at all. Only the humble ass who had said nothing, for he thought he was too humble to be used at all, looked with mild brown eyes at the mother and her child as Mary crooned over the manger-cradle the baby's first lullaby . . .

But after all, it was on the humble ass that the King rode into His city in the end.

W.E. Orchard

119

That there was no room in the inn was symbolic of what was to happen to Jesus. The only place where there was room for him was on the Cross.

William Barclay

120

Light looked down and beheld Darkness:
'Thither will I go,' said Light.
Peace looked down and beheld War:
'Thither will I go,' said Peace.
Love looked down and beheld Hatred:

'Thither will I go,' said Love.
So came Light and shone.
So came Peace and gave rest.
So came Love and brought life.
And the Word was made flesh and dwelt among us.

Laurence Housman

121

I think, therefore, that the purpose and cause of the Incarnation was that he might illuminate the world by his wisdom and excite it to the love of himself.

Peter Abelard

122

The Russians have for centuries told a legend about a young medieval prince, Alexis, who lived (as Russian princes commonly did) in a sumptuous palace, while all around, in filthy hovels, lived hundreds of poor peasants. The Prince was moved with compassion for these poor folk and determined to better their lot. So he began to visit them. But as he moved in and out among them he found that he'd got absolutely no point of contact with them. They treated him with enormous respect, almost worship; but he was never able to win their confidences, still less their affection, and he returned to the palace a defeated and disappointed young man.

Then one day a very different man came among the people. He was a rough and ready young doctor who also wanted to devote his life to serving the poor. He started by renting a filthy rat-ridden shack in one of the back streets. He made no pretence of being superior – his clothes (like theirs) were old and tattered and he lived simply on the plainest food, often without knowing where the next meal was coming from. He made no money from his profession because he treated most people free and gave away his medicines. Before long this young doctor had won the respect and affection of all those people as Prince Alexis had never succeeded in doing. He was one of them. And little by little he transformed the whole spirit of the place, settling quarrels, reconciling enemies, helping people to live decent lives. No one ever guessed that this young doctor was in fact the Prince himself, who had abandoned his palace and gone down among his people to become one of them. That's just what God did on that first Christmas day. He came right down side by side with us to help us to become the sort of beings he intends us to be.

John Williams

123

In the British Commonwealth and in the United States, 'Good King Wenceslas' is the most popular of all Christmas carols. Yet, while the carol is both modern and Protestant, Wenceslas was a Catholic saint who was martyred more than 1,000 years ago.

Why is it, therefore, that millions of Anglo-Saxon voices of all denominations are raised in praise of a king of whom probably not more than one in 10,000 knows more than the mere name?

The words of the carol were written over 100 years ago by the Rev. J.M. Neale, the English hymn writer and author of 'Jerusalem the Golden'. The carol was based on one of many legends which surround Wenceslas and was set to a beautiful medieval tune.

Born in AD 907, Wenceslas was the grandson of Borivoj, the first Christian prince of Bohemia. His father, Wratislav, died in AD 920 while fighting the Hungarians, and during Wenceslas' minority the reins of power lay in the hands of his mother, Drahomina.

Ambitious, and a lover of power, Drahomina was no ordinary woman. Although nominally a Christian, she sided with pagan nobles and bore the responsibility of the murder of her much respected mother-in-law.

On reaching the age of eighteen, in AD 925, Wenceslas assumed control of his Principality; his most important contribution to history was the peace treaty he made which saved the Slavs of Central Europe from extinction. Yet, Wenceslas was too progressive for his times, and his brother, Boleslav, backed by the pagans, determined to murder him.

He invited Wenceslas to a banquet at which he and his co-conspirators planned to kill him. Thrice they drew their swords and thrice they drew back in the face of the holy Prince.

The next day Boleslav and his supporters tried again as Wenceslas was on his way to church. Having bolted the church doors so that he could not find sanctuary, they struck him down with their swords and spears.

There are countless stories of Wenceslas' saintliness: how he vowed himself to life-long chastity, how he wore a hair shirt under his princely robes, his assiduous attendance at Divine Office and how he gathered and threshed the wheat and pressed the grapes with his own hands to prepare the bread and wine for Communion.

The story of his pilgrimages to the poor dates back to earliest chronicles. Disguised as a forester, and accompanied by his faithful page, Podevin, he would go into the forest and cut wood for the needy. It is this legend which inspired the English carol.

Robin B. Lockhart

124
A Child my Choice

Let Folly praise that fancy loves, I praise and love that Child

Whose heart no thought, Whose tongue no word, Whose
  hand no deed defiled.
I praise Him most, I love Him best, all praise and love is
  His:
While Him I love, in Him I live, and cannot live amiss.
Love's sweetest mark, laud's highest theme, man's most
  desired light,
To love Him life; to leave Him death; to live in Him delight.
He mine by gift, I his by debt, thus each to other due,
First friend He was, best friend He is, all times will try Him
  true.
Though young, yet wise, though small, yet strong, though
  man, yet God he is
As wise He knows, as strong He can, as God He loves to
  bless.
His knowledge rules, His strength defends, His love doth
  cherish all;
His birth our joy, His life our light, His death our end of
  thrall.
Alas! He weeps, He sighs, He pants, yet do His angels sing;
Out of His tears, His sighs and throbs, doth bud a joyful
  spring.
Almighty Babe, Whose tender arms can force all foes to fly,
Correct my faults, protect my life, direct me when I die.

Robert Southwell

125

Into this world, this demented inn, in which there is
absolutely no room for him at all, Christ has come
uninvited. But because he cannot be at home in it, because
he is out of place in it, his place is with those others for
whom there is no room, with those who are rejected,
discredited, denied the status as persons, tortured, bombed
and exterminated.

Thomas Merton

126

The Puritans ruled the country, and they strongly dis-
approved of keeping any day special – except Sunday, 'the
Lord's Day'. So they passed an Act of Parliament to cancel
Christmas 1652, and to show they meant it, they decided
that Parliament would sit just as on any other day of the
year. Everything was banned – from mince-pies to church
attendance. John Evelyn, the diarist, defied the ban and
went with his wife to church. He recorded what happened.
As they were receiving communion, a party of musketeers
broke in. They waited till the service was over, then
arrested the worshippers. They soon let them go, unsure
how to punish people for going to church.

No one is likely to cancel Christmas again, but perhaps
for many the real Christmas *is* cancelled. The true cause for
celebration has been forgotten.

Anon.

127

Little Jennie was being taught that it was the proper thing
to do to write a 'thank-you' letter to those persons who sent
her gifts at Christmas. She seemed to do pretty well until it
came to Aunt Martha's gift. Finally she finished her note
which read: 'Thank you for your Christmas present. I
always wanted a pin-cushion, although not very much.'

Anon.

128

The first Christmas that little Linda learned to read, she
was allowed to distribute the family gifts on Christmas Eve.

According to the family custom, the one who distributed
the gifts could open the first package. After all the gifts were
distributed with loving care, Linda kept looking and
looking around the tree and among the branches. Finally
Father asked, 'What are you looking for, dear?' To which

Linda replied, 'I thought Christmas was Jesus' birthday, and I was just wondering where his present is. I guess everyone forgot him.'

Anon.

Church

129

The word *Church* used in most of the North European languages comes from the Greek *Kyriakē oikia*, 'the family of the Lord'. It is significant that when people sought a word to describe the reality of what it means to be Church, the word they chose meant 'family of the Lord'.

Leonard Doohan

130

What matters in the Church is not religion but the form of Christ, and its taking form amidst a band of men.

Dietrich Bonhoeffer

131

The Church of Christ is not an institution; it is a new life with Christ and in Christ, guided by the Holy Spirit.

Sergius Belgakov

132

A child on the way home from school decided to call in the church to have a look around. When he arrived home he told his grandmother he had been to God's house.

'Oh,' said grandma, did you see God?'

'No' replied the little boy, 'but I did see his wife scrubbing the floor.'

Anon.

133

For where the Church is, there is the Spirit of God; and where the Spirit of God is, there is the Church and every form of grace, for the Spirit is truth.

Irenaeus

134

Some churches are like lighthouses, built of stone, so strong that the thunder of the sea cannot move them – with no light at the top. That which is the light of the world in the Church is not its largeness, nor its services celebrated with pomp and beauty; not its music, nor the influences in it that touch the taste or instruct the understanding: it is the Christlikeness of its individual members.

Henry Ward Beecher

Church for Sinners

135

Wherever we see the Word of God purely preached and heard, there a church of God exists, even if it swarms with many faults.

John Calvin

136

The Church is the only institution in the world that has lower entrance requirements than those for getting on a bus.

William Laroe

137

A minister was called to a certain church in America. He was warned that the congregation was dead, but nevertheless he regarded the call as a challenge and he decided to accept it. He soon discovered that the church was dead. No planning, no toil, no exhortation, no urging could kindle a spark of life or waken any response.

He told the congregation that they were dead, and that he proposed to carry out the funeral of the church. A day was fixed. Into the church there was brought a coffin; the church was decked with mourning wreaths.

The time of the 'burial service' came. The church was crowded as it had not been for years. The minister carried out the 'burial service'. Then, at the end, as a last token of respect, he invited the congregation to file past the open coffin. As they did so, they received a shock. The coffin was open, and empty. But the bottom of the coffin was not wood; it was a mirror. As each person looked into the coffin of the dead they saw themselves.

Anon.

138
There are many sheep without, many wolves within.

Augustine of Hippo

139
Among the regulations for the tenants of a new block of flats near Marble Arch, occurs the injunction 'No religious services or immorality permitted in these flats.'

Anon.

140
The Church exists for the sake of those outside it.

William Temple

141

The retiring usher was instructing his youthful successor in the details of his office. 'And remember, my boy, that we have nothing but good, kind Christians in this church – until you try to put someone else in their pew!'

Anon.

142

Don't stay away from church because there are so many hypocrites. There's always room for one more.

A.R. Adams

143

This was posted on a Bronx, New York, church notice board: 'Do come in – trespassers will be forgiven.'

Anon.

Citizenship

144

Few people are aware that the word 'govern' comes from the Latin term 'guberno' meaning 'to steer a ship'.

This thought was graphically illustrated by one man who said that a 'dictatorship is like a high-powered ocean liner. It can go straight ahead at a fast clip. The danger is that it may hit an iceberg.

'Democracy', he added, 'is like a log raft. You can't guide the thing very well; you wallow all over the place; your feet are always wet.

'But you can never sink a log raft', he concluded, 'and if you keep trying you eventually get there. That's what we've got to do, keep trying.'

The inefficiencies of self-government are often exasperating. But it is within the power of citizens, thank God, to right most wrongs.

Anon.

145
We are justified, from the point of view of exegesis, in regarding the democratic conception of the State as an expansion of the thought of the New Testament.

Karl Barth

146
The story is told of a king who placed a heavy stone in the road and then hid and watched to see who would remove it. Men of various classes came and worked their way round it, some loudly blaming the king for not keeping the highways clear, but all dodging the duty of getting it out of the way. At last a poor peasant on his way to town with his burden of vegetables for sale came, and contemplating the stone, laid down his load, and rolled the stone into the gutter. Then, turning round, he spied a purse that had lain right under the stone. He opened it and found it full of gold pieces with a note from the king saying it was for the one who should remove the stone.

'Indian Christian'

147
Whatever makes men good Christians makes them good citizens.

Daniel Webster

148

Bishops and Christians generally should beware of simply following politicians. A politician has an excuse for compromising, but it seems to me a christian bishop has not.

Archbishop T.D. Roberts

149

When my father visited me he never asked, 'How's business?' or even 'How are the children?' He'd pull cuttings out of his pockets and say angrily, 'Did you see that editorial in this morning's papers? Let's answer it!' My father was involved in mankind, and that is why he lived into his eighties. A man is like a tree: he dies on top first.

Harry Golden

150

Nothing is politically right which is morally wrong.

Daniel O'Connell

151

We have all laughed at the reputed story of Pat Murphy at the battle of Trafalgar, whose version of the battle was as follows: 'Lord Nelson came on deck and said "Is Pat Murphy on board?" And I said "Here I am, m'Lord." Then said his lordship. "Let the battle proceed."'

And yet, while this was written for a joke, there is more to it than we are apt to think. For if it had not been for the Pat Murphys, or John Joneses or Tom Smiths and others who were on hand doing their duty, there would have been no victories for Nelson, Wellington, Napoleon or Grant who now live in history as great commanders.

A.W. Graham

Communication

152
We are bombarded by messages. One study says that we
receive between 1,700 and 2,500 messages a day. We
remember only about 65 of them. Another study suggests
that: We remember 10 per cent of what we read. We retain
20 per cent of what we hear. We retain 30 per cent of what
we see. We retain 50 per cent of what we see and hear.

Anon.

153
The genius of communication is the ability to be both
totally honest and totally kind at the same time.

John Powell

154
In ancient Sparta, the citizens were stoical, military-
minded and noted for their economy of speech. Legend has
it that when Philip of Macedonia was storming the gates of
Sparta, he sent a message to the besieged king saying, 'If we
capture your city we will burn it to the ground.' A one-word
answer came back: 'If.'

Norman Lewis

155
Anyone who would cultivate the art of conversation should
learn that listening to others is often more important than
talking to them. These words of wisdom deserve reflection:
1. Nature has given to man one tongue, but two ears, that
we may hear from others as much as we speak. (*Epictetus*)
2. It takes a great man to make a good listener. (*Helps*)

3. A good listener is not only popular everywhere but after a while he knows something. (*Mizner*)

4. To be a judicious and sympathetic listener will go far toward making you an agreeable companion, self-forgetful, self-possessed, but not selfish enough to monopolize the conversation. (*Jack*)

Community

156

The church is never a place, but always a people; never a fold, but always a flock; never a sacred building, but always a believing assembly. The church is you who pray, not where you pray. A structure of brick or marble can no more be a church than your clothes of serge or satin can be you. There is in this world, nothing sacred but man, no sanctuary of God but the soul. ·

Anon.

157

A community is only a community when the majority of its members are making the transition from 'the community for myself' to 'myself for the community'.

Jean Vanier

158

Our generation is remarkable . . . for the number of people who must believe something but do not know what.

Evelyn Underhill

159

There was once a family who brought their youngest child, a girl, to be baptised. When it came time for the baptism, the family went forward, including a very happy three-year-old brother. When the baptism was over, the minister carried the baby into the middle of the congregation, expressing what a delight it was to welcome this child into the larger family, the Church. The three-year-old brother had noticed a grandpa-aged man sitting and smiling with a very happy smile. In a voice that all could hear, the little boy said, 'Would you like to touch our baby?' 'I would,' said the elderly man.

So the minister gently held out the baby for the man to touch. The man seemed so pleased that the little boy said, 'Maybe someone else would like to touch her.'

The minister walked down the aisle, and hands reached out to touch the baby. 'Now,' said the minister, 'those of you who have touched this child should pass that loving touch to others around you, until all have been touched.' And so it happened. People were so thrilled with that service that they asked if the same thing might not be done at each baptism.

John Ambrose

160

One Sunday morning, a man entered the church and sat down at the front with his hat on. Noting the man, one of the ushers spoke to him, asking him if he knew he had forgotten to remove his hat.

'Yes,' the man replied, 'I realise I have my hat on. I've been coming to this church for two months and this is the only way I could get anyone to speak to me!'

Anon.

Compassion

161
Certainty is the sin of bigots, terrorists and pharisees.
Compassion makes us think we may be wrong.

Anon.

162
Compassion will cure more sins than condemnation.

Henry Ward Beecher

163
Man is never nearer the Divine than in his compassionate
moments.

Joseph H. Hertz

164
Mercy and compassion are the great virtues which bring
with them our rewards, for they are recompensed with
mercy and loving-kindness from the mercy-seat of God.

The Midrash

Conscience

165
And I will place within them as a guide,
My umpire Conscience, whom if they will hear,
Light after light well used they shall attain,
And to the end persisting, safe arrive.

John Milton

166

Conscience is God's presence in man.

Emmanuel Swedenborg

167

Most of us follow our conscience as we follow a wheelbarrow. We push it in front of us in the direction we want to go.

Billy Graham

168

Cowardice asks, Is it safe?
Expediency asks, Is it politic?
Vanity asks, Is it popular?
But Conscience asks, Is it right?

W. Morley Punshon

169

'Oh, yes,' said the Indian, 'I know what my conscience is. It is a little three-cornered thing in here', he laid his hand on his heart, 'that stands still when I am good; but when I am bad, it turns round, and the corners hurt very much. But if I keep on doing wrong, by-and-by the corners wear off and it doesn't hurt any more.'

J. Ellis

170

Conscience warns us as a friend before it punishes us as a judge.

King Stanislaus I

171

A writer on Russia recorded that when it was discovered

that the word for God had been printed with a capital letter in some school books, the initial was changed to lower case in each of a million copies before the edition was allowed to reach the pupils. But it is not only in Russia that it is a political crime to spell God with a capital G, but in every place where the state is elevated to supremacy over conscience.

Halford E. Luccock

172
A brave man risks his life but not his conscience.

J.C.F. von Schiller

173
An old Sioux Indian once asked a white man to give him some tobacco for his pipe. The man gave him a loose handful from his pocket. The next day the Indian came back and asked for the white man. 'For', said he, 'I found a quarter of a dollar among the tobacco.' 'Why don't you keep it?' asked a person standing by. 'I've got a good man and a bad man here,' said the Indian pointing to his breast, 'and the bad one say, "Never mind, you got it, and it is your own now." The good man, "No, no! You must not keep it." So I didn't know what to do; and I thought to go to sleep; but the good man and the bad man kept talking all night, and troubled me; and when I bring the money back, I feel good.'

Anon.

174
My conscience is captive to the Word of God.

Martin Luther

175

Two men once visited a holy man to ask his advice. 'We have done wrong actions,' they said, 'and our consciences are troubled. Can you tell us what we must do so that we may be forgiven and feel clear of our guilt?'

'Tell me of your wrong doings, my sons,' said the old man.

The first man said, 'I have committed a great and grievous sin.'

'What about you?' the holy man asked the second.

'Oh,' said he, 'I have done quite a number of wrong things, but they are all quite small, and not at all important.'

The holy man considered for a while. 'This is what you must do,' he said at last. 'Each of you must go and bring me a stone for each of his misdeeds.'

Off went the men: and presently the first came back staggering with an enormous boulder, so heavy that he could hardly lift it, and with a groan he let it fall at the feet of the holy man. Then along came the second, cheerfully carrying a bag of small pebbles. This he also laid at the feet of the saint.

'Now,' said the holy man, 'take all those stones and put them back where you found them.'

The first man shouldered his rock again, and staggered back to the place from which he had brought it. But the second man could only remember where a few of his pebbles had lain. After some time, he came back, and said that the task was too difficult.

'You must know, my son,' said the old man, 'that sins are like these stones. If a man has committed a great sin, it lies like a heavy stone on his conscience; but if he is truly sorry, he is forgiven and the load is taken away. But if a man is constantly doing small things that are wrong, he does not feel any very great load of guilt, and so he is not sorry, and remains a sinner. So, you see, my son, it is as important to avoid little sins as big ones.'

Anon.

Courage

176

The word 'courage' takes on added meaning if you keep in mind that it is derived from the Latin term *cor* meaning 'heart'.

The dictionary defines it as a 'quality which enables one to pursue a course deemed right, through which one may incur contempt, disapproval or opprobrium.'

Some 300 years ago, La Rochefoucauld went a step further when he said: 'Perfect courage is to do unwitnessed what we should be capable of doing before all men.'

Anon.

177

Fear can keep a man out of danger, but courage can support him in it.

Thomas Fuller

178

One Friday morning in February 1975, an underground train, with 300 people on it, crashed against a stone wall at Moorgate station killing forty-one people. Among the passengers was a nineteen-year-old girl, named Margaret, who had just become a policewoman. When the train hit the wall, she found herself sitting on the floor with one of her legs under her body and a man on top of her. Neither could move without hurting the other. It was completely dark. The man on top said to her, 'You are being very brave.' 'I have to be,' she said, 'I am a policewoman.' For many hours, fireman tried to pull them out. Then they found that Margaret's left leg was trapped under a huge steel girder. The firemen marvelled that she could still laugh and joke. They could do nothing more to get her out.

Then a surgeon came and told her that she was going to be put to sleep so that she could be got out. 'That's fine,' she said, 'who's going to take me?' Five minutes later, the surgeon took Margaret's left foot off above the ankle. Within two days she was sitting up in hospital, chatting cheerfully to visitors. She received more than 2,000 gifts and cards from all over the world.

M. Nassan

179

Courage consists not in blindly overlooking danger, but in seeing it and conquering.

Jean Paul Richter

180

One of the most famous stories of unselfishness and courage is the epic of Captain L.E. Oates, of the Inniskilling Dragoons, who marched with Scott to the South Pole. It was an ill-fated expedition. One disaster after another overtook the little party of men struggling over hundreds of miles of snow and ice in temperatures as low as minus 46, without machines or dogs to help them. Captain Oates was badly afflicted by frostbite; he could hardly hobble along, let alone pull his share of the weight of the sledge and stores. March 17, 1912 was his birthday and, in the evening, he quietly left his tent and walked out into the blizzard knowing that without him to hamper them, his companions had a better chance of survival. His sacrifice was unavailing but is none the less memorable for that. Today in the Antarctic wastes, now crossed and recrossed by scientists with all their latest modern equipment, there is still a cairn and a cross and a plaque which begins, 'Hereabouts died a very gallant gentleman . . .'

R.C. Macrobie

181

Kathy Miller swayed slightly at the lectern and there were long hesitations in the southern drawl.

But she kept her nerve under the harsh television lights and the heraldic devices and the stony gaze of the Duke of Wellington and forced the last words out in a rush.

'Most of all I'd like to thank the good Lord, you know, for keeping me alive. I'm here as his representative, I guess.'

In cold print it must look about the schmalziest paragraph we've printed since Mr Billy Graham came to save all our souls, but you wouldn't hold that, would you, against a fourteen-year-old girl addressing 500 people in the ancient Guildhall of London?

Nor, surely, against a child who exactly this time last year was as good as dead after being struck by a car in her home town of Scottsdale, Arizona?

If it was something short of classic oratory it remained a remarkable achievement by a girl who has still consciously to think each time she puts one foot after another or an adjective before a noun or a spoon towards her mouth.

After ten weeks in a deep coma last year she is still feeling her way slowly back into the world we take for granted, but not so slowly that yesterday it prevented her from receiving the International Award for Valour in Sport in succession to Niki Lauda.

There were more than 500 nominations, including many famous names in world sport, but Miss Miller won it on the flat earth of Arizona by getting out of hospital, running in a 10,000 metres and coming third out of seventy-five in a girls' marathon.

From time to time she lost her balance and fell. Once in training she spun over and broke her nose. She got up and ran on and yesterday, 6,000 miles from home, she negotiated the eight stairs to the right of the Guildhall's stage with great determination and received a gold laurel crown from Prince Michael of Kent.

Ian Wooldridge

182

Have plenty of courage. God is stronger than the devil. We are on the winning side.

John Chapman

183

Courage is almost a contradiction in terms. It means a stong desire to live taking the form of a readiness to die.

G.K. Chesterton

Creation

184

The first creature of God, in the works of the Days, was the light of the sense; the last was the light of reason; and his Sabbath work ever since is the illumination of his Spirit. First he breathed light upon the face of the matter, or chaos; then he breathed light into the face of man; and still he breatheth and inspireth light into the face of his chosen.

Francis Bacon

185

When God at first made man,
Having a glass of blessings standing by,
'Let us', said he, 'pour on him all we can;
Let the world's riches, which dispersed lie,
Contract into a span.'

So strength first made a way,
Then beauty flowed, then wisdom, honour, pleasure;
When almost all was out, God made a stay,
Perceiving that, alone of all his treasure,
Rest in the bottom lay.

'For if I should', said he,
'Bestow this jewel also on my creature,
He would adore my gifts instead of me,
And rest in Nature, not the God of Nature:
So both should losers be.

'Yet let him keep the rest,
But keep them with repining restlessness;
Let him be rich and weary, that at least,
If goodness lead him not, yet weariness
May toss him to my breast.'

George Herbert

(This beautiful and oft-quoted poem was written by the
saintly George Herbert (1593–1633) under the curious title
of 'The Pulley' – an allusion to man's need, at last, to be
drawn up to God.)

186

And I dream that these garden closes
    With their glades and their sun-flecked sod
And their lilies and bowers of roses
    Were laid by the hand of God.

The kiss of the sun for pardon,
The song of birds for mirth,
One is nearer God's heart in a garden
Than anywhere else on Earth.

Dorothy Frances Gurney

187

Trees are the oldest living things in time, brooding
witnesses of man and his queer ways – of the rise and fall of
empires, the birth, progress and decay of what we call
civilisation. There are two English oak trees in Norfolk, for

example, which were 700 years old when William the Conqueror landed at Pevensey.

The oldest tree in the world – probably the oldest living thing – is the mighty Cypress tree in Chapultepec, Mexico, which has a trunk 118 feet in circumference and is believed to be more than 6,000 years old.

John Clement

188

In a little church in the far South of Ireland, every window but one is of stained glass, representing Christ and his saints. Through the one window which is plain glass may be seen a breath-taking view: a lake of deepest blue, studded with green islets, and backed by range after range of purple hills. Under the window is the inscription: 'The heavens declare the glory of God, and the firmament showeth His handiwork.'

Robert Gibbings

189

A little girl who lived in a remote part of the country was receiving her first Bible instruction at the hands of her elderly grandmother, and the old lady was reading the child the story of the creation. After the story had been finished the little girl seemed lost in thought.

'Well, dear,' said the grandmother, 'what do you think of it?'

'Oh, I love it. It's so exciting,' exclaimed the youngster. 'You never know what God is going to do next!'

Anon.

Death

190

The Church is the only society on earth that never loses a
member through death! As a Christian I believe, not just in
life *after* death but in life *through* death. In the words of a
Russian Christian, 'The moment of death will be in the
inrush of timelessness.'

David Watson

191

For those who have put their trust in Christ now, death
means that we shall be perfectly with him, more alive than
ever, and free from pain, sickness, anxiety, depression and
sin. On the memorial of Martin Luther King are these
simple words:

Rev Martin Luther King Jr
1929 – 1968
'Free at last, free at last,
Thank God Almighty, I'm free at last.'

Anon.

192

For the Christian death interrupts nothing; it destroys
nothing; it liberates, not from the body, but from the
empire of sin.

Robert Gleason

193

The final entry in Scott of the Antarctic's diary:
'We are pegging out in a very comfortless spot. Hoping this
letter may be found and sent to you. I write you a word of
farewell. I want you to think well of me and my end. [After

some private instructions too intimate to read, he goes on]
Goodbye – I am not at all afraid of the end, but sad to miss
many a simple pleasure which I had planned for the future
in our long marches . . . We are in a desperate state – feet
frozen, etc., no fuel, and a long way from food, but it would
do your heart good to be in our tent, to hear our songs and
our cheery conversation . . . [Later – it is here that the
words become difficult] We are very near the end . . . We
did intend to finish ourselves when things proved like this,
but we have decided to die naturally without.'

I think it may uplift you all to stand for a moment by that
tent and listen, as he says, to their songs and cheery
conversation.

J.M. Barrie

194
Christ leads me through no darker rooms
    Than he went through before;
He that unto God's kingdom comes,
    Must enter by this door.

My knowledge of that life is small,
    The eye of faith is dim
But 'tis enough that Christ knows all,
    And I shall be with him.

Richard Baxter

195
Death does not take the old but the ripe.

Russian proverb

196
When a man dies he clutches in his hands only that which
he has given away in his lifetime.

Jean Jacques Rousseau

197

The practice of using flowers at funerals has its origin in antiquity; not only did they smell sweet to disguise the odour of the corpse but they were also regarded as protective against infection. When the plague was at its height, Dekker in *Wonderful Yeare*, 1603, records that rosemary, which could normally be bought at a price of twelve pence an armful, rose to six shillings a handful.
The traditional funeral emblematic flowers and trees are:
Oak – signifying virtue and majesty
Ivy – immortality
Passion flower – the crucifixion
White lily – futurity
Palm – martyrdom
Rosemary – remembrance
Cypress – symbol of life
Rosemary was regarded by ancient and classical authorities as the most highly esteemed among flowers because it was believed to retard putrefaction.

Don Lewis

198

Death is nothing at all
I have only slipped away into the next room.
I am I and you are you:
whatever we were to each other we are still.

Call me by my old familiar name.
Speak to me in the easy way which you always used.
Put no difference into your tone.
Wear no forced air of solemnity or sorrow.
Laugh as we always laughed at the little jokes we enjoyed
    together.
Play, smile, think of me, pray for me.

Let my name be the household word that it always was,

let it be spoken without effect,
without the ghost of a shadow on it.

Life means all that it ever meant.
It is the same as it ever was.
There is absolutely unbroken continuity.

What is death but a negligible accident?
Why should I be out of mind because I am out of sight?
I am but waiting for you,
for an interval,
somewhere very near,
just around the corner.

All is well.

Canon Scott Holland

199

I have seen death too often to believe in death.
It is not ending – but a withdrawal.
As one who finished a long journey,
Stills the motor,
Turns off the lights,
Steps from his car,
And walks up the path to the home that awaits him.

W. Blanding

200

Once you accept your own death, all of a sudden you're free
to live. You no longer care about your reputation, you no
longer care except so far as your life can be used for others.

Saul Alinsky

201

A rich and mighty Persian once walked in his garden with
one of his servants. The servant cried that he had just

encountered Death, who had threatened him. He begged
his master to give him his fastest horse so that he could
make haste and flee to Teheran, which he could reach that
same evening. The master consented and the servant
galloped off on the horse. On returning to his house the
master himself met Death, and questioned him, 'Why did
you terrify and threaten my servant?' 'I did not threaten
him; I only showed him surprise in still finding him here
when I planned to meet him tonight in Teheran,' said
Death.

Viktor Frankl

202

In different countries and societies, death is associated with
different colours. In the West, mourners traditionally wear
black. In China, white has always been acceptable because
it represents happiness and prosperity in the next world.
Gypsies used to wear red at funerals to symbolise physical
life and energy. Red was also the colour representing death
in the Celtic world and foretelling disaster. Moslems
believe that the souls of the just assume the form of white
birds. This idea spread to Europe in the Middle Ages, and
mourners in England wore white for centuries before black
became the fashion.

Anon.

203

There is an old story of a jester who sometimes made very
wise utterances, One day, the jester had said something so
foolish that the king, handing him a staff, said to him, 'Take
this, and keep it till you find a bigger fool than yourself.'

Some years later, the king was very ill, and lay on his
deathbed. His courtiers were called; his family and servants
also stood round his bedside. The king, addressing them,
said, 'I am about to leave you. I am going on a very long

journey, and I shall not return again to this place: so I have
called you all to say "Goodbye".' Then his jester stepped
forward and, addressing the king, said, 'Your Majesty, may
I ask a question? When you have journeyed abroad visiting
your people, staying with your nobles, or paying diplomatic
visits to other courts, your heralds and servants always
went before you, making preparations for you. May I ask
what preparations your Majesty has made for this long
journey that he is about to take?'

'Alas!' replied the king, 'I have made no preparations.'

'Then', said the jester, 'take this staff with you, for now I
have found a bigger fool than myself.'

Anon.

204

If I should never see the moon again
  Rising red gold across the harvest field,
Or feel the stinging of soft April rain,
  As the brown earth her hidden treasures yield.

If I should never taste the salt sea spray
  As the ship beats her course against the breeze,
Or smell the dog-rose and the new mown hay,
  Or moss and primroses beneath the tree.

If I should never hear the thrushes wake
  Long before sunrise in the glimmering dawn
Or watch the huge Atlantic rollers break
  Against the rugged cliffs in baffling scorn.

If I have said goodbye to stream and wood,
  To the wide ocean and the green clad hill,
I know that He who made this world so good
  Has somewhere made a heaven better still.

This I bear witness with my latest breath
Knowing the love of God, I fear not death.

(Lines found in the Bible of Major Malcolm Boyle, killed in
action after the landing on D-Day, June 1944.)

205

We understand death for the first time when he puts his
hand upon one whom we love.

Mme de Stael

206

The ageing but still active French comedian, Maurice
Chevalier, was asked how he felt about old age. 'I prefer it',
he said, 'to the alternative.'

K. Edwards

207

He was surprised to read the announcement of his death in
the morning paper, a confusion of similar names having
taken place. Ringing up his friend Brown, he enquired,
'Did you see the announcement of my death in the paper
this morning?' 'Yes,' was the unexpected answer, 'where
are you speaking from?'

Anon.

208

The goldfish died after living in a bowl that was in the
family lounge. The first time the baby-sitter came over after
the fish died she immediately noticed the empty bowl.
'Where's the fish?' she asked. Without hesitation, the
family's three-year-old shot back, 'Oh, he's swimming with
God.'

Anon.

Decision

209

There is an old legend which tells of a powerful genius who
promised a beautiful maiden a gift of rare value if she would

go through a field of corn and select the largest and ripest ear, and in doing so she was not to pause nor go backward nor wander hither and thither. The value of the gift was to be in proportion to the size and perfection of the ear. The maiden passed by many fine ears, but so anxious was she to get the largest and most perfect that she kept on without plucking any. Then the ears began to grow smaller and smaller, until finally they became so stunted that she was ashamed to pluck any, and not being allowed to go backward, she came out on the other side without any. For lack of decision she missed the very gift she coveted.

Tena F. Best

Depression

210

The devil asks only for sadness and melancholy, and as he is sad and melancholy himself, and will be so eternally, he wishes that every one should become like him.

Francis of Sales

211

When you find yourself overpowered as it were by melancholy, the best way is to go out, and do something kind to somebody or other.

John Keble

Determination

212

Few missionaries have caught the popular imagination more than Gladys Aylward who, but for her own determination, would never have got to China.

'You've been with us now for three months, I see, Miss Aylward?' he said.

'Yes, sir.'

'Theology, now . . .?'

'I wasn't very good at Theology, was I?' she said quietly.
He had looked up under his eyebrows. 'No, you weren't.
Not good at all . . . She knew she could never make him
understand. She knew she lacked the persuasiveness to
argue with him or the education to pass his examinations
. . .

'You see, Miss Aylward, all these scholastic short-
comings are important,' he said sympathetically, 'but most
important of all is your age. If you stayed at the China
Inland Mission Centre for another three years and then we
sent you out, you would be about thirty by the time you
arrived.' He had shaken his head doubtfully . . . 'You will
understand, I'm sure,' he continued, 'that there seems to be
little point in your continuing your studies here.'

Alan Burgess

Dignity – Human

213

I cannot bear the universal categorisation of human beings:
'bourgeois', 'bolshevist', 'capitalist', 'nigger', 'hippie', 'pig',
'imperialist'. The one so labelled may be reviled, imprisoned,
tortured, killed or exiled because he is no longer a human
being, but a symbol. He does not bleed when pricked; his
heart does not cry in the night. By this conjuring trick,
conscience is made to disappear. It is, perhaps, the
profoundest corruption of our time.

Eric Sevareid

214

My first visit to the Third World, changed me. You cannot
look into the eyes of a starving child and remain the same.

The first relief camp I was able to visit . . . was Quiha.

The camp was enormous and hundreds of women and children were sitting in groups trying to keep warm with only simple ragged shawls. Many people were just lying on the ground and I sought as a simple priest to give comfort to many who were obviously close to death.

By the next morning in this one camp 300 people had died. I still have a vision of a small boy in another centre who took my fingers and rubbed them against his face, and put his fingers in his mouth to show he was hungry. He had only a loin cloth around him. He would not let go of my hand. I thought this child is craving for food, craving for love. There in a very simple, uncluttered way, I realised once again the fundamental needs of human beings. They need food just to live, and they need love, to be valued.

Basil Hume

215
A whole bushel of wheat is made up of single grains.

Thomas Fuller

216
The morning came, but my servant appeared not. Doors were all open, the water was not drawn from the well, my servant had been out all night. My morning meal was not ready; my clothes were all lying unfolded.

As the hours passed by my anger grew, and I devised hard punishments for him. At last he came, late in the morning, and bowed low. I called out angrily: 'Go forth from my presence and never see my face again.'

He looked at me, and remained silent, and then said in a low, husky voice: 'My little daughter died last night.' And without another word he went to his daily task.

Rabindranath Tagore

217
Even one ear of corn is not exactly like another.

Talmud

218

Have you not heard how a bird from the sea
Was blown inshore and landed
Outside the capital of Lu?

The Prince ordered a solemn reception,
Offered the sea bird wine in the sacred precinct,
Called for musicians
To play the compositions of Shun,
Slaughtered cattle to nourish it:
Dazed with symphonies, the unhappy sea bird
Died of despair.

How should you treat a bird?
As yourself
Or as a bird?

Thomas Merton

219

The Sunday school teacher had ended her Bible story and
was asking questions of her primary tots. 'Why, do you
think, does God love us all so very much?' she asked. There
was a momentary silence as the children wrinkled their
little brows and 'thought hard' for the proper answer. 'Why
does God love us – so very much?'

Suddenly little Kristin's hand shot up. And without the
slightest doubt about the correctness of her answer she
blurted: 'Because he has only one of each of us.'

Only one of each of us!

Anon.

220

It is only people of small moral stature who have to stand
on their dignity.

Arnold Bennett

Discipleship

221

He comes to us as One unknown, without a name, as of old, by the lakeside, He came to those men who knew him not. He speaks to us the same word 'Follow thou me!' and sets us to the tasks which He has to fulfil for our time. He commands. And to those who obey him, whether they be wise or simple, He will reveal himself in the toils, the conflicts, the sufferings which they shall pass through in his fellowship, and as an ineffable mystery, they shall learn in their own experience who He is.

Albert Schweitzer

222

The world around us will recognise us as disciples of Jesus when they see our prayers being answered.

Colin Urquhart

223

There are two words used a great deal by Jesus in the Gospels. One is 'Come' and the other is 'Go'. It's no use coming unless you go, and it's no use going unless you come.

Anon.

224

Happy are they who know that discipleship simply means the life which springs from grace, and that grace simply means discipleship.

Dietrich Bonhoeffer

225

If we were willing to learn the meaning of real discipleship
and actually to become disciples, the Church in the West
would be transformed, and the resultant impact on society
would be staggering.

David Watson

Divine Providence

226

God's providence is not in baskets lowered from the sky,
but through the hands and hearts of those who love him.
The lad without food and without shoes made the proper
answer to the cruel-minded woman who asked, 'But if God
loved you, wouldn't he send you food and shoes?'
   The boy replied, 'God told someone, but he forgot.'

George Arthur Buttrick

227

In all created things discern the providence and wisdom of
God, and in all things give Him thanks.

Teresa of Avila

228

I saw a delicate flower had grown up two feet high, between
the horses' path and the wheel-track. An inch more to the
right or left had sealed its fate, or an inch higher; and yet it
lived to flourish as much as if it had a thousand acres of
untrodden space around it, and never knew the danger it
incurred. It did not borrow trouble, nor invite an evil fate
by apprehending it.

Henry David Thoreau

229

This life rests upon God's providence and on your faith, since he has promised to be your God and sustain you. Therefore you should not say: No matter what I do, I cannot hinder the will of God, so that because of my conduct less happens than God has determined. For this is the language of the devil and it is forever damned.

Martin Luther

230

Not God alone in the still calm we find;
He mounts the storm, and walks upon the wind.

Alexander Pope

231

Confide ye aye in Providence, for Providence is kind,
And bear ye a' life's changes wi' a calm and tranquil mind;
Tho' press'd and hemm'd on ev'ry side, ha'e faith and ye'll
    win through,
For ilka blade o' grass keps its ain drap o' dew.

James Ballantine

232

One evening when Luther saw a little bird perched on a tree, to roost there for the night, he said, 'This little bird has had its supper, and now it is getting ready to go to sleep here, quite secure and content, never troubling itself what its food will be, or where its lodging on the morrow. Like David, it "abides under the shadow of the Almighty". It sits on its little twig content, and lets God take care.'

Anon.

233

The story is told of the devout Irishman, who, when his

house was caught in a great flood, climbed for safety to the roof. Along came a rescue launch and offered to take him off. 'No thanks,' he said, 'I believe God will save me.' The rescuers on the launch could not persuade him and went away. The water rose and covered the roof and the Irishman climbed onto the chimney. A helicopter arrived and lowered a crewman. 'No thanks,' Paddy said, 'I believe God will save me.' He drowned. On arrival in heaven he met God and asked, 'Why didn't you save me?' 'I don't know what went wrong,' God replied. 'I sent a launch and a helicopter!'

Anon.

Doubt

234

When unhappy, one doubts everything, when happy, one doubts nothing.

Joseph Rowe

235

Seeing the immense design of the world, one image of wonder mirrored by another image of wonder – the pattern of fern and of feather echoed by the frost of the window-pane, the six rays of the snowflake mirrored by the rock crystal's six-rayed eternity – I ask myself, 'Were those shapes moulded by blindness? Who, then, shall teach me doubt?'

Edith Sitwell

236

General Sherman used to say that when he was at the front, on the firing-line, leading and directing his troops, he was always full of hope. He felt sure that the victory would be won. When he was at the rear, where the wounded were being brought back, where the stragglers and deserters were in evidence, he was filled with fear and depression.

If you really want to overcome your doubt and discouragement, if you want to 'greet the unseen with a cheer', always with a cheer, get into the fight against the evil in the world.

Anon.

237

If there is a lesson
In the history of religious experience
in modern times,
It is the quest for certainty
is self-defeating.

The more earnestly a man
seeks for certainty,
the more uncertain he becomes;
the more strenuously
he tries to remove all doubt
the more doubt he experiences.

John S. Dunne

238

It is when God appears to have abandoned us that we must abandon ourselves most wholly to God.

François Fénelon

239

A man went to stay with a friend in Cornwall, in a part where there were a large number of deep holes in the ground. These were disused mine-shafts, some of which had no rails round them. He went for a walk one day and got lost. Darkness came and he realised that he was near these holes and it was dangerous to walk in the dark. But it was too cold to sit down and wait till morning, so he walked on with great care. In spite of this, his feet slipped and he started to slide down a mine-shaft. He managed to grasp a rock that was sticking out of the side of the shaft. There he hung terrified, with his feet dangling. He managed to hang on for about twenty minutes, but the agony in his arms got so great that he knew he would soon have to let go and plunge to his death. He was about to let go when he saw, to his immense relief, a little light in the distance which began to grow greater and he knew that help was coming. He shouted loud with all the energy he had left. When the rescuers arrived and shone their light down on him the first thing they saw was that his feet were dangling within a foot of solid earth. This mine-shaft had been filled in! All his agony and fears had been for nothing.

M. Nassan

Dreams

240

Once upon a time in a forest, three young trees were growing side by side. As they grew, they shared with one another their dreams of what they would become when they grew to be big trees. The first tree said, 'My dream is to become part of a luxurious home where many famous people come and go and admire the grain and colour of my wood.'

The second tree said, 'My dream is to become the tall mast of an elegant sailing vessel that journeys to the seven seas.'

And the third said, 'My dream is to become part of a great tower, so high that it will inspire people who look at it. People will come from all over the world to see it.'

And so the young trees dreamed. Eventually the trees grew to maturity and were cut down The first didn't become a part of a luxurious home, as it had dreamed, but instead some of its wood was fashioned into a simple manger, a wooden trough to hold the hay that animals ate. The second tree didn't become the tall mast of an elegant ship, as it had dreamed, but instead it became the sides of an ordinary fishing boat like many others on the Sea of Galilee. The third didn't become part of a tall tower, as it had dreamed, but was fashioned into the beams of a cross and used for a crucifixion.

William Bausch

241

I seek Thee in my dreams,
And lo, Thy glory seems
To pass before me, as of old, the cloud
Descended in his sight, who heard
The music of Thy spoken word.
Then from my couch I spring, and cry aloud,
'Blest be the glory of Thy name, O Lord.'

Judah Halevi

Easter

242

The word Easter derives from *Eostre*, the pagan goddess of Spring, and to the Saxons, April was 'ostermonud' – the month of the ost-end wind (wind, that is, from the east) so that Easter became by association the April feast, which lasted eight days.

But Easter Sunday nowadays is the first Sunday after the first full moon following 21st March, and can therefore fall as early as 22nd March, or as late as 25th April. For many

years in earlier times, it was quite a popular belief that the
Sun danced on Easter day. Sir John Suckling (1609–1642)
wrote:

> But oh, she dances such a way,
> No sun upon an Easter day
> Is half so fine a sight.

We do not believe that any longer, but we still have an
affection for the 'Easter Egg'. The presentation of eggs at
Eastertime is a practice that goes back to Persian times,
when it was held that there were two contending forces.
The Jews, Egyptians and Hindus also clung to the idea and
made symbolic presentations of eggs to each other. In due
course, Christians adopted the custom, signifying by the
new life within the egg the resurrection of Christ. They also
coloured eggs they gave red, so as to represent to their
friends the Blood of the Redemption.

W. A. Dickins

243

The little white or violet-veined wood sorrel is sometimes
called 'Hallelujah' because it blooms about Easter, the time
of the singing of Alleluias.

Anon.

244

Rise, Heir of fresh Eternity,
From thy Virgin Tomb:
Rise mighty man of wonders, and thy world with thee
Thy Tomb, the universal East,
Nature's new womb,
Thy tomb, faire Immortalities perfumed Nest.

Of all the Glories make Noone gay
This is the Morn.

This rock buds forth the fountain of the streames of Day.
In joyes white Annals live this hour,
When life was borne,
No cloud scowl on his radiant lids no tempest lower.

Life, by this light's Nativity
All creatures have,
Death onely by this Day's just Doom is forc't to Die
Nor is Death forc't; for may he lie
Thron'd in thy Grave;
Death will on this condition be content to Die.

Richard Crashaw

245

The kindergarten-age child came home from Sunday school
Easter Sunday and told his mother he could understand
about Christ but not about the roses and asked his mother,
'Why was Christ a rose?'

Anon.

Elderly

246

There was once a very old man, whose eyes had become
dim, his ears dull of hearing, his knees trembled, and when
he sat at table he could hardly hold the spoon, and spilt the
broth upon the table-cloth or let it run out of his mouth. His
son and his son's wife were disgusted at this, so the old
grandfather at last had to sit in the corner behind the stove,
and they gave him his food in an earthenware bowl, and not
even enough of it. And he used to look towards the table
with his eyes full of tears. Once, too, his trembling hands
could not hold the bowl, and it fell to the ground and broke.
The young wife scolded him, but he said nothing and only
sighed. Then they bought him a wooden bowl for a few
half-pence out of which he had to eat.

They were once sitting thus when the little grandson of four years old began to gather together some bits of wood upon the ground. 'What are you doing there?' asked the father. 'I am making a little trough', answered the child, 'for father and mother to eat out of when I am big.' The man and his wife looked at each other for a while, and presently began to cry. Then they took the old grandfather to the table, and henceforth always let him eat with them, and likewise said nothing if he did spill a little of anything.

J.L.K. and W.K. Grimm

Emmanuel

247

In the house alongside the City Road chapel, made forever memorable by the preaching of John Wesley, they show you the room where Wesley died, on a March day in 1791. Some time before his death, he had been trying vainly to make those who stood by his bed understand what he would say. He kept silent for a few moments and then, gathering all his strength, uttered in a clear, loud voice those words which have become a watchword of the Church he founded, 'The best of all – God is with us.'

Clarence E. Macartney

248

It is unbelievable that men could take a word like 'Bethlehem', so glorious and beautiful, and make out of it a synonym for confusion and disorder. Yet this is what happened. St Mary of Bethlehem was founded as a hospital in England in 1247. Two centuries later it was turned into a hospital for the insane. The noise and confusion of that institution became known throughout the country. The original name, through contraction and corruption, was changed to Bedlam.

Anon.

249

One Christmas, Santa Claus brought me a toy engine. I took it with me to the convent, and played with it while mother and the nuns discussed old times. But it was a young nun who brought us in to see the crib. When I saw the Holy Child in the manger, I was distressed because little as I had, he had nothing at all. For me it was fresh proof of the incompetence of Santa Claus. I asked the young nun politely if the Holy Child didn't like toys, and she replied composedly enough, 'Oh, he does but his mother is too poor to afford them.' That settled it. My mother was poor too, but at Christmas she at least managed to buy me something even if it was only a box of crayons. I distinctly remember getting into the crib and putting the engine between his outstretched arms. I probably showed him how to wind it as well, because a small baby like that would not be clever enough to know. I remember too the tearful feeling of reckless generosity with which I left him there in the nightly darkness of the chapel, clutching my toy engine to his chest.

Frank O'Connor

250

Dialogue from a church nativity play, written, directed and acted by a class of nine-year-olds, opens with the scene at the inn. Joseph and Mary ask for a room overlooking Bethlehem.

Innkeeper: Can't you see the 'No Vacancy' sign?

Joseph: Yes, but can't you see that my wife is expecting a baby any minute?

Innkeeper: Well, that's not my fault.

Joseph: Well it's not mine either!

Anon.

251

A Nativity play was to be performed in the church hall and a country vicar went to town to get a streamer for display. Unfortunately, he forgot the measurements so he wired his wife for details. The telegraph clerk at the other end nearly had a fit when the reply message was received. It read: 'Unto us a Child is Born – seven feet six by one foot three.'

Anon.

Enemies

252

A certain king, after conquering his enemies, took them into his favour and had them about his court. His courtiers remonstrated with him, saying that he should have destroyed them. 'But I destroy my enemies in the most effective way of all', he answered, 'when I make them my friends.'

Anon.

253

I owe much to my friends, but all things considered, it strikes me that I owe even more to my enemies. The real person springs to life under a sling, even better than under a caress.

André Gide

254

In 1941, Mama took me back to Moscow. There I saw our enemy for the first time. If my memory is right, nearly 20,000 German war prisoners were to be marched in a single column through the streets of Moscow. The pavements swarmed with onlookers, cordoned off by soldiers and police. The crowd were mostly women. Russian women with hands roughened by hard work, lips untouched by lipstick and thin hunched shoulders which had borne half the burden of the war. Every one of them must have had a father or a husband or a brother or a son killed by the Germans.

They gazed with hatred in the direction from which the column was to appear. At last we saw it.

The generals marched at the head, massive chins stuck out, lips folded disdainfully, their whole demeanour meant to show superiority over their plebeian victors . . .

The women were clenching their fists. The soldiers and policemen had all they could do to hold them back.

All at once something happened to them.

They saw German soldiers, thin, unshaven, wearing dirty, bloodstained bandages, hobbling on crutches or leaning on the shoulders of their comrades; the soldiers walked with their heads down.

The street became dead silent – the only sound was the shuffling of boots and the thumping of crutches.

Then I saw an elderly woman in broken-down boots push herself forward and touch a policeman's shoulder, saying: 'Let me through.' There must have been something about her that made him step aside.

She went up to the column, took from inside her coat something wrapped in a coloured handkerchief and unfolded it. It was a crust of black bread. She pushed it awkwardly into the pocket of a soldier, so exhausted that he was tottering on his feet. And now suddenly from every side women were running towards the soldiers, pushing into their hands bread, cigarettes, whatever they had.

The soldiers were no longer enemies They were people.

Yevgeny Yevtushenko

255
There is so much good in the worst of us,
And so much bad in the best of us,
That it ill behoves any of us,
To find fault with the rest of us.

Anon.

256
A British soldier wrote to a German mother: 'As a member
of a Commando unit raiding a village in France, it became
my duty to kill your son ... I earnestly ask for your
forgiveness, for I am a Christian ... I hope I may, some
day after the war is over, talk with you face to face.'

This German mother received the note several months
later, and she wrote to the English soldier in turn: 'I find it
in my heart to forgive you, even you who killed my son; for
I too am a Christian ... If we are living after the war is
over I hope you will come to Germany to visit me, that you
may take the place in my home, if only for a time, of my son
whom you killed.'

Edwin A. Goldsworthy

257
Love your enemies, for they tell you your faults.

Benjamin Franklin

Equality
258
He who treats as equal those who are far below him in
strength really makes them a gift of the quality of human
beings, of which fate has deprived them.

Simone Weil

259

The Lord so constituted everybody that no matter what colour you are, you require the same amount of nourishment.

Will Rogers

260

I have a dream that one day this nation will rise up and live out the true meaning of its creed: 'We hold these truths to be self-evident; that all men were created equal.'. . .

I have a dream that one day every valley shall be exalted, every hill and mountain shall be made low, the rough places will be made plain, and the crooked places will be made straight and the glory of the Lord shall be revealed and all flesh shall see it together. This is our hope. This is the faith that I go back to the South with. With this faith, we will be able to hew out of the mountain of despair a stone of hope. With this faith, we will be able to transform the jangling discords of our nation into a beautiful symphony of brotherhood. With this faith we will be able to work together, to pray together, to struggle together, to go to jail together, knowing that we will be free one day.

Martin Luther King

261

'Can you find no other way?' asks Sir Arthur Wardour of the beggar when the two men were cut off by the tide. I'll give you a farm . . . I'll make you rich.' 'Our riches will soon be equal,' says the beggar, and looks out across the advancing sea.

Sir Walter Scott

262

The two farm hands were having an argument and Garge, who had 'discovered' the amazing new principle that all

Example   95

men were equals, was having great difficulty in making
Willum understand the principles of his new found creed.
'It's share and share alike,' he said. 'If you've got
something someone else hasn't, then you give them half.'
Willum seemed to be getting the general drift of it. 'I see,'
he said. 'You mean that if you had a thousand pounds and
I hadn't you give I half?' Garge nodded. 'That's the ticket,'
he said. Said Willum, 'And if you had two moty cars, then
you'd give I one?' Again Garge nodded. Said Willum, 'And
if you had a pig and I hadn't, then you'd give I half?' Garge
thought that one out quickly. Then he said, 'No ruddy fear
– I've *got* a pig.'

Anon.

263

One night a Negro was walking along Forty-Second Street
in New York, from the railway to the hotel, carrying a
heavy suitcase and a heavier valise. Suddenly a hand took
hold of the valise and a pleasant voice said: 'Pretty heavy,
brother! Suppose you let me take one. I'm going your way.'
The Negro resisted but finally allowed the young white
man to assist him in carrying his burden, and for several
blocks they walked along, chatting together like cronies.
'And that', said Booker T. Washington, years afterwards,
'was the first time I ever saw Theodore Roosevelt.'

'Onward'

Example

264

Men will not attend to what we say, but examine into what
we do; and will say, 'Do you first obey your own words, and
then exhort others.' This is the great battle, this is the
unanswerable demonstration, which is made by our acts.

John Chrysostom

265

Example is not the main thing in influencing others – it is the only thing.

Albert Schweitzer

266

I knew a miller who went from his work, his clothes covered with flour, to the post office, and edged his way through the crowd. He left his mark on every one he touched. As Christians we should leave a mark for Christ on every one with whom we come in contact.

H. B. Gibbard

267

There is not enough darkness in all the world to put out the light of one small candle.

Anon.

268

A group of women teachers from a Christian school had fled to an outlying village in another part of Burma, when their town was invaded. It was during the disastrous days of our retreat. Stragglers from our forces came staggering in, British lads, with blistered feet and torn clothing. Famished, parched and sleepless, they were done. These women, both Burmese and Karen, took them in . . . There were some in the neighbourhood ready to inform against the women. Armed men surrounded the house. 'You have been helping the enemy,' they said. 'You shall die.' Then they said, 'If we must die, give us a moment to get ready.' The company of them knelt in prayer, and were cut to pieces. One of them was a girl of seventeen. When the Japanese were gone, and the Bishop held his first confir-

Example 97

mation, he recognised a Burmese who had been a prominent anti-Christian leader.

'My friend,' said the Bishop, 'how did you come to be baptised?'

'It was the way those girls in that village died two years ago,' he said. 'I knew they had something which I had not.'

John Foster

269

A holy life will produce the deepest impression. Lighthouses blow no horns; they only shine.

D.L. Moody

270

An American teacher was employed in Japan on the understanding that during school hours he should not utter a word on the subject of Christianity. The engagement was faithfully kept, and he lived before his students the Christian life, but never spoke of it to them. Not a word was said to influence the young men committed to his care. But so beautiful was his character, and so blameless his example, that forty of the students, unknown to him, met in a grove and signed a secret covenant to abandon idolatry. Twenty-five of them entered the Kyoto Christian Training School, and some of them are now preaching the Gospel which their teacher had unconsciously commended.

Anon.

271

There are two ways of spreading light; to be a candle, or the mirror that reflects it.

Edith Wharton

272

The tree is made manifest by its fruit; so they who profess themselves to be Christians are known by what they do. For Christianity is not the work of an outward profession, but shows itself in the power of faith, if a man be found faithful unto the end. It is better for a man to hold his peace, and be, than to say he is a Christian and not to be.

Ignatius of Antioch

273

In the nursery the children were shouting and making a din. Mother went in and asked what they were quarrelling about. 'We're not quarrelling,' said the eldest, 'we're just playing Mummy and Daddy.'

Anon.

Failure

274

If there is any single factor that makes for success in living, it is the ability to draw dividends from defeat. Every success I know has been reached because the person was able to analyse defeat and actually profit by it in his next undertaking . . .

Defeats are nothing to be ashamed of. They are routine incidents in the life of every man who achieves. But defeat is a dead loss unless you face it without humiliation, analyse it and learn why you failed to make your objective . . .

If you exploit the power which defeat gives, you can accomplish with it far more than you are capable of when all is serene.

William Moulton Marston

275

Failure doesn't mean you are a failure;
It *does* mean you haven't yet succeeded.
Failure doesn't mean you have accomplished nothing;
It *does* mean you have learned something.
Failure doesn't mean that you have been a fool;
It *does* mean you have a lot of faith.
Failure doesn't mean you have been disgraced;
It *does* mean you were willing to try.
Failure doesn't mean you don't have it;
It *does* mean you have to do something in a different way.
Failure doesn't mean you are inferior;
It *does* mean you are not perfect.
Failure doesn't mean you've wasted your life;
It *does* mean you have a reason to start afresh.
Failure doesn't mean you should give up;
It *does* mean you must try harder.
Failure doesn't mean you will never make it;
It *does* mean it will take a little longer.
Failure doesn't mean God has abandoned you;
It *does* mean God has a better way.

Anon.

Faith

276

Bruce Larson tells a story in his book *Edge of Adventure*. It's
about a letter found in a baking-powder tin wired to the
handle of an old pump, which offered the only hope of
drinking water on a very long and seldom-used trail across
the Amargosa Desert in the USA; the letter read as follows:

This pump is alright as of June 1932. I put the new leather
sucker washer into it, and it ought to last several years. But
this leather washer dries out and the pump has got to be

primed. Under the white rock, I buried a bottle of water.
There's enough water in it to prime the pump, but not if
you drink some first. Pour in about one quarter, and let her
soak to wet the leather. Then pour in the rest, medium fast
and pump like crazy. You'll get water. The well has never
run dry. Have faith. When you get watered up, fill the
bottle and put it back like you found it for the next feller.
(Signed) Desert Pete.
P.S. Don't go drinking up the water first. Prime the pump
with it first, and you'll get all you can hold.

277

All I have seen teaches me to trust the Creator for all I have
not seen.

Ralph Waldo Emerson

278

If a man believes and knows God, he can no longer ask,
'What is the meaning of my life?' But by believing he
actually lives the meaning of his life.

Karl Barth

279

Was it Archimedes who said, 'Give me a lever long enough
and a place to put it on, and I will move the world'? There
is such a lever, and it is called 'Faith'; there is a place to put
it on, and it is called 'God'; and there is a power that can
swing that lever, and it is called 'man'.

Richard M. Steiner

280

One of the few famous and enduring slogans from World
War II was coined by an Army Chaplain in the Philippines,
namely: 'There are no atheists in foxholes.'

Anon.

281

There is no love without hope, no hope without love, and neither hope nor love without faith.

Augustine of Hippo

282

I do not want merely to possess a faith, I want a faith that possesses me.

Charles Kingsley

283

A vicar ran out of petrol, but the filling station was only 100 yards away. He hadn't an empty can, so he used the baby's potty that was in his car, to put the petrol in. As he was pouring it into the tank, one of his parishioners passed by. 'Heavens, Vicar,' he said, 'you've more faith than I have!'

Anon.

284

Ultimately, faith is the only key to the universe. The final meaning of human existence, and the answers to the questions on which all our happiness depends cannot be found in any other way.

Thomas Merton

Faithfulness

285

In sepulchral effigies of early times the dog is frequently introduced lying at the feet of married women. In such cases it represents fidelity – the faithful watcher and defender of the home, quick to warn of the approach of danger, ready to defend to the death the friend who is attacked. It is this same suggestion of fidelity which led Greek artists to paint a dog chained to the outside post of houses, and place over them – as in the well-known picture at Pompeii – the motto '*Cave-Canem*' ('Beware the dog'). One of the most touching incidents in ancient history is the joy of the old dog Argus, who expires at the feet of his master, Ulysses, when he returns after an absence of twenty years.

Anon.

286

Polycarp lived to be eighty-six, and the story of his martyrdom at that great age illustrates his Christian fortitude and calmness. He was Bishop of Smyrna, and was therefore by far the most prominent of the Christians in that city. From time to time, if the weather spoiled the harvests, or if floods damaged the towns, or if the Roman army suffered defeat, a cry would be raised that the disaster was sent by the gods who were angry because Christians were allowed to live. Then a furious mob would attack the Christians, and the Roman governors, instead of forbidding the outrage, would regulate and guide it, so that hundreds of Christians would be cruelly put to death.

One of these periodical outbursts took place in Smyrna in AD 155. Knowing that their beloved Bishop would be marked out for attack, the Christians urged him to leave the city. He did so, much against his will, but one of his attendants was tortured by the pagans until he disclosed his master's hiding place. When soldiers arrived to arrest him, Polycarp welcomed them, ordered refreshments to be provided for them, and only asked that he might be allowed time for prayer before they took him away.

Polycarp was then conducted to the race-course, where a vast crowd had assembled to watch the Christians die. He must have been well known, at least by sight, to many of

them, for as soon as he appeared a shout like a clap of
thunder burst from the mob demanding that Polycarp
should die.

The Governor of the city pitied and admired the old
man, and urged him to save himself; giving a condition:

'Only say that the Emperor is God, and I will set you
free.'

Polycarp refused.

'Then', pleaded the Governor, 'say one word to show
that you will give up Christ, and your life shall be spared.'

The old man shook his head. 'Eighty and six years', he
replied, 'I have served Christ, and He hath done me no
wrong. How, then, can I speak evil of my King who saved
me?'

Finding that no persuasions would change the Bishop's
mind, the Governor gave orders that he should be burnt.

So ended one of the noblest lives in the history of the
Church.

Maud Higham

Family

287

A humble Methodist itinerant minister was often discouraged. The work was hard. The compensation meagre. How
many times he was tempted to give it up! Three daughters
grew up to young womanhood in that home. In course of
time all three were married. One became the mother of a
celebrated artist; one was the mother of Stanley Baldwin,
Prime Minister; the other was the mother of Rudyard
Kipling.

Anon.

288

Where does the family start? It starts with a young man falling in love with a girl – no superior alternative has yet been found.

Winston Churchill

289

Few are born to do the great work of the world, but the work that all can do is to make a small home circle brighter and better.

George Eliot

290

Once a little boy of five was left alone with his father at bedtime. It had never happened before. After some manoeuvring and a lot of fun, the father finally got the little fellow into his night clothes, and was about to lift him into bed when the child said, 'But daddy, I have to say my prayers.' He knelt down beside his bed, joined his hands, raised his eyes to heaven and prayed: 'Now I lay me down to sleep, I pray the Lord my soul to keep; if I should die before I wake, I pray the Lord my soul to take.' That was his usual prayer, but tonight he looked up at his dad, then raised his eyes to heaven and prayed, 'Dear God, make me a great big good man, like my daddy, Amen.' In a moment he was in bed and in five minutes asleep. And then the father knelt by his son's bedside and prayed, 'Dear Lord, make me a great big good man like my boy thinks I am.'

P. Fontaine

291

Children are very adept at comprehending modern statistics. When they say, 'Everyone else is allowed,' it is usually based on a survey of one.

Paul Sweeney

292

A woman got on a bus with seven children. The conductor asked 'Are these all yours, lady, or is it a picnic?'

'They're all mine,' came the reply, 'and it's no picnic.'

Anon.

293

Dad volunteered to babysit one night so Mum could have an evening out. At bedtime he sent the youngsters upstairs to bed and settled down to look at the newspapers. One child kept creeping down the stairs, but Dad kept sending him back. At 9 p.m. the doorbell rang, it was the next-door neighbour, Mrs Smith, asking whether her son was there. The father brusquely replied, 'No!' Just then a little head appeared over the bannister and a voice shouted, 'I'm here, Mum, but he won't let me go home!'

Anon.

Family of God

294

Tolstoy tells the story of a man who stopped to give alms to a beggar. To his dismay he found that he had left his money at home. Stammering his explanation, he said, 'I am sorry, brother, but I have nothing.' 'Never mind, brother,' was the beggar's answer, 'that too was a gift.' The one word 'brother' meant more to him than money.

John Schmidt

295

The word *Church* used in most of the Northern European languages comes from the Greek *kyriake oikia*, 'the family of the Lord'.

Leonard Doohan

296
To the Unknown Many

I raise no glass to the man whose fame
   Has spread from coast to coast,
Whose talents have served to place his name
   With those men honour most.

My toast is not for the lady fair,
   Whose grace and charming ways
Have set men marvelling everywhere
   And won her kindly praise.

I raise no glass to the hero who
   Has won deserved applause,
Who has done as the brave alone may do
   In a daring, righteous cause.

I drink no health to the one whose voice
   Mankind shall ne'er forget,
Whose genius has made the world rejoice
   And left it in her debt.

I raise my glass to the silent horde
   Spread o'er the world's expanse,
The unknown many who might have soared
   But never had a chance.

Anon.

297

The Grand Rabbi of Lyons was a Jewish Chaplain to the
French forces in the 1914–1918 war. One day, a wounded
man staggered into a trench and told the Rabbi that a
Roman Catholic was on the point of death in no-man's-
land, and was begging that his padre should come to him
with a crucifix. The padre could not be quickly found. The
Jew rapidly improvised a cross, ran out with it into no-
man's-land and was seen to hold it before the dying man's

eyes. He was almost immediately shot by a sniper; the
bodies of the Catholic and the Jew were found together.

Victor Gollancz

Fatherhood of God

298

Father in Heaven, when the thought of Thee wakes in our
hearts, let it not awaken like a frightened bird that flies
about in dismay, but like a child waking from its sleep with
a heavenly smile.

Sören Kierkegaard

299

Have you ever realised that the words 'I', 'my' and 'me' do
not occur once in the Lord's Prayer?

Yet while saying 'Our Father', it is easy to mean only
'my Father'; to utter the words 'give us this day our daily
bread' and still think only in terms of 'give me my daily
bread'.

These lines of Charles Thompson may help you avoid the
tendency to be self-centred while praying:

> You cannot pray the Lord's Prayer,
>   And even once say 'I',
> You cannot pray the Lord's Prayer,
>   And even once say 'my'.
> Nor can you pray the Lord's Prayer,
>   And not pray for another;
> For when you ask for daily bread,
>   You must include your brother.
> For others are included
>   In each and every plea:
> From the beginning to the end of it,
>   It does not once say 'me'.

Anon.

300

The daughter of Karl Marx once confessed to a friend that she had never been brought up in any religion and had never been religious. 'But', she said, 'the other day I came across a beautiful little prayer which I very much wish could be true.' 'And what was the prayer?' she was asked. Slowly the daughter of Karl Marx began repeating in German, 'Our Father, which art in heaven . . .'

Robert Latham

301

The Father is our fount and origin, in whom our life and being is begun.

John of Ruysbroeck

302

When we pray to God, says Cyprian, with entire assurance, it is Himself who has given us the spirit of our prayer. Then it is the Father listening to the words of his child; it is He who dwells in the depths of our hearts, teaching us how to pray.

François Fénelon

303

It was well past midnight. Little four-year-old Tommy had been asleep for hours. Suddenly he awoke from a bad dream. Not knowing whether he was alone in the large, dark bedroom, he whispered into the darkness: 'Daddy, are you there?'

From the other side of the room came the comforting voice: 'Yes, Tommy, Daddy's here.' For a moment Tommy lay silent, still not quite sure his bad dream was imagined. Once more he whispered: 'Daddy, is your face towards me?' And once more the kind voice of his father assured

him: 'Yes, Tommy, my face is towards your bed.' With that
assurance the little fellow turned over, closed his eyes, and
drifted back to peaceful slumber.

Anon.

304

Cyril was a young man who became a Christian at
Caesarea in Cappadocia, in the third century. His rich
pagan father reviled him, beat him, and at last turned him
out of the house; but nothing could quench the joy in his
heart, and he won many other boys to a Christian life also.

Soon he was brought before the tribunal as a Christian.
Threats failed to move him. Then the magistrate offered to
release him if he would return to his home and inheritance.
'Leaving home did not trouble me,' he answered, 'There is
a real home waiting for me, much grander and more
beautiful, where my Father in heaven lives.'

They took him to the fire as if for execution, then back to
the tribunal. 'Why don't you get on with it?' he asked. As
nothing could shake his firmness, he was led forth again to
die. Some Christians around were weeping, but Cyril said:
'You ought to be a joyful escort for me. Evidently you do
not know the City where I am going to live!' He watched
the fire being kindled, and died in it brave to the last, with
his mind fixed on his heavenly home.

F.H. Drinkwater

305

Bishop Brooks taught me no special creed or dogma; but he
impressed upon my mind two great ideas – the fatherhood
of God and the brotherhood of man – and made me feel that
these truths underlie all creeds and forms of worship. God
is love, God is our father, we are his children; therefore the
darkest clouds will break, and though right be worsted,
wrong shall not triumph.

Helen Keller

306

Our Heavenly Father never takes anything from his children unless He means to give them something better.

George Mueller

307

John Chrysostom, summoned before the Roman Emperor Arcadius, and threatened with banishment, is said to have replied: 'Thou can'st not banish me, for the world is my Father's house.'

'Then I will slay thee,' exclaimed the Emperor wrathfully.

'Nay, but thou can'st not, for my life is hid with Christ in God.'

'Your treasures shall be confiscated,' was the grim reply.

'Sire, that cannot be. My treasures are in heaven, as my heart is there.'

'But I will drive thee from men and thou shalt have no friends left.'

'That you cannot do either, sire, for I have a Friend in heaven Who has said, "I will never leave thee nor forsake thee." '

Anon.

308

In the timber mountains of the Northwest of the USA a five-year-old boy was lost. Night came. The citizens and rangers searched frantically every cave and mountainside. Snow began to fall. Blanket upon blanket covered the forest floor, but no Bobby could be found. The next morning the father, fatigued from an all-night search, kicked against what seemed to be a log in the path, but when the snow fell loose, a small boy sat up, stretched, yawned, and exclaimed: 'Oh Daddy! I've found you at last!'

Anon.

Fear

309

Fear imprisons, faith liberates; fear paralyzes, faith empowers; fear disheartens, faith encourages; fear sickens, faith heals; fear makes useless, faith makes serviceable – and, most of all, fear puts hopelessness at the heart of life, while faith rejoices in its God.

Harry Emerson Fosdick

310

If you fear God, cast yourself into his arms and then his hands cannot strike you.

Augustine of Hippo

311

Let then our first act
every morning be to
make the following resolve for the day:
I shall not fear anyone on earth.
I shall fear only God.
I shall not bear ill-will toward anyone.
I shall not submit to injustice from anyone.
I shall conquer untruth by truth.
And in resisting untruth I shall put up with all suffering.

Mahatma Gandhi

312

Being afraid of God is different from fearing God. The fear of God is a fruit of love, but being afraid of Him is the seed of hatred. Therefore, we should not be afraid of God but should fear Him so that we do not hate Him whom we should love.

Martin Luther

313

When two years ago I spoke at the funeral of a sixteen-year-old girl who died in our dale, I said that God was to be found in the cancer as much as in the sunset. That I firmly believed, but it was an intellectual statement. Now I have had to ask if I can say it of myself, which is a much greater test.

When I said it from the pulpit, I gather it produced quite a shock wave. I guess this was for two reasons. First I had mentioned the word openly in public and even among Christians it is (or was: much has happened in a short time since) the great unmentionable. 'Humankind', said Eliot, 'cannot bear very much reality.' It is difficult for me to comprehend that there are people who just do not want to know whether they have got cancer. But above all, there is a conspiracy of silence ostensibly to protect others. We think they cannot face it, though in my experience they usually know deep down; and obviously how they can face other realities and above all how they are told and who tells them (and of course whether they really need to know) is critical.

But what we are much more likely to be doing is mutually protecting ourselves – and also that goes often (though less and less) for doctors. For we dare not face it ourselves or talk about it at the levels of reality that it might open up.

But Christians above all are those who should be able to bear reality and show others how to bear it. Or what are they to say about the cross, the central reality of our faith?

John H. Robinson

Feeding the Hungry

314

Your poverty is greater than ours ... the spiritual poverty of the West is much greater than the physical poverty of the

East. In the West, there are millions of people who suffer
loneliness and emptiness, who feel unloved and unwanted.
They are not the hungry in the physical sense; what is
missing is a relationship with God and each other.

Mother Teresa

315

The road to Jericho today, the road to the Good Samaritan,
runs through every under-developed country.

Michel Quoist

316

If you give a man a fish, he will eat once.
If you teach a man to fish, he will eat for the rest of his life.
If you are thinking a year ahead, sow seed.
If you are thinking ten years ahead, plant a tree.
If you are thinking one hundred years ahead, educate the
   people.
By sowing seed, you will harvest once.
By planting a tree, you will harvest tenfold.
By educating the people you will harvest one hundredfold.

Kuantzu

317

It is the easiest thing in the world to buy a slave child. To
prove the point I bought one in Colombo last month. He is
Raju, aged eight, from Nawalapittiya, near Kandy.
   The sale was conducted among mounds of onions,
chillies and coconuts in Colombo's crowded Wellawatta
junction. Raju, wearing only a tattered sarong, was getting
what food he could from a half-eaten coconut which he had
found on the road. Raju's mother, looking incredibly worn
out, was standing by, waiting to be paid. I asked her why
she did it. The staccato answer had a familiar ring: 'Dry

season. Very little work. No food for many days. Now we buy some. At least this one' (shot a glance at Raju) 'will not starve.'

Anthony Mascarenhas

318

During a persistent famine in 980, Ethelwold, Bishop of Winchester, sold the gold and silver vessels of his cathedral church in order to relieve the poor; saying, 'There is no reason that the senseless temples of God should abound in riches, and the living temples of the Holy Spirit starve.'

Anon.

319

Victor Hugo, in *Ninety-Three*, tells the story of a French mother who, after the Revolution, had been driven from her home with her two children. She had wandered through the woods and fields for several days; she and her two children had lived on roots and leaves. On the third morning they had hidden in some bushes on the approach of two soldiers, a captain and a sergeant. The captain ordered the sergeant to find out what was stirring the bushes; he prodded the mother and her two children out. They were brought to the captain's side, and he saw in an instant that they were starving; he gave them a long loaf of brown French bread. The mother took it eagerly, like a famished animal, broke it into two pieces giving one piece to one child and the other to the second child. The sergeant looked up to the captain and said, 'Is it because the mother is not hungry?' The captain replied, 'No, sergeant, it is because she is a mother!'

Homiletic Review

320

A little Japanese boy called at the house of a retired

gentleman and offered some picture postcards for sale at 10p each.

'What are you going to do with the money?' he asked him.

'I am raising one million pounds for the earthquake relief,' he answered, gravely, and he was so tiny and the sum he named was so large that the gentleman had to laugh.

'One million pounds?' he cried. 'Do you expect to raise it all by yourself?'

'No, sir,' he replied gravely 'There's another little boy helping me.'

Anon.

Forgiveness

321

During the times of persecution in the early Church, Sulpicius, a presbyter of Antioch, was arrested and brought before the Imperial Legate, who asked him, 'Of what family art thou?'

'I am a Christian.'

'Know that all who call themselves Christians will be put to the torture unless they sacrifice to the immortal gods.'

'We Christians', answered Sulpicius, 'have for our King Christ, who is also God.'

He was then tortured and led away to be beheaded. As he was on his way to execution a Christian called Nicephorus rushed forward and fell at his feet. Between him and Sulpicius there had been a bitter quarrel, and Nicephorus felt that he must win his forgiveness while there was yet time.

'Martyr of Christ,' he cried, 'forgive me for I have wronged thee.'

Sulpicius did not reply, and even at the place of

execution maintained the same silence. Then followed a scene which struck the beholders with astonishment and the Christians with awe.

Sulpicius, who had not flinched under torture, was seen to be growing paler as he was told to kneel down under the sword of the executioner.

'Do not strike me,' he cried. 'I will obey the Emperor, I *will* sacrifice to the gods.'

Once more Nicephorus rushed forward, but this time it was to implore Sulpicius not to forfeit the martyr's crown which he had well-nigh won, but it was in vain.

'Then', said Nicephorus, 'tell the Legate I will take his place, I am a Christian,' and he was forthwith taken at his words.

The fall of Sulpicius was quoted by the early Church to show that the sacrifice of life itself is not accepted on high when offered by those who have not learnt from their Saviour to pardon injuries.

Anon.

322

The man who is truly forgiven and knows it, is a man who forgives.

Martyn Lloyd-Jones

323

Almost hidden in a secluded corner of a New York cemetery is a small gravestone polished smooth by the wind and weather of many years. The stone bears no name, nor is there any date inscribed on it. Still legible on the face of the stone, however, in letters that neither wind nor weather have been able to erase, is one solitary word, 'forgiven'. No monument, no obelisk, no vaulted mausoleum marks the final resting place of the anonymous person who lies buried there – only a simple stone – and the single word 'forgiven'.

O man, forgive thy mortal foe,
Nor ever strike him blow for blow;
For all the souls on earth that live,
To be forgiven must forgive;
Forgive him seventy times and seven,
For all the blessed souls in heaven
Are both forgivers and forgiven.

Anon.

324

'I can forgive, but I cannot forget' is only another way of saying 'I cannot forgive.'

Henry Ward Beecher

325

A minister tells the story of a clergyman who was given a flowery introduction before a speech. When he stood up to present his address, he said, 'May the Lord forgive this man for his excesses, and me for enjoying them so much.'

Alice Murray

326

Only one petition in the Lord's Prayer has any condition attached to it; it is the petition for forgiveness.

William Temple

327

Humanity is never so beautiful as when praying for forgiveness or else forgiving another.

Jean Paul Richter

Freedom

328

In Budapest a man went to the police station to ask for permission to emigrate to Western Europe.

'Aren't you happy here?' the police asked.

'I have no complaints,' said the Hungarian.

'Are you dissatisfied with your work?'

'I have no complaints.'

'Are you discontented with the living conditions?'

'I have no complaints.'

'Then why do you want to go to the West?'

'Because there I can have complaints,' explained the man.

'Times', Hong Kong

329

God forces no one, for love cannot compel, and God's service, therefore, is a thing of perfect freedom.

Hans Denk

330

During the early days of the nineteenth century a wealthy plantation owner was attracted by the heartbreaking sobs of a slave girl who was about to step up to the auction block to be sold. Moved by a momentary impulse of compassion, he bought her at a very high price and then disappeared into the crowd.

When the auction was over, the clerk came to the sobbing girl and handed her her bill of sale. To her astonishment, the unknown plantation owner had written 'Free' over the paper that should have delivered her to him as his possession. She stood speechless, as one by one the other slaves were claimed by their owners and dragged

away. Suddenly, she threw herself at the feet of the clerk
and exclaimed: 'Where is the man who bought me? I must
find him! He has set me free! I must serve him as long as I
live!'

Anon.

331

A Christian man is the most free lord of all, and subject to
none; a Christian man is the most dutiful servant of all, and
subject to everyone.

Martin Luther

332

Spirit is man's whole creative act. Spirit is freedom and
freedom has its roots in the depths of pre-existential being.

Nikolai Berdyaev

333

There are two freedoms – the false, where a man is free to
do what he likes; the true, where a man is free to do what he
ought.

Charles Kingsley

334

Harriet Tubman, who became known as the Moses of her
people, was born in 1820 on a plantation in Bucktown,
Maryland in the USA. While still a girl, she, like many
black Americans in those days, was hired out to do
housework. Later she became a field hand. In her teens,
Harriet was struck on the head by an overseer as she tried
to help a fellow slave escape. For the rest of her life she
suffered blackouts from this blow.

In 1849, fearing that she would be sold further south,

Harriet escaped from slavery. With the help of the Underground Railroad, a secret network of people that helped fugitive slaves flee to the Northern States and Canada, she reached Philadelphia. There she earned money which she used to help rescue her family.

In December 1850 Harriet made her first hazardous return to Maryland to free members of her family. Between 1850 and the outbreak of the Civil War, she made nineteen daring journeys back into the slave states. These journeys freed over 300 slaves. Due to her head injury she sometimes blacked out during these expeditions. But the slaves, hidden in forests or fields, waited until she regained consciousness and could lead them north. As an outstanding 'conductor' of the Underground Railroad, Harriet at one time had a price on her head of 40,000 dollars.

Anon.

335

Sir Winston Churchill had a pet budgerigar – Toby – which travelled with him everywhere and was allowed much freedom. One day, while Sir Winston was staying in Monte Carlo, Toby flew out of the window into the bright beckoning sunshine – and he never returned. His master reflected sadly, but philosophically, 'Freedom is the birthright of all God's creatures.'

Anon.

Free Will

336

The difference between a 'weak' will and a 'strong' will lies not so much in the weakened will itself as in the lack of a strong deeply loved master purpose or ideal to direct the will.

Fulton Sheen

337

There are no galley slaves in the royal vessel of divine love –
every man works his oar voluntarily.

Jean Pierre Camus

338

Cherish no hate for thy brother who offends, because you
have not offended like him. If your fellow man possessed
your nature he might not have sinned. If you possessed his
nature you might have offended as he has done. A man's
trangressions depend not entirely upon his free choice, but
often upon many other circumstances.

A Hasidic Rabbi

339

God is omnipotent – but powerless still
To stop my heart from wishing what it will.

Angelus Silesius

340

The old clergyman was without doubt the world's worst
golfer. One day on a fairly long straight hole he uncorked a
towering drive straight towards the pin. The ball started to
roll and as if drawn by a magnet continued to roll – over the
apron – across the green – hit the pin and dropped into the
hole.

The astounded clergyman turned his eyes towards
heaven. 'Lord,' he begged, 'I'd rather do it *myself.*'

Cecil Bateman

341

We glorify rugged wills; but the greatest things are done by
timid people who work with simple trust.

John La Farge

Friendship

342

A true friend is one who will recognise me when necessity compels me to wear shabby clothes; who will take my hand when I am sliding downhill, instead of giving me a push to hasten my descent; who will lend me a dollar when I really need it, without demanding two dollars security; who will come to me when I am sick; who will pull off his coat and fight for me when the odds are two to one against me; who will talk of me behind my back as he talks to my face.

Anon.

343

So long as we love, we serve; so long as we are loved by others I would almost say that we are indispensable; and no man is useless while he has a friend.

Robert Louis Stevenson

344

Two boys, strangers to one another, but both ten years of age, were moved to the same small side ward of a general hospital. Simon, placed by the only window, was the more active although, like Martin, he was confined to bed.

At first Martin was very poorly and depressed but Simon succeeded in cheering him up. As he gained in strength Martin was daily entertained ·by his new friend, who brightened each day with vivid descriptions of what he could see from the window alongside his bed. Through the Spring and into the early Summer Simon told Martin of the daffodils coming out in the park across the street; told him about the children playing on the swings and roundabout; he spoke of the old and young people that passed in the street below.

The sad day came when the boys were parted. Simon was sent off on convalescence and Martin asked to be moved to the bed by the window. Sister would not permit it; she gave good reasons but that did not stop Martin from asking again and again. One day a new Sister was put on the ward. Martin seized the opportunity and asked her. He was moved. With eager anticipation Martin looked out of the window. He looked and looked again in stunned disbelief; there was nothing there but a blank brick wall and a squalid yard with a row of dustbins! For two months Simon had worked hard, hour after hour, to enliven his friend's day with his vivid imagination.

Anon.

345

Every man will be thy friend
Whilst thou hast wherewith to spend;
But if store of crowns can be scant,
No man will supply thy want.

He that is thy friend indeed,
He will help thee in thy need;
If thou sorrow, he will weep;
If thou wake, he cannot sleep.

Thus of every grief in heart
He with thee doth bear a part.
These are certain signs to know
Faithful friend from flattering foe.

Richard Barnfield

346

True friendship is a plant of slow growth, and must undergo and withstand the shocks of adversity before it is entitled to the appellation.

George Washington

Gardening

347

Gardening, by the grace of God, is one of the few things in which perfection can never be achieved. With all the gold in the world to spend, and all the world in which to choose a site, though a man might labour all his life, and his children, and his children's children, the finished garden would still fall short of the paradise he planned . . . That is as it should be, for thus we strive, and in our striving find happiness. Fortunately, as a garden is something which no machine can make, we find relief from the whirr of wheels that will, in the end, grind men down to the dust from whence they came. Everything else may bow to the lust for speed, but a garden must ever run its course the seasons round, bearing its flowers in its own appointed spring-time and its fruits as the days draw in.

W.E. Johns

Generosity

348

Alexander the Great had a famous but poor philosopher in his court. Being pressed for money, the philosopher made application to his patron for relief. Alexander had commissioned him to draw whatever cash he needed from the Treasury, so the philosopher presented a request for a very large sum. The Treasurer refused to honour the draft until he consulted his royal master, adding that he thought the amount exhorbitant. Alexander replied, 'Pay the money at once. The philosopher has done me a singular honour. By the largeness of his request he shows the idea he has conceived both of my wealth and my generosity.'

Anon.

349

It is possible to give without loving, but it is impossible to love without giving.

Richard Braunstein

350

The best thing to give . . .
   to your enemy is forgiveness;
   to an opponent, tolerance;
   to a friend, your heart;
   to your child, a good example;
   to a father, deference;
   to your mother, conduct that will make her proud of you;
   to yourself, respect;
   to all men, charity.

Lord A.J. Balfour

351

One of the most difficult things to give away is kindness – it is usually returned.

C. Flint

352

There is a legend about the boy who gave up his five barley loaves and two small fishes so that Christ could feed the multitude. It tells how the boy hurried home, after all the fragments had been gathered, and told his mother about the exciting incident.

With eyes still big with wonder, he told her how his five little barley cakes and two dried fishes had multiplied in the Saviour's hand until there was enough to satisfy 5,000 hungry people. And then, with a wistful look, he added: 'I wonder, Mother, whether it would be that way with *everything* you gave him!'

Anon.

353

A generous heart suffers for the misfortunes of others as much as though it had caused them.

Marquis de Vauvenargues

354

I know a ranch in Colorado at the base of a mountain. From snow fields hundreds of feet above, two streams trickle down and divide. One grows until its waters are caught up by skilled engineers and made to irrigate a thousand ranches. The other runs into a blind valley and spreads into a lake with no outlet. There it poisons itself. In it are the carcases of cattle, who, thirsty and eager, have come to drink of the tainted flood. Some of them still stand upright in the miry bottom, their heads bent into the bitter tide, the flesh falling from their bones. The first lake has an outlet. It loses itself on a mesa and gives drink to the homes of men. The other turns in upon itself and kills everything that touches it. One loses life and finds it again in generosity – the other loses life in stagnation, never to find it again.

George Stewart

355

I enjoyed the tale of the elderly money-lender and the Salvation Army lass. She accosted him in Bond Street in Self-Denial Week, and said,

'Will you give a shilling to the Lord?'

'How old are you?' said he, and she answered, 'Nineteen.'

'Well,' said the money-lender, 'I am seventy-five, so I shall be seeing Him before you do, so I'll give it to him.'

Anon.

356

A minister was once preaching at a little chapel on the

subject of 'Giving'. During the sermon he was delighted
when he saw a member of the congregation go to the side of
the chapel and place a coin in a box, and a little later
another did the same. Surely, the minister thought, his
sermon had never before met with such practical response.
On leaving he was stopped by one of the men, who said: 'I
hope we didn't disturb you, sir, but ours is a shilling-in-a-
slot meter, and we should have been in darkness if we
hadn't attended to it!'

London Evening Standard

357

A pig was lamenting his lack of popularity. He complained
to the cow that people were always talking about the cow's
gentleness and kind eyes, whereas his name was used as an
insult. The pig admitted that the cow gave milk and cream,
but maintained that pigs gave more. 'Why,' the animal
complained, 'we pigs give bacon and ham and bristles and
people even pickle our feet, I don't see why you cows are
esteemed so much more.' The cow thought awhile and said
gently, 'Maybe it's because we give while we're still living.'

Anon.

Gentleness

358

It was winter and Martin was riding with his regiment
through the snow and slush into the fourth century city of
Amiens. Crowds had gathered to watch the soldiers coming
in, worn and weary, with sodden equipment, perishing with
cold, in spite of thick, warm military cloaks and uniform.
As they pass through the city gate a young officer
dismounts. He has seen among the crowd a poor man, well-
nigh naked, blue with cold, holding out a trembling hand

for alms to buy bread. The officer flings off his cloak, and, having drawn his sword, he cuts the cloak in two – gently and courteously he wraps one half of it round the shivering shoulders of the beggar . . . Perhaps a great laugh goes up as the crowd see the surprised old beggar-man decked out in the smart purple-blue cloak, and Martin, laughing with the rest, wraps the other half round himself, remounts and rides on. That night, as he lay asleep in his billet, he saw a vision. He saw the half of a military cloak. And he heard a voice which bade him look well at it, and asked him if he had seen the cloak before. And as he looked upon it he expected to see beneath it the features of his shivering friend at the city gate, but he saw the figure of no beggar-man, but the strong and gracious face and form of Jesus Himself. And as in adoring silence Martin listened for the voice to speak again, the laughing crowd of peasants seemed to change into groups of the Heavenly Host . . .

J.A. Bouquet

359
The gentle mind by gentle deeds is known.

Edmund Spenser

360
Did any bird come flying
    After Adam and Eve,
When the door was shut against them
    And they sat down to grieve?

I think not Eve's peacock
    Splendid to see,
And I think not Adam's eagle;
    But a dove, maybe.

Did any beast come pushing
    Through the thorny hedge
Into the thorny thistly world,
    Out from Eden's edge?

I think not a lion,
    Though his strength is such;
But an innocent loving lamb
    May have done as much.

Christina Rossetti

361

The smile that you send out returns to you.

Indian wisdom

362

The Wind and the Sun once had a quarrel. The Wind boasted that he was much stronger than the Sun. He said, 'I'll show you I'm stronger; see that old man over there with a big coat on? I bet I can make him take his coat off much quicker than you can.' 'All right,' said the Sun, 'we'll see.' So the Sun went behind a cloud, but left a little hole so that he could peep through and see what the Wind did. The Wind blew and blew as hard as he could, causing a terrible storm, but the harder he blew the tighter the old man wrapped his coat about him. In the end the poor old Wind had to become calm and give in. Then it was the Sun's turn. He came out from behind the cloud and smiled with sunshine at the old man. After a while, the old man began to mop his brow, then he pulled his coat off. So the Sun beat the Wind.

Maurice Nassan

Giving

363

May your bounty teach me greatness of heart. May your magnificence stop me being mean. Seeing you a prodigal and open-handed giver, let me give unstintingly like a king's son, like God's own.

Helder Camara

Glory to God

364

On the margin of many of his masterpieces, Johann Sebastian Bach jotted down the words: 'To God Alone the Glory.'

And indeed, the prodigious quantity and sublime quality of his music, literally woven of religious contemplation and exaltation, reflect his lofty intention.

Although Bach was one of the greatest German organists of the eighteenth century, few besides his family and pupils knew of his genius in musical composition. At his death in 1750, after a lifetime of total dedication, poverty, and struggle, many of his priceless works were lost.

Music lovers today owe the 'rediscovery' of Bach to Felix Mendelssohn. As a young boy, he was enraptured by Bach's manuscript of the *St Matthew Passion*. At the age of twenty he gave a private performance of it. As a result, Bach's genius was widely acclaimed.

Anon.

365

Grace is but glory begun, and glory is but grace perfected.

Jonathan Edwards

366

There is a legend that Jerome, who lived for many years in a cave near Bethlehem, was visited by the Christ Child and talked with him. One day Jerome asked: 'What may I give to Thee, O Christ Child?' But the Holy Child replied: 'I need nought but that thou should'st sing, "Glory to God in the highest, and on earth peace, goodwill." ' But Jerome persisted: 'I would give thee gifts – money.' 'Nay,' repeated the Child. 'I need no money, give it to my poor, for my sake. Thus shalt thou be giving to me.'

Anon.

367

By faith we know his existence, in glory we shall know his nature.

Blaise Pascal

368

But true glory and holy joy is to glory in Thee and not in one's self; to rejoice in Thy name, and not to be delighted in one's own virtue, not in any creature, save only for Thy sake.

Thomas à Kempis

369

I AM is the unqualified fullness of being
    is the supreme indication of presence
    is the one statement that cannot be uttered without
      being completely true
    is the one completely and immediately personal
      statement
    is the presupposed in every intelligible utterance
    is true equally of God and man
    is true in every time and place
    is the name of God.

T.S. Gregory

370

In 1828, the Anglican priest, William Broughton, was sent out to Australia as Archdeacon of that island continent, which was then part of the diocese of Calcutta! Eight years later he was made Australia's first Bishop, and his work and energy and spiritual leadership in carrying out his vast task were marvellous. There are many stories associated with that great man. Here is one of them.

When the great gold rush came, although he was an already ageing man, Bishop Broughton joined himself to the amazing exodus, arrived at the diggings and collected a great crowd of miners for service on Sunday, when he told them that on the following Wednesday, at six a.m., the building of their church was to begin.

At six o'clock precisely, the Bishop, attended by a large crowd, was at the ground. He first delivered a truly great sermon, which concluded by saying that he would set an example of what it meant that they should dig together for the honour and glory of God. Then being supplied with a pick, he began to open the ground where the north-east support of the building was to stand. The example was contagious; in a few minutes all who could obtain tools were digging, so that before eight-thirty more than half the holes were dug to the required depth. By midday the carpenters were at work; by evening the church was apparent in outline; and in four days' time was furnished and ready for consecration.

Anon.

Good Friday

371

Nature Legends linked with the Cross

Nature, as well as the Church, can turn men's thoughts to the cross of Christ, as is illustrated by many pretty legends. Here are some:

1. *The Crossbill* This little bird is said to have pecked at the nails in our Lord's hands and feet, striving to remove them, and thus twisting its bill, and receiving forever the blood-red marks on its plumage.

2. *The Aspen* The cross of Calvary was said to have been made from the wood of this tree. Remembering that one of their number took part in so awful a crime, all aspen trees, since then, have quivered and trembled for fear.

3. *The Weeping Willow* It is said that the soldiers who scourged our Lord had made their scourges from branches of the willow, and that is why the weeping willows bow their heads today, in shame and sorrow, because of the wounding of the body of Christ by one of them.

4. *The Dwarf Birch* In certain parts of Scotland a stunted birch tree grows, attaining no greater height than three feet. A native of those parts would tell you that the soldiers' scourges were made (not of willow, as just described) but of this particular kind of birch, which in those days grew as tall as its relations, but for its share in that shameful day's work it was doomed to become, and remain, a dwarf.

5. *The Wood-sorrel* It is said that some of the drops of the blood of our Lord fell upon this small white flower, as it grew at the foot of the Cross, giving it its present stain.

6. *The Wild-rose* Once, legend tells us, its flowers were meagre and insignificant; but the soldiers seeking a crown for our Lord, found this, and ever since it has borne its beautiful blossoms in memory of the day on which it was so honoured.

Maud Higham

372

Nicaragua; Good Friday 1987 I had hoped to finish this letter in a major key of optimism. However, a nun of this Diocese, Sandra Price from California, gave me a written report yesterday. The following excerpts need no comment from me.

'On March 25 a group of terrorists took one of our Catholic catechists, Donato Mendoza, from his home; two kilometers further on they castrated him, gouged out his eyes, pulled out his finger-nails, cut the flesh from his legs, broke every bone in his body, and shot him . . .

'Three days later, on Good Friday, his naked and mutilated body was found. Donato had always worn a chain and cross as a distinctive mark of his position in the Church. He said he had lost the cross a few days before while working. It was this chain without a cross that identified his dead body. He no longer wore a cross of metal; his life had taken on the passion and death of Jesus.

'On Easter Sunday we celebrated Mass with Donato's family: mother, brothers, sister, wife, nine children, two grandchildren. On the altar was the chain, matted with blood and dirt. There was no cross. As Christ's life did not terminate on the cross but in the victory of the resurrection, so too we believe that Donato has conquered death and suffering, and lives on by the power of this same God whom he served faithfully during the forty years of his life.'

John Medcalf

373

Take the Cross *he* sends, as it is, and not as *you* imagine it to be.

Cornelia Connelly

Good and Evil

374

The problem of the relation between good and evil is a very difficult one to settle, especially if we keep it away from the conviction that we ourselves are sinners. I don't think we should consider the problem at all until we realise that we are sinners.

Vincent McNabb

375

I find, from talking to atheists, that the real objection they have to God is that He doesn't destroy free will. While there is free will, you and I can sin, and it is most unreasonable to lay the blame on God. The Chosen People never did that. They knew that God permitted sin. If ever you have had the government of other human beings, if you teach children, you know there are a great many things you have to permit, because you have to train them. You may even let them burn themselves because it is the only way of teaching them to leave fire alone.

Vincent McNabb

Good Shepherd

376

Some years ago a great actor was asked at a drawing-room function to recite for the pleasure of his fellow guests. He consented and asked if there was anything they specially wanted to hear. After a minute's pause, an old minister asked for Psalm 23. A strange look came over the actor's face. He paused for a moment, then said, 'I will, on one condition – that after I have recited it, you, my friend, will do the same.'

'I!' said the preacher, in surprise, 'I am not an elocutionist, but, if you wish it, I shall do so.'

Impressively, the actor began the Psalm. His voice and intonation were perfect. He held his audience spellbound, and, as he finished, a great burst of applause broke from his guests. As it died away, the old man rose and began to declaim the same psalm. His voice was not remarkable, his tone was not faultless, but, when he finished, there was not a dry eye in the room.

The actor rose and his voice quivered as he said, 'Ladies and gentlemen, I reached your eyes and ears; he has reached your hearts. The difference is just this: I know the psalm but he knows the Shepherd.'

Anon.

377

When a shepherd in Scotland was asked if his sheep would follow the voice of a stranger, he replied: 'Yes, when they are sick; but never when they are well. A sick sheep will follow anybody.'

Anon.

378

One evening General Garibaldi met a Sardinian shepherd who had lost a lamb out of his flock and was in great distress because he could not find it. Garibaldi became deeply interested in the man and proposed to his staff that they should scour the mountains and help to find the lost lamb. A search was organised, lanterns were brought, and these old soldiers started off full of eager earnestness to look for the fugitive. The quest was in vain, however, and by-and-by all the soldiers returned to their quarters. Next morning Garibaldi's attendant found the General in bed fast asleep long after his usual hour for rising. The servant aroused him at length, and the General rubbed his eyes and then took from under his bed coverings the lost lamb, bidding the attendant carry it to the shepherd. Garibaldi had kept up the search through the night until he had found the lamb.

F.H. Drinkwater

379

One night, a tall American doctor told me a story of
Commissioner Lord, of the Salvation Army, also a prisoner
of the Chinese in Korea.

'We were dead beat. Another terrible day's march lay
ahead. The men were lying cold and half-starved in the
lousy shacks waiting for the command to get going. A lot of
those guys had thought they couldn't make it – they felt
they'd had it. Suddenly old Commissioner Lord appeared
in the doorway of our shack. He seemed very confidential
about something. "Boys," he said, "boys, I've got news for
you – great news – listen." We all took notice. We all
thought, "What's with this guy?" That old Commissioner,
why he just stood among us and said, "The Lord is my
Shepherd; I shall not want," and he went right through
that psalm, like it was God's personal message to us.
Chaplain, I'm telling you, you could hear the silence. I
never felt so moved in all my life. Then the guards came – it
was get going or die. Those men rose like they had new
strength. Can't tell you where they got it from. They
marched and they stuck it out.'

S. J. Davies

Good Works

380

In the history of the Scout Movement, pride of place is
given to the 'Good Turn' performed by a London newspaper boy. This scout, meeting Mr William Boyce, the
American newspaper proprietor, in Fleet Street during a
London fog, piloted him to his West End destination,
refusing any reward. Mr Boyce was so impressed that, on
his return to America, he transplanted the Boy Scout
movement there in 1910. Millions of American boys have
since enjoyed Scout training as a result.

Anon.

381

We do the works, but God works in us the doing of the works.

Augustine of Hippo

382

A teamster sought the Rabbi of Berditchev's advice as to whether he should give up his occupation because it interfered with regular attendance at the synagogue.

'Do you carry poor travellers free of charge?' asked the Rabbi.

'Yes,' answered the teamster.

'Then you serve the Lord in your occupation just as faithfully as you would be frequenting the synagogue.'

Hasidic Story

383

The Christian should resemble a fruit tree, not a christmas tree! For the gaudy decorations of a christmas tree are only tied on, whereas fruit grows on a fruit tree.

John R.W. Stott

384

A little girl told a friend who was visiting her father that her brothers set traps to catch the birds. He asked her what she did. She replied 'I prayed that the traps might not catch the birds.' 'Anything else?' 'Yes,' she said. 'I prayed that God would keep the birds out of the traps.' 'Anything else?' 'Yes, then I went and kicked the traps all to pieces.'

'Christian Leader'

Gospel – Good News

385

It should never be forgotten that Christianity did not come into the world through the editorial page; it came through the news columns. It was a news event – front page, stop-the-press news. Something happened. 'The Word became flesh and dwelt among us.' The Gospel was first preached as news. Whenever it has dwindled down to mere advice, become merely editorial Christianity, it has evaporated into a cloud as vague as fog.

Halford E. Luccock

386

The glory of the Gospel is that when the Church is absolutely different from the world, she invariably attracts it.

Martin Lloyd-Jones

387

Author Lloyd Douglas used to tell how he loved to visit an old violin teacher who had a homely wisdom that refreshed him. One morning, Douglas walked in and said 'Well, what's the good news today?' Putting down his violin, the teacher stepped over to a tuning fork suspended from a cord and struck it.

'There is the good news for today,' he said. 'That, my friend, is the musical note A. It was A all day yesterday, will be A next week and for a thousand years.'

Purnell Bailey

388

GOOD North
        East
        West
        South FOR ALL.

Anon.

389

Ruskin says that many people read the Scriptures as the hedgehog gets grapes. The old monks said that this animal rolled over among the grapes and carried what happened to stick to its spines or quills. So the 'hedgehoggy' readers roll themselves over on a portion of the Scriptures and get only what happens to stick. But you can get only the skins of Bible verses that way. If we want the juice, we must press them in clusters.

Anon.

390

You are writing a Gospel,
   A chapter each day,
By the deeds that you do,
   And the words that you say.

Men read what you write,
   If it's false or it's true.
Now what is the Gospel
   According to you?

Anon.

391

Our reading of the Gospel story can be and should be an act of personal communion with the living Lord.

William Temple

392

That the Gospel is to be opposed is inevitable –
That the Gospel is to be disbelieved is to be expected –
But that it should be made dull is intolerable!

Gerald Kennedy

393

God writes the gospel not in the Bible alone, but on trees,
and flowers, and clouds, and stars.

Martin Luther

394

The curate stepped into the pulpit to preach with all the
apprehension of a young man recently ordained. He
hesitated for a moment. Then his face broke into a wide
grin as he shared with us the message someone had left near
his notes. 'Give 'em Heaven!'

M.L. Rogness

Gossip

395

Aesop has a fable of three bulls in a field together in the
greatest peace and safety. A lion had long watched them in
the hope of making prey of them, but found little chance so
long as they kept together. He therefore began secretly to
spread evil and slanderous reports of one against another
till he fermented jealousy and distrust among them. Soon
they began to avoid each other and each took to feeding
alone. This gave the lion the opportunity it had been
wanting. He fell on them singly and made an easy prey of
them all.

Aesop

396

A real Christian is a person who can give his pet parrot to the town gossip.

Billy Graham

397

'When this pen flows too freely,' run the instructions given with a fountain pen, 'it is a sign that it is nearly empty, and should be filled.' The caution would seem to apply to human beings. Gossip, slander, idle chatter, all testify to the emptiness of the mind and are a damaging sign.

'Forward'

398

Socrates in an anonymous anecdote about gossip:
   'Have you heard, O Socrates –'
   'Just a moment friend,' said the sage. 'Have you made sure that all you are going to tell me is true?'
   'Well, no. I just heard others say it.'
   'I see. Then we can scarcely bother with it unless it is something good. Will it stand the test of goodness?'
   'Oh, no, indeed. On the contrary'.
   'Hmm. Perhaps it is necessary that I know this in order to prevent harm to others.'
   'Well, no –'
   'Very well, then', said Socrates. 'Let us forget about it. There are so many worthwhile things in life; we can't afford to bother with what is so worthless as to be neither true nor good nor needful.'

'The Liguorian'

399

The slanderous tongue kills three; the slandered, the slanderer, and him who listens to the slander.

The Talmud

400

Mrs Brown (very annoyed): 'Look here, Mrs Green, Mrs Gray told me that you told her the secret I told you not to tell her.'
Mrs Green: 'Oh, the mean creature, and I told her not to tell you that I told her.'
Mrs Brown: 'Well look here. Don't you tell her that I told you she told me.'

Anon.

401

Gossip specialist: 'I won't go into all the details; in fact, I've already told you more about it than I heard myself.'

Anon.

Grace

402

'There, but for the grace of God, goes . . .'
   Who used these famous words? They have been attributed to several saintly men, including John Bunyan, but the story is rightly told of John Bradford, the Protestant martyr, who was burnt at Smithfield on Sunday 30th June, 1555. The story is that once, on seeing some criminals being taken to execution, he exclaimed, 'There, but for the grace of God, goes John Bradford.'

Anon.

403

As the earth can produce nothing unless it is fertilised by the sun, so we can do nothing without the grace of God.

John Vianney

404

To produce real moral freedom, God's grace and man's will must co-operate. As God is the prime mover of nature, so also he creates free impulses toward himself and to all good things. Grace renders the will free that it may do everything with God's help, working with grace as with an instrument which belongs to it. So the will arrives at freedom through love, nay, becomes itself love, for love unites with God.

Meister Eckhart

405

Grace is not sought nor bought nor wrought. It is a free gift of Almighty God to needy mankind.

Billy Graham

406

In Nottingham is the Wesleyan chapel where William Booth, founder of the Salvation Army, was converted. A memorial tablet keeps fresh in recollection the fact that there this notable friend of the friendless received his baptism of spiritual power. Naturally, the chapel has become a shrine of pilgrimage for Salvation Army leaders from around the world.

One day an aged black man in the uniform of the Army was found by the minister of the chapel standing with uplifted eyes before the table. 'Can a man say his prayers here?' he asked. 'Of course,' was the minister's answer. And the old Salvation Army officer went down on his knees, and lifting his hands before the tablet prayed: 'O God, do it again! Do it again!'

That prayer is the touchstone of abiding reality in religion; awareness that it is God, by his grace, who is the author of all good actions.

Anon.

Grandparents

407
Written by a seven-year-old boy:
A grandmother is a lady who has no children of her own, so
she likes other people's boys and girls. Grandmothers don't
have anything to do but be there. If they take us for walks
they slow up past pretty leaves and caterpillars. They never
say 'Hurry up'.

Usually they are pretty fat, but not too fat to tie our
shoes. Most times they wear glasses, and most of them can
take their teeth out. They can answer many questions, like:
'Why do dogs hate cats?' and 'Why isn't God married?'
When they read to us they don't skip words or mind if it's
the same story again.

Everyone should have a grandmother, especially if they
haven't got a TV. I don't know where you can buy one,
they just seem to be there, because grandmothers are the
only people who have time.

Anon.

Grief

408
Facing and accepting a loss is the first step of managing
bereavement. Only life which deliberately picks up and
starts again is victorious.

James Gordon Gilkey

409
A missionary translator, labouring amongst a tribe in the
mountains of Mexico, found it hard to get the right word for
'comfort'. One day his helper asked for a week's leave, and
explained that his uncle had died and he wanted some days

off to visit his bereaved aunt 'to help her heart around the corner'. That was just the expression this missionary needed.

Anon.

410

Sorrow makes us all children again, destroys all differences in intellect. The wisest knows nothing.

Ralph Waldo Emerson

411

The Arabs have a saying that all sunshine makes the desert. It is even so. Just as sun and shower are alike needful for the development of the flower, so are joy and grief for the culture of the soul.

From vintages of sorrow are deepest joys distilled;
And the cup outstretched for healing is oft at March filled.
God leads to joy, through weeping; to quietness, through
    strife;
Through yielding, unto conquest; through death, to endless
    life.

Henry Durbanville

412

Only when grief finds its work done can God dispense us from it. Trial then only stops when it is useless; that is why it scarcely ever stops. Faith in the justice and love of the Father is the best and indeed the only support under the sufferings of this life.

Henri Frederic Amiel

413

A little girl came home from a neighbour's house where her little friend had died. 'Why did you go?' questioned her father.

'To comfort her mother,' replied the child.

'What could you do to comfort her?' the father continued.

'I climbed into her lap and cried with her,' answered the child.

Anon.

Growth – Personal

414

Traditionally the task of correction has been limited to criticism, to finding the fault, repeating the accusation and passing judgement, all of which is meant to induce guilt, a sense of badness and fear.

In fact this merely adds insult to injury. Most people know when they are in the wrong and suffer enough from the consequences without additional burdens of guilt.

Our journey of growth is through insight to change. We have to help each other to understand behaviour in terms of deficiencies and limitations, not of badness. We do not encourage change when we impoverish the other's self-esteem. We ask for change out of love. When people change for the better everybody gains by becoming more loving.

Jack Dominion

415

Not long ago an elderly teacher at a little Church Primary School in Somerset resigned. She was sixty-five and she first went to that village school when she was three. She began to teach there as a young woman. She left after forty-one years' service.

That doesn't strike you as a successful career. She never married. Every morning, week after week, year after year, she walked to school, called the register, got on with the lessons. Many of her pupils must have done much more spectacular things when they grew up. But on her last day the 129 children at the school each brought her a posy of flowers. And the village put a plaque on a chestnut tree which she had grown from a seed brought by a pupil thirty years ago. The plaque simply said, 'Miss Davies' tree'. That tree was exactly the right symbol. Miss Davies made something good grow in other people's lives, and that is success.

Fred Martin

Habit

416

There is a story of a smith of the Middle Ages who was taken prisoner and confined in a dungeon. Because of the knowledge his craft had taught him he carefully examined the heavy links that bound him, expecting somewhere to find a flaw that would show him a weak place which could soon be made to yield. But presently he dropped his hands hopelessly. Certain marks told him that the chain was of his own making, and it had always been his boast that one of his workmanship could not be broken. There are truly no chains so hard to break as those of our own forging, but they are not hopeless. The worst possible habits will yield to human resolution and strength from above.

D. Williamson

Healing

417

The good Instructor, the Wisdom, the Word of the Father,

who made man, cares for the whole nature of his creature.
The all-sufficient physician of humanity, the saviour,
heals both our body and soul, which are the proper man.

Clement of Alexandria

418

He is a path, if any be misled;
   He is a robe, if any naked be;
If any chance to hunger, he is bread;
   If any be a bondman, he is free;
   If any be but weak, how strong is he!
To dead men life he is, to sick men health,
To blind men sight, and to the needy wealth; –
A pleasure without loss, a treasure without stealth.

Giles Fletcher

419

Health means wholeness. It is concerned not simply with
cure but with healing of the whole person in all his or her
relationship; and this is what the Communion service is
about.

Healing cannot be confined to any, or indeed every, level
of human understanding or expectation. That is why too it
shows up those twin deceivers, pessimism amd optimism,
as so shallow. The Christian takes his stand not on
optimism but on hope. This is based not on rosy prognosis
(from the human point of view mine is bleak, showing I'm
dying of cancer) but, as Paul says, on suffering. This, he
says, trains us to endure, and endurance brings proof that
we have stood the test, and this proof is the ground of hope
in the God who can bring resurrection out and through the
other side of death; though we carry death with us in our
bodies (all of us) we never cease to be confident.

John H. Robinson

Heaven

420

Heaven is the soul finding its own perfect personality in God.

Phillips Brooks

421

One day, in my despair, I threw myself into a chair in the consulting room and groaned out, 'What a blockhead I was to come out here to doctor savages like these!' Whereupon Joseph quietly remarked, 'Yes, doctor, here on earth you are a great blockhead, but not in heaven.'

Albert Schweitzer

422

Blessed are they that are homesick for they shall come at last to their father's house.

Jean Paul Richter

423

Here lies a woman who was always tired,
She lived in a house where help was not hired,
Her last words on earth were: 'Dear friends, I am going
Where washing ain't done, nor sweeping, nor sewing;
But everything there is exact to my wishes;
For where they don't eat, there's no washing of dishes.
I'll be where loud anthems will always be ringing,
But having no voice, I'll be clear of the singing.
Don't mourn for me now, don't mourn for me never –
I'm going to do nothing for ever and ever.'

Anon.

424

A little girl was walking with her father along a country

road. The night was clear, and the child was enthralled by the splendour of the sky, all lit up with twinkling stars from one end to the other. After moments of reflection she suddenly looked up to her father and said: 'Daddy, I was just thinking, if the wrong side of heaven is so beautiful, how wonderful the right side must be!'

Anon.

425

There was a great plague in the world which killed off all the mice. When they went to heaven, they were amazed how beautiful and plentiful it was.

After a few days, God was doing his rounds and came across the mice. 'How are you doing?' he asked, 'Have you got everything you need?'

The mice replied what a wonderful place this heaven was and thank you, yes, they had everything they needed.

'There is one thing we could use some help with,' spoke up one small mouse.

'What's that?' asked God.

'Well,' the mouse replied, 'this is such a vast place and with our tiny legs, we find it difficult to get around and see everything. I don't suppose you could fix us up with some sort of transport? Nothing elaborate, in fact, a skateboard will do nicely.'

God smiled and immediately set Joseph the carpenter about the task of producing a skateboard.

Some time later there was another great plague and this time all the cats died. They in turn went to heaven and again in turn met God whilst he was doing his rounds.

'What do you think of heaven?' asked God.

'What a wonderful place!' answered the cats. 'It's absolutely delightful and so well organised. Especially the meals on wheels!'

Anon.

Hell

426

Hell is full of long speeches that say nothing. In heaven, one Word means everything.

In hell they talk a lot about love. In heaven they just do it.

Hell is an unending church service without God. Heaven is God without a church service.

In hell, everything is pornographic and no one is excited. In heaven everything is exciting and there is no pornography.

In hell there is sex without pleasure. In heaven there is pleasure without sex.

In heaven, a drill is a dance. In hell, a dance is a drill.

Hell is grey and so are its inhabitants. Heaven is full of colours and all colours of people.

Hell is a bad dream from which you never wake. Heaven is waking from which you never need to sleep.

Hell is full of clocks and telephones.

In heaven they laugh at philosophy. In hell they philosophize about laughter.

You will have in heaven only those earthly possessions that you gave away on earth.

C.S. Lewis

Holiness

427

Holiness is the architectural plan upon which God buildeth up His living temple.

Charles Haddon Spurgeon

428

Growing in holiness is like riding a bike. If you stop pedalling, you fall off.

Rob Warner

429

Being holy means getting up immediately every time you fall, with humility and joy. It doesn't mean never falling into sin. It means being able to say, 'Yes, Lord, I have fallen one thousand times. But thanks to you I've got up one thousand and one times.'

Helder Camara

430

To obtain the gift of Christian holiness is the work of a lifetime.

John H. Newman

431

O think me worth your anger, punish me,
Burn off my rusts and my deformity,
Restore your Image, so much, by your grace,
That you may know me and I'll turn my face.

John Donne

Holy Spirit

432

Pure and genuine love always desires above all to dwell wholly in the truth, whatever it may be, unconditionally. Every other sort of love desire, before anything else, means satisfaction, and for this reason is a source of error and falsehood. Pure and genuine love is in itself spirit of truth. It is the Holy Spirit. The Greek word, which is translated spirit, means literally fiery breath, breath mingled with fire, and it represented, in antiquity, the notion which science represents today by the word energy. What we translate by 'spirit of truth' signifies the energy of truth, truth as an active force. Pure love is this active force, the love that will not at any price, under any condition, have anything to do with either falsehood or error.

Simone Weil

433
Only through Jesus' death and resurrection is the Spirit poured out. Only through repentance and faith in Christ is the Spirit received. Life in the Spirit comes through the Lord of the Spirit.

Rob Warner

434
I have a glove here in my hand. The glove cannot do anything by itself, but when my hand is in it, it can do many things. True, it is not the glove, but my hand in the glove that acts. We are gloves. It is the Holy Spirit in us who is the hand, who does the job. We have to make room for the hand so that every finger is filled.

The question on Pentecost is not whether God is blessing our own plans and programmes but whether we are open to the great opportunities to which his Spirit calls us.

Corrie ten Boom

435
We may possibly think that the vegetables and fruits of the earth have always existed in their present state for the use of man. But that is not the case. The wild plant is generally

of little use as food, and only becomes valuable through our care.

The wild cabbage as it grows on some ocean cliff has a long stalk and a few raw green leaves with a sharp and unpleasant taste. It has by the long cultivation of man been brought up to its present state. The wild pear tree is an ugly bush, bristling with fierce thorns and bearing a rough, hard, and bitter fruit, in no way comparable with the delicious mellow pear of some cared-for country orchard today. It is not without care and cultivation that the fruits of the Spirit can be gained.

Anon.

Hope

436

Sir Walter Raleigh is believed to have written this poem in the Tower of London on the night before his execution:

> Even such time, that takes in trust
>   Our youth, our joys, our all we have,
> And pays us but with earth and dust;
>   Who, in the dark and silent grave,
> When we have wandered all our ways,
> Shuts up the story of our days,
>   But from this earth, this grave, this dust,
>   My God shall raise me up, I trust.

Anon.

437

Everything that is done in the world is done by hope.

Martin Luther

438

Hope is the best possession. None are completely wretched but those who are without hope, and few are reduced so low as that.

William Hazlitt

439

Love means to love that which is unlovable, or it is no virtue at all; forgiving means to pardon the unpardonable, or it is no virtue at all; faith means believing the unbelievable, or it is no virtue at all. And to hope means hoping when things are hopeless, or it is no virtue at all.

G.K. Chesterton

440

To be a sinner is our distress, but to know it is our hope.

Fulton Sheen

441

Bill: 'Have you ever realised any of your childhood hopes?'
Pete: 'Yes; when mother used to comb my hair, I often wished I didn't have any.'

Anon.

Human Rights

442

All human beings are born free and equal in dignity and rights.

Adopted by UNO 10th December, 1948

443

We hold these truths to be self-evident – that all men are created equal; that they are endowed by their Creator with certain unalienable rights; that among these are life, liberty, and the pursuit of happiness.

Thomas Jefferson

444
The Tree of Liberty

Without this tree, alake this life
  Is but a vale o' woe, man;
A scene o' sorrow mixed wi' strife,
  Nae real joys we know, man.
We labour soon, we labour late.
  To feed the titled knave, man;
And a' the comfort we're to get
  Is that ayont the grave, man.

Wi' plenty o' sic trees, I trow,
  The world would live in peace, man;
The sword would help to make a plough,
  The din o' war wad cease, man.
Like brethren in a common cause,
  We'd on each other smile, man;
And equal rights and equal laws
  Wad gladden every isle, man.

Robert Burns

445

To shelter or give medical aid to a man on the run from a police force which will torture and perhaps kill him, is an act of Christian love demanded by Christ in the Gospel and is no more a political act than giving first aid and a cup of tea to a Member of Parliament who has a car smash outside your door.

Sheila Cassidy

446

I have the audacity to believe that peoples everywhere can have three meals a day for their bodies, education and culture for their minds, and dignity, equality and freedom for their spirits. I believe that what self-centred men have torn down, other-centred can build up. I still believe that one day mankind will bow down before the altars of God and be crowned triumphant over war and bloodshed, and nonviolent redemptive good will proclaim the rule of the land. 'And the lion and the lamb shall lie down together and every man shall sit under his own vine and fig tree and none shall be afraid.' I still believe that we shall overcome.

Martin Luther King

447

Rights that do not flow from duty well performed are not worth having.

Mahatma Gandhi

448

No one can be perfectly free till all are free; no one can be perfectly moral till all are moral; no one can be perfectly happy till all are happy.

Herbert Spencer

449

John Newton wrote a great hymn which the Church sings – 'Glorious things of thee are spoken'. When he wrote it he was sitting in the sunshine on a ship's deck while in the hatches slaves were groaning in anguish, shackled and being taken to be sold in some hellhole in London or America. We might call Newton a hypocrite. But he wasn't. He was morally asleep. Now is the time for good people everywhere to awake from their moral slumber, else some

future generation will look upon us as insensitive to the
evils around us as was John Newton who described the
voyage as one of sweet communion with Jesus. The
opportunity is here, let's not let it pass.

Anon.

Humility

450

There is a story told of Mr Gladstone who invited his
tenants and workers to dinner. It was a very good dinner,
served in the very best style, complete with napkins and
finger bowls.

One man who had never been at such a dinner before
started drinking from his finger bowl. Some guests who
knew the real purpose of the bowls started sniggering,
whereupon Mr Gladstone immediately lifted his finger
bowl and drank from it.

Anon.

451

The only wisdom we can hope to acquire is the wisdom of
humility – humility is endless.

T.S. Eliot

452

A rather pompous landowner met a local farmer one
morning and said to him. 'Why, Brown, you're getting
quite bent. Why don't you stand up straight like me?'

In reply, Farmer Brown said: 'Do you see yon field of
corn?' And when the other nodded, went on. 'Well, you'll
notice that the full heads hang down, and the empty ones
stand up.'

Anon.

453

If you want to realise your own importance, put your finger into a bowl of water, take it out and look at the hole.

Robert Burdette

454

Some American tourists one day visited the home of Beethoven. A young woman among them sat down at the great composer's piano and began to play his Moonlight Sonata. After she had finished, she turned to the old caretaker and said: 'I presume a great many musicians visit this place every year.' 'Yes,' he replied. 'Paderewski was here last year.' 'And did he play on Beethoven's piano?' 'No! He said he wasn't worthy.'

Anon.

455

True humility makes no pretence of being humble, and scarcely ever utters words of humility.

Francis of Sales

456

There is a beautiful legend which tells of a saintly man who was greatly beloved of the angels, who had seen much of his godly life on earth.

The angels asked God to give this man some mark of the divine favour, some new gift which would make him still more useful. They were told to see the man and ask him what special power he would like to have. The angels came and asked him what gift he would choose. He said that he was content, and wanted nothing more. They continued to urge him to choose. Would he not like to have power to perform miracles? He said no, that was Christ's work. Would he not like power to lead a great many souls to

Christ? He answered no, for it was the work of the Holy Spirit to convert souls. The angels still begged him to have something which they might ask God to grant to him.

He answered at last, that if he must make a choice, he would like power to do a great deal of good among men without even knowing it. So it was from that day that his shadow, when it fell behind him, where he could not see it, had wondrous healing power, but when it fell before him, where he could see it, had no such power. This is the spirit of true holiness, nothing for self, everything for God. God loves to use the life that will keep itself out of sight and only honour Him.

Anon.

457

There is a story of a rabbi and a cantor and a humble synagogue cleaner who were preparing for the Day of Atonement. The rabbi beat his breast and said 'I am nothing, I am nothing.' The cantor beat his breast and said, 'I am nothing, I am nothing.' The cleaner beat his breast and said 'I am nothing, I am nothing.' And the rabbi said to the cantor, 'Look who thinks he's nothing.'

Alan Paton

458

Humility has no act of its own. It is a quality of other acts. You can't go out into the streets and be humble. I have to be a humble minister, think humbly, speak humbly. I can't just go and perform an act of humility. It is the same with freedom. We must freely get on a train or help somebody else, but we can't just perform an act of freedom. So with the virtue of humility, we must humbly do this action or the other. The greatest difficulty is to do great things humbly. I don't think the greatest achievement is to do little things humbly – that *is* an achievement – but to do great things humbly is humility's greatest achievement.

Vincent McNabb

459

If ever I'm disappointed with my lot in life, I stop and think about little Jamie Scott. Jamie was trying for a part in his school play. His mother told me that he'd set his heart on being in it, though she feared he would not be chosen.

On the day the parts were awarded, I went with her to collect him after school. Jamie rushed up, eyes shining with pride and excitement.

Then he said those words that remain a lesson to me: 'I've been chosen to clap and cheer.'

Marie Curling

Hunger

460

Mother Teresa has shared her experience of one parent's response to this dilemma. 'Some time ago a gentleman came to our house and said "There is a Hindu family with eight children that have not eaten for some time. Kindly go and see them." I took rice with me and I went, and when I arrived I could see the children's faces shining with hunger. I gave the rice to their mother. She divided it into two and she went out. When she came back I asked her: "Where did you go and what did you do?" And the only answer she gave me was, "They are hungry also."

"Who are *they*?" I asked.

She said: "A Muslim family next door."

I was struck very much; not so much by what she did as by the fact she knew they were hungry; that she saw their hunger, she felt their hunger and therefore she had the courage to share with them. This is the greatness of poor people. Love, to be true, has to hurt.'

Dr Ittyerah

461

If you're put on bread and water, it's a punishment. The image conjures up visions of imprisonment and bare survival. In Africa these words mean exactly the opposite; bread and water means freedom – escape from the prison of starvation and death.

'Tear Fund'

Hypocrisy

462

There's not much practical Christianity in the man who lives on better terms with angels and seraphs than with his children, and neighbours.

Henry Ward Beecher

463

An architect who had worked for a large company for many years was called in one day by the board of directors and given plans for a fine house to be built in the best quarter of the town. The chairman instructed him to spare no expense, using the finest materials and best builders. As the house began to go up, the architect began to think, 'No expense spared? Why use such costly materials?' So he began to use poor materials and to hire poor quality workmen, and he put the difference in the cost into his own pocket. When the house was finished, it looked very fine on the outside, but it certainly would not last long. Shortly after it was finished, the board of directors held another meeting to which the architect was called. The chairman made a speech, thanking the architect for his long service to the company, as a reward for which they were making him a present of the house!

Anon.

464

We hand folks over to God's mercy, and show none ourselves.

George Eliot

465

God knows, I'm no' the thing I should be,
Nor am I even the thing I could be,
But twenty times I rather would be
    An atheist clean,
Than under gospel colours hid
    Just for a screen.

Robert Burns

466

A Pharisee is a man who prays publicly and preys privately.

Don Marquis

Indwelling

467

The difference between a good and a bad man does not lie in this, that the one wills that which is good and the other does not, but solely in this, that the one concurs with the

living, inspiring Spirit of God within him, and the other
resists it, and can be chargeable with evil only because he
resists it.

William Law

468

As the Spirit is the loving presence between the Father and
the Son, he can be present to us only by his work of love.

George A. Maloney

469

However well of Christ
    you talk and preach,
unless He lives within,
    He is beyond your reach.

Angelus Silesius

470

There was a blind boy who was flying his kite and enjoying
this pastime along with others of his own age. A passer-by,
knowing him and wanting to give him a gentle teasing,
said, 'Where's your kite? You don't know whether it is on
the ground or up in the sky.' 'Oh yes!' said the blind lad, 'I
do know. It is quite a fair height up in the air.' 'How do you
know that?' asked his friend, 'you can't see it.' 'No!' replied
the boy, 'I can't see it, it is true, but I can feel the tug of the
string every now and again.'

Anon.

471

This indwelling Holy Spirit teaches us how to pray deeply
in the heart. He leads us beyond our idols constructed

about God to live in the mystery of the circular movement
of the Father, Son and Spirit, inter-love relationships.

George A. Maloney

472

It isn't the Devil in humanity that makes man a lonely
creature, it's his Godlikeness. It's the fullness, of the good
that can't get out or can't find its proper 'other place' that
makes for loneliness.

Fynn

Integrity

473

Some years ago, a young businessman, who had risen to a
position of importance, fell in love with a well-known and
highly respected actress. For many months he was constantly in her company, escorting her to all 'the right
places'. Eventually he decided to marry the young lady.
Before doing so, however, he hired a private detective to
investigate her. The task was assigned to a special agent,
who had no knowledge of the identity of his client.

Finally, the agent's report was sent to him. It read:

'Miss — has an excellent reputation. Her past is spotless,
her associates beyond reproach. The only hint of scandal is
that in recent months she has been seen in the company of a
businessman of doubtful reputation.'

Anon.

474

No Mirabeau, Napoleon, Burns, Cromwell, no man adequate to do anything, but is first of all in right earnest about
it; what I call a sincere man. I should say sincerity, a deep,

great, genuine sincerity, is the first characteristic of all men in any way heroic. A little man may have it; it is competent to all men that God has made; but a great man cannot be without it.

Thomas Carlyle

475

I am not bound to win,
but I am bound to be true.
I am not bound to succeed,
but I am bound to live up to the light I have.
I must stand with anybody that stands right,
stand with him while he is right,
and part with him when he goes wrong.

Abraham Lincoln

476

In Napoleon's expedition to Russia, a Russian peasant was captured, forced into Napoleon's service and branded on the arm with the letter 'N'. When he understood what it meant, he chopped off the arm that had been branded, rather than serve his country's enemy.

Anon.

477

'My boy,' said the business man to his son, 'there are two things that are essential if you are to succeed in business.'
    'What are they, Dad?' asked the boy.
    'Integrity and sagacity.'
    'What is integrity?'
    'Always, no matter what, always keep your word.'
    'And sagacity?'
    'Never give your word!'

Anon.

Jesus

478

Sir Ernest Shackleton (who died in 1922), the leader of the famous Antarctic expedition, writes in *The Presence*:

When I look back upon those days, with all their anxiety and peril, I cannot doubt that our party was divinely guided both over the snowfields and across the storm-swept sea. I know that during that long and racking march of thirty-six hours over the unnamed mountains and glaciers of South Georgia, it seemed to me often that we were not three, but four. I said nothing to my companions on the point, but afterwards Worsley said to me: 'Boss, I had a curious feeling on the march that there was another Person with us.'

479

They borrowed a bed to lay His head
    When Christ the Lord came down;
They borrowed an ass in the mountain pass
    For Him to ride to town;
But the crown He wore and the cross He bore
    Were his own
    The cross was His own.

Anon.

480

Life is filled with meaning as soon as Jesus Christ enters into it.

Stephen Neill

481

A missionary who laboured on the east coast of Africa tells this story: One day a little black boy came to him and said,

'Was Jesus a white man or a black man?' The missionary was going to say right away that Jesus was a white man, but he happened to guess what was in the black boy's mind. He knew that if he said Jesus was a white man the boy would turn away with a sad look, thinking that everything that was good had been given to the white man. So the missionary thought a moment. He remembered that Jesus lived, when on earth, in a very warm country, that the people there were dark-skinned, though not black. So he answered, 'No, Jesus was not a white man, nor a black man but sort of between the two. He was kind of brown.' 'Oh, then he belongs to both of us, doesn't he?' exclaimed the little fellow with delight.

Anon.

482

Jesus did not come to explain away suffering or remove it. He came to fill it with his presence.

Paul Claudel

483

We have all heard the nursery rhyme: 'Humpty Dumpty'. A Christian mother had just repeated this rhyme to her four-year-old son. The boy thought for a moment, then as if having suddenly come up with a solution, he said with bright-eyed confidence: 'Jesus could have done it!'

Anon.

Jewish People

484

There are three impudent creatures: among beasts, the dog; among birds, the cock; among people, Israel. But Rabbi

Ammi added 'Do not consider this as blame; it is praise, for
to be a Jew means to be ready to be martyred.'

Midrash: Exodus Rabbah

485

In the closing days of World War II a group of American
prisoners in Europe showed their Nazi captors a sample of
faith in action. The rumour spread within the camp that
the Jewish soldiers among them were to be separated from
the others for 'special treatment'. All the men in the camp
were talking about it. The Jewish boys urged their buddies
not to stick their necks out for them.

The following day when the command was given, 'All
prisioners of Jewish blood step forward,' every single
soldier stepped out!

Anon.

486

Frederick the Great of Prussia asked his chaplain to prove
the authenticity of the Bible in two words, and the chaplain
immediately replied, 'The Jews, your Majesty!'

Anon.

487

Pride and humiliation hand in hand
  Walked with them through the world where'er they
    went;
Trampled and beaten were they as the sand,
  And yet unshaken as the continent.

H.W. Longfellow

488

Because He was a man
As well as He was God

He loved his own goat-nibbled hills,
His crumbling Jewish sod.
He bowed to Roman rule
And dared none to rebel
But Oh the windflowers out of Nain
We know He loved them well!
He must have loved its tongue,
His Aramaic brogue,
As much as any Norman loves
The accents of La Hogue.
Discountried and diskinged
And watched from pole to pole,
A Jew at heart remains a Jew –
His nation is his soul.
Had He upon that day
Of headlong cloaks and boughs
Surrendered all mankind to race
And lifted David's brows,
They would not on his cross
Have writ as mocking news
That He the man from Nazareth
Was monarch of the Jews.
As heifers' to their young
Christ's bowels yearned to his sod.
He was the very Jew of Jews
And yet since He was God –
Oh you with frontiered hearts,
Conceive it if you can –
It was not life alone He gave,
But country up for man.

Eileen Duggan

489

The Jew's home has rarely been his 'castle'; throughout the
ages it has been something far higher – his sanctuary.

Joseph H. Hertz

Joy

490

Joy is distinctly a Christian word and a Christian thing. It is the reverse of happiness. Happiness is the result of what happens of an agreeable sort. Joy has its springs deep down inside, and that spring never runs dry, no matter what happens. Only Jesus gives that joy. He had joy, singing its music within, even under the shade of the cross. It is an unknown word and thing except as He has sway within.

Samuel Gordon

491

Joy is the echo of God's life within us.

Joseph Marmion

492

Can we not say to the young apprentice who has just learnt the use of a high precision lathe, and is thrilled at his new ability to use so apparently heavy and bulky a machine to prepare a piece of metal to a given shape with an accuracy of one ten-thousandth of an inch, that God is equally thrilled, and that this sheer joy in the situation is not wholly different from that of the angels who behold God's glory and rejoice?

C. A. Coulson

493

Joy is prayer – Joy is strength – Joy is love – Joy is a net of love by which you can catch souls.

Mother Teresa

494

Health enough to make work a pleasure.
Wealth enough to support your needs.
Strength to battle with difficulties and overcome them.
Grace enough to confess your sins and forsake them.
Patience enough to toil until some good is accomplished.
Charity enough to see some good in your neighbour.
Love enough to move you to be useful and helpful to others.
Faith enough to make real the things of God.
Hope enough to remove all anxious fears concerning the
   future.

Johann Wolfgang von Goethe

495

Those who bring sunshine to the lives of others cannot keep
it from themselves.

J.M. Barrie

496

There was a medieval king who regularly used the advice of
a wise man. This sage was summoned to the king's
presence. The monarch asked him how to get rid of his
anxiety and depression of spirits, how he might be really
happy, for he was sick in body and mind. The sage replied,
'There is but one cure for the king. Your Majesty must
sleep one night in the shirt of a happy man.'

Messengers were dispatched throughout the realm to
search for a man who was truly happy. But everyone who
was approached had some cause for misery, something that
robbed them of true and complete happiness. At last they
found a man – a poor beggar – who sat smiling by the
roadside and, when they asked him if he was really happy
and had no sorrows, he confessed that he was a truly happy
man. Then they told him what they wanted. The king must
sleep one night in the shirt of a happy man, and had given

them a large sum of money to procure such a shirt. Would he sell them his shirt that the king might wear it? The beggar burst into uncontrollable laughter, and replied, 'I am sorry I cannot oblige the king. I haven't a shirt on my back.'

Anon.

497
Happiness is the practice of the virtues.

Clement of Alexandria

498
'There was a little Indian girl at school today,' announced my son proudly. 'Does she speak English?' I asked. 'No,' came the reply, 'But it doesn't matter because she laughs in English.'

Anon.

499
There is a story of an Irishman who died suddenly and went up for divine judgment, feeling extremely uneasy. He didn't think he had done much good on earth! There was a queue ahead of him, so he settled down to look and listen. After consulting his big book, Christ said to the first man in the queue: 'I see here that I was hungry and you gave me to eat. Good man! Go on into Heaven.' To the second he said: 'I was thirsty and you gave me to drink,' and to the third: 'I was in prison and you visited me.' And so it went on. As each man ahead of him was sent to Heaven the Irishman examined his conscience and felt he had a great deal to fear. He'd never given anyone food or drink, he hadn't visited prisoners or the sick. Then his turn came. Trembling he watched Christ examining the book. Then Christ looked up and said: 'Well there's not much written here, but you did

do something: I was sad and discouraged and depressed;
you came and told me funny stories, made me laugh and
cheered me up. Get along to Heaven!'

That story makes the point that no form of charity should
be neglected or undervalued.

Anon.

500

Recently I visited a man, a fervent agnostic, whose wife and
children are devout Christians. He was affable, easy to talk
to, and when I asked him if his family had moved him to
wonder about their faith he answered with candour. 'I've
no time for any religion.' 'Why?' I asked. 'Because it makes
them melancholy. It makes my wife melancholy, it makes
my children melancholy.'

Anon.

501

An Englishman, a Frenchman and a Russian were trying to
define true happiness. 'True happiness', said the Englishman, 'is when you return home tired after work and find a
gin and tonic waiting for you.' 'You English have no
romance,' countered the Frenchman. 'True happiness is
when you go on a business trip, find a pretty girl who
entertains you, and then you part without regrets.' 'You are
both wrong,' concluded the Russian. 'Real true happiness
is when you are home in bed at four o'clock in the morning
and there is a hammering at the front door and there stand
members of the Secret Police who say to you, "Ivan
Ivanovitch, you are under arrest," and you are able to
reply, "Sorry! Ivan Ivanovitch lives next door!" '

Anon.

502

Joy is never in our power, and pleasure is. I doubt whether

anyone who has tasted joy would ever, if both were in his power, exchange it for all the pleasure in the world.

C.S. Lewis

503
We are all strings in the concert of his joy.

Jakob Boehme

504
Happiness is a butterfly, which, when pursued is always beyond our grasp, but which, if you will sit down quietly, may alight upon you.

Nathaniel Hawthorne

505
The sweet mark of a Christian is not faith, or even love, but joy.

Samuel M. Shoemaker

506
Christian Joy is the flag which is flown high from the castle of the heart when the King is in residence there.

P. Raimy

Kindness

507
One day, so says an old legend, God gave a banquet for all his servants, and a really grand feast it was. All the virtues came and had a fine time. Humility was there, sitting in the lowest place at the table. Patience was there and didn't mind at all being served last. Faith and Hope sat together. Everyone was having a wonderful time.

At the height of the banquet, Charity noticed that two of

the virtues were strangers to each other. He was surprised because he thought they were always together and he had purposely placed them side by side for just that reason. He came down to them and asked each one whether she had met her partner before. When they said that they had not, Charity introduced them: 'Kindness, I want you to meet Gratitude.' Both the virtues were so surprised to find out who the other was, Kindness said to Gratitude: 'We are supposed to be always together. Where one of us is, the other should be. Isn't it a pity that we have never really met before?'

P. Fontaine

508

Kindness has converted more sinners than zeal, eloquence and learning.

Frederick W. Faber

509

There are ten strong things. Iron is strong, but fire melts it. Fire is strong, but water quenches it. Water is strong but the clouds evaporate it. Clouds are strong, but wind drives them away. Man is strong but fears cast him down. Fear is strong, but sleep overcomes it. Sleep is strong, yet death is stronger. But loving kindness survives death.

The Talmud

510

Life is mostly froth and bubble,
  Two things stand like stone;
Kindness in another's trouble:
  Courage in your own.

Adam L. Gordon

511

John Wesley, on one of his countless travels, discovered he was sharing a carriage with an army officer. Their conversation was lively and interesting but the officer's contribution was punctuated by swear words and blasphemies. The gentle Wesley was most disturbed by this language but made an effort not to show his displeasure.

When they stopped to change the coach horses, Wesley seized the opportunity to have a word with the officer. 'I wonder if I might ask you a favour,' Wesley asked. The officer, pleasantly surprised, agreed. 'We will be travelling some distance together,' Wesley said, 'and if I should forget myself and use a swear word in front of the ladies, perhaps you would kindly correct me?' The officer immediately took the point, and Wesley's method of reproof worked perfectly.

Anon.

The Kingdom of God

512

Everybody in this room has been taught to pray 'Thy kingdom come'. Now, if we hear a man swear in the streets, we think it very wrong, and say he 'takes God's name in vain'. But there's a twenty-times worse way of taking His name in vain than that. It is to *ask God for what we don't want.* He doesn't like that sort of prayer. If you don't want a thing, don't ask for it ... If you do not wish for His kingdom, don't pray for it. But if you do, you must do more than pray for it; you must work for it.

J. Ruskin

513

Power in complete subordination to love – that is something like a definition of the Kingdom of God.

William Temple

514

A Russian youth who had become a conscientious objector to war through the reading of Tolstoy and the New Testament was brought before a magistrate. With the strength of conviction he told the judge of the life which loves its enemies, which does good to those who despitefully use it, which overcomes evil with good, and which refuses war.

'Yes,' said the judge, 'I understand. But you must be realistic. These laws you are talking about are the laws of the kingdom of God; and it has not come yet.'

The young man straightened and said, 'Sir, I recognise that it has not come for you, nor yet for Russia or the world. But the kingdom of God has come for me! I cannot go on hating and killing as though it had not come.'

Neil S. Swanson

515

This life, this Kingdom of God, this simplicity of absolute existence, is hard to enter. How hard? As hard as the master of salvation could find words to express the hardness.

George MacDonald

516

Christ looked at the people.
He saw them assailed by fear:
He saw the locked door;
He saw the knife in the hand;
He saw the buried coin;
He saw the unworn coat,
consumed by moth;
He saw the stagnant water
drawn and kept in the pitcher,
the musty bread in the bin –

the defended,
the unshared,
the ungiven.
He told them then
of the love
that casts out fear,
of the love that is four walls
and a roof over the head:
of the knife in the sheath,
of the coin in the open hand,
of the coin given
warm with the giver's life,
of the water poured in the cup,
of the table spread –
the undefended,
the shared,
the given –
the Kingdom of Heaven.

Caryll Houselander

517

'Where are you going your Royal Highness?'

'Wherever the king goes.'

'But do you know exactly where the king is going?'

'He has told me in a general way, but I'm not anxious to know. I only want to go with him.'

'So, your Majesty, you have no idea about this journey?'

'No, I have no idea, except that it will be in the company of my dear lord and husband.'

'Your husband is going to Egypt, and stopping at Acre, and many other places. Don't you mean to go there too your Majesty?'

'No, not really. All I want is to be near my king. It is quite unimportant to me where he goes, except in so far as he will be there. I'm not so much going as following him. I don't want to make this journey, but the king's presence is enough for me.'

Francis of Sales

518

To accept his kingdom and to enter in brings blessedness, because the best conceivable thing is that we should be in obedience to the will of God.

C.H. Dodd

519
The Donkey

When fishes flew and forests walkèd
And figs grew upon thorn,
Some moment when the moon was blood,
Then surely I was born;
With monstrous head and sickening cry
And ears like errant wings,
The devil's walking parody,
On all four-footed things.
The tattered outlaw of the earth,
Of ancient crooked will;
Starve, scourge, deride me: I am dumb,
I keep my secret still.
Fools! for I also had my hour;
One far fierce hour and sweet:
There was a shout about my ears,
And palms before my feet.

G.K. Chesterton

520

Wherever God rules over the human heart as King, there is the Kingdom of God established.

Paul W. Harrison

Last Judgment

521

The last judgment is not fable or allegory, but vision. Vision or imagination is a representation of what eternally exists, really and unchangeably. Fable or allegory is formed by the daughters of memory. Imagination is surrounded by the daughters of inspiration.

The Hebrew Bible and the Gospel of Jesus are not allegory, but eternal vision or imagination of all that exists.

William Blake

522

Judgment cannot be pronounced on a man until he has run his course.

Thomas Aquinas

523

Then one of the soldiers, without waiting for orders and without a qualm for the terrible consequences of his action but urged on by some unseen force, snatched up a blazing piece of wood, and climbing on another soldier's back, hurled the brand through a golden aperture giving access on the north side to the chambers built round the Sanctuary . . . A runner brought the news to Titus as he was resting in his tent after the battle. He leapt up as he was and ran to the Sanctuary to extinguish the blaze . . . Thus the Sanctuary, in defiance of Caesar's wishes, was set on fire.

Josephus

524

And when the last Great Scorer comes,
To write against your name,

He'll ask not if you won or lost,
But how you played the game.

Anon.

525

A 200-seater amphitheatre, costing £20,000, was built overlooking Sydney Harbour, Australia, in 1925, for the Second Coming of Christ. Members of the Order of the Star of the East, led by Hindu mystic Krishnamurti, believed that Christ would soon return to earth in human form and walk across the Pacific Ocean to the amphitheatre. When he did not arrive by 1929, the group dissolved, and a block of flats now occupies the site.

Anon.

526

If we have to answer for our lives after death, those people who have made other people unhappy will be the ones really in trouble with the Boss.

Jimmy Savile

Law

527

Under the blue laws of the seventeenth and eighteenth centuries Puritans administered religion to unwilling subjects by means of the whipping post, the ducking stool, the stocks, fines and prisons. Mrs Alice Morse Earle's history, *The Sabbath in Puritan New England*, lists such examples:
Two lovers, John Lewis and Sarah Chapman, were accused and tried for sitting together on the Lord's day under an apple tree. A Dunstable soldier, for wetting a piece of old hat to put in his shoe to protect his foot, was fined forty

shillings for doing this heavy work. Captain Kemble of Boston in 1656 was put in public stocks for two hours for his 'lewd and unseemly behaviour' which consisted of kissing his wife in public on the Sabbath on the door-step of his house after his return from a three-year voyage. A man who had fallen into the water absented himself from church to dry his only suit of clothes; he was found guilty and publicly whipped.

Anon.

528
Wherever law ends, tyranny begins.

John Locke

529
During the Second World War, in the mountain village of Giazza, north of Verona, German paratroopers were going to execute some villagers, presumably for showing resistance. The parish priest, Fr Domenico Mercante, offered himself as a hostage. The Germans accepted his offer, and decided to shoot him. When the time came, one of the firing-party refused to obey orders. 'I can't shoot a priest,' he said. He was placed at the priest's side, and both were shot together. The soldier's name is unknown. Fifteen years later, the Bishop of Verona unveiled a simple white monument commemorating the two heroes. The German Embassy in Rome was represented, and the Italian Minister of Justice gave an address. He said, 'The example of a priest and a soldier dying by the same rifle-fire, in order that not only the written law but the unwritten law too should be respected, provides an example of great moral value. It gives rise to the hope that the cause of peace amongst men may find its strongest protection in the conscience of humble but heroic spirits.'

F.H. Drinkwater

530

Alice: While you talk, he's gone.

More: And go he should, if he were the Devil himself, until he broke the law!

Roper: So now you'd give the Devil benefit of law?

More: Yes. What would you do? Cut a great road through the law to get after the Devil?

Roper: I'd cut down every law in England to do that.

More: Oh? And when the last law was down, and the Devil turned round on you – where would you hide, Roper, the laws all being flat? This country's planted thick with laws from coast to coast – Man's laws, not God's – and if you cut them down – and you are just the man to do it – d'you really think you could stand upright in the winds that would blow then? Yes, I'd give the Devil benefit of law, for my own safety's sake.

Robert Bolt, 'A Man for all Seasons'

Law – Mosaic

531

There are seventy ways of studying Torah; one is in silence.

Rabbi Tcharkover

532

When Rabbis of Judaism used the word 'Torah' or Law, a complicated concept was involved.

(1) Technically the Torah refers to the Pentateuch or 'the Five Books of Moses'.

(2) In another sense 'the Torah' designates the actual scroll containing the Five Books of Moses.

(3) In a general sense, 'Torah' is all of Jewish Law.

(4) In the widest use of the word, 'Torah' refers to Judaism
     as a religion or philosophy.

Anon.

533
What is hateful to you, do not to your fellow: that is the
whole Law: all the rest is interpretation.

Rabbi Hillel

Life

534
To be alive, and not half-dead seek Jesus who is alive. Seek
Him even if you seem to have lost Him. He loves you.
Finding Him you will find everything: love, peace, trust.
Then life is worth living.

Roger Schultz

535
There was the character who discovered at a tender age
that life was a deck-chair, hard to assemble into a coherent,
useful or permanent shape, and even if assembled, liable to
collapse without notice at any moment. Jesus did not come
to take away all the troubles that chance and change fling
against us. He came to teach us his way of living, which is a
rock to stand on. He came to show us the truth, which gives
us balance. He came to offer life eternal, which gives us
perspective.

He'll help you with your deck-chair, but mind your
fingers.

Timothy Rice

536

She lay dying. On a rough board, in a cold barracks at Dachau, surrounded by other coughing, crying prisoners. A harried doctor, also an inmate of the prison, bent over her. The old Jewish lady looked up, 'How are you today?' he asked. Her eyes lit up. She smiled.

'How can she be smiling,' the doctor thought, 'in her condition, in this hell-hole?'

She glanced up over his shoulder, towards a small window high up in the wall. The doctor followed her eyes, and through the window saw a solitary branch with a green leaf.

'I've been listening to that branch all morning,' she whispered. He bent lower, worried that she was hallucinating.

'The leaf was talking to you?' he asked.

'Yes.' A smile softened her pain-worn face.

'What did the leaf tell you?'

Very softly she confided, 'Over and over it said: Life . . . life . . . new life.'

Soon after, the old woman died. The doctor, Victor Frankl, survived and became a world famous psychiatrist. He recalled this experience in his book *Man's Search for Meaning*.

537

That wonderful Dutch Christian Corrie ten Boom grew up in a shop full of clocks. Her father was a watchmaker and she was the first woman in Holland officially licensed to follow the same trade.

She tells the Dutch parable of the clock that had just been made and was put on a shelf between two old clocks.

One of the old clocks said to the newcomer: 'So you have started out in life. I am sorry for you. If you'll just think ahead and see how many ticks it takes to tick through one year, you will never make it. It would have been better had the maker never wound you up and set your pendulum.'

So the new clock began to count up the ticks.

'Each second requires two ticks, which means 120 ticks per minute,' he calculated.

'That's 7,200 ticks per hour; 172,800 ticks per day; 1,209,600 ticks per week for 52 weeks, which makes a total of 62,899,200 ticks per year. Horrors.' The clock immediately had a nervous breakdown and stopped ticking!

But the wise old clock on the other side said, 'Pay no attention to him. Just think. How many ticks do you have to tick at a time?'

'Why, only one, I guess,' the new clock answered.

'There now. That's not so hard, is it? Try it along with me. Just one tick at a time.'

Seventy-five years later the clock was still ticking perfectly one tick at a time!

Similarly, no man sinks under the burden of the day. It is only when yesterday's guilt is added to tomorrow's anxiety that our legs buckle and our backs break.

Anon.

538

'I thank God for my handicaps for through them I have found myself, my work and my God.'

These are the words of Helen Keller, who in over eighty years of existence lived three distinct lives, milestones in the triumph of the human spirit over affliction, utter isolation and despair.

Stricken by a strange disease that left her so that she could not hear or see when she was almost nineteen months old, Helen Keller began a life of loneliness in the sudden silence and blackness of a strange world that cut her off from all she knew and loved. As her young mind developed, she fought furiously to free herself.

Anne Sullivan arrived at the Keller homestead in Alabama early in 1887 and through patience and perseverance finally roused the first spark in the child's mind by teaching her the meaning of words attached to things and how to talk and express her thoughts with her fingers.

In time though, Helen Keller was able to earn her own livelihood through lecturing and writing.

But Helen Keller's third life was the most important and dearest to her heart – her tireless efforts over four decades in creating better understanding of the deaf and blind everywhere on earth.

She visited every state in the USA, covered every continent and nearly every country during six gruelling world tours, and raised vast sums to provide better care and education for those afflicted as she was. In this great and unselfish crusade she did more for the silent and the sightless of the world than anyone who ever lived.

And this is the statement Helen Keller made long ago: 'Life is an exciting business and most exciting when lived for others.'

Richard Harrity and Ralph G. Martin

Life After Death

539

Eternal Life – there is no end to it! It is life without end. The government was trying to make a treaty with the Indians, and in one place put the word, 'forever'. The Indians did not like the word 'forever', and said, 'No, put it, "as long as water runs and grass grows".' The Indians could understand that.

Dwight L. Moody

540

I know as much about the afterlife as you do – nothing. I must wait and see.

William Inge

541

Over the triple doorway of the Cathedral of Milan, there are three inscriptions spanning the splendid arches. Over one is carved a beautiful wreath of roses, and underneath is the legend: 'All that pleases is but for a moment.'

Over the other is sculptured a cross, and these are the words beneath: 'All that troubles is but for a moment.'

But underneath the great central entrance in the main aisle is the inscription 'That only is important which is eternal.'

Anon.

542

For a small living, men run a great way; for eternal life, many will scarce move a single foot from the ground.

Thomas à Kempis

543

· Ancient British practices demanded that mourners had to carry branches of yew and throw them into the grave after the body had been committed. It was thought that they would shoot and they were thus regarded as symbolic of the resurrection of the body, as well as the immortality of the soul.

Don Lewis

544

To be immortal is to share in Divinity.

Clement of Alexandria

545

There was a meeting of the board of directors going on in Hell. Satan was concerned over the fact that business was not increasing. He wanted to reach as many people as possible and draw them into Hell.

One demon jumped up and said: 'I'll go back to earth and convince the people that there is no Heaven.'

'That won't do,' said Satan, 'We've tried it before and it doesn't work.'

'I'll convince them that there is no Hell,' offered a second demon.

'No – that doesn't work either,' said Satan.

A wise old veteran in the back of the room rose and said, 'If you let me go back to earth, I can fill this place. I'll just convince them that there is no hurry.'

Anon.

546

One of my favourite stories is about the golfer who goes to hell and is astonished to find himself on the most beautiful golf course he has ever seen. A little horned caddy brings him the most magnificent and deadly golf clubs he has ever handled. He takes a few practice swings with the driver and it cuts the air with the authority of a practised sword. Power surges through his muscles. 'OK, caddy, put down a ball.' 'I'm sorry, sir. That's the hell of it. There are no balls.'

Eamon Andrews

Light of the World

547

'The Light of the World' is the title of a famous picture by Holman Hunt painted in 1854. It portrays Christ, thorn-crowned, and carrying a lantern, knocking at a closed door.

When the artist showed the completed picture to some friends, one pointed out what seemed to be an omission.

'You have put no handle on the door,' he said to Holman Hunt. The artist relied, 'We must open to the Light – the handle is on the inside.'

Anon.

548

That Light whose smile kindles the Universe.
That Beauty in which all things work and more . . .

Percy Bysshe Shelley

549

Two legends enhance the lustre of the Koh-i-Noor diamond; that is that it must never be worn by a man, and its owner will rule the world. The diamond's name means 'Mountain of Light'. It flashed among the possessions of the Mogul Emperor Mohammed when he fell to Nadir, the Shah of Persia, who in turn died in a palace revolt of 1747. One hundred years later, it was the brightest jewel in the male-dominated Sikh empire that was conquered by the British Empire. Since then it has been worn by three English queens, but never by an English king.

Anon.

550

There is a famous cave, some sixty miles from Auckland in New Zealand. It is known as the cave of the glow-worms. You reach it in a boat pulled by a wire for silence. As you glide down the stream, you suddenly come across a soft light gleaming in the distance; then you enter a magic world of fairyland. From the top of the cave, thousands of threads hang down from the glowing insects. So great is the light that it is possible to read a book there. But if there is the slightest noise, the bright light dies out, just as if a switch had been turned off.

Anon.

551

A man was flying his single-engine airplane towards a small country airport. It was late in the day, and before he could get the plane into position to land, dusk fell and he could not see the hazy field below. He had no lights on his plane and there was no one on duty at the airport. He began circling, but the darkness deepened, and for two hours he flew that plane around and around, knowing that he would certainly crash when his fuel was expended.

Then a miracle occurred. Someone on the ground heard his engine and realised his plight. A man drove his car back and forth on the runway, to show where the airstrip was and then shone the headlights from the far end of the strip to guide the pilot to a safe landing.

Christ is the Light and the Way for our lives. There is safety in the lighted area of his path for us. But disaster lies in the darkness to the left or the right.

James Dobson

552

The Spirit in man is the candle of the Lord,
lighted by God, and lighting men to God.

Benjamin Whichcote

553

The story goes that a little girl was with her family in a party being shown around one of our great cathedrals. As the guide was explaining an historic tomb nearby, the girl was staring at a great stained glass window through which the summer sun was streaming, bathing the cathedral floor in colour. As the group was about to move on she asked the guide in a shrill clear voice, 'Who are those people in the pretty window?' 'Those are the saints,' the man replied.

That night as she was undressing for bed she told her mother, 'I know who the saints are.'

'Do you dear?' replied her mother. 'Who are they?'
'They're the people who let the light shine through.'

Anon.

554

It is said that Tennyson was walking one day in a beautiful
garden where many flowers were blooming. A friend who
accompanied him said: 'Mr Tennyson, you speak so often
of Jesus. Will you tell me what Christ really means to you?'
Tennyson stopped, thought a moment and then, pointing
down to a beautiful flower, said: 'What the sun is to the
flower, Jesus Christ is to my soul.'

Anon.

Little Things

555

Over 10,000 people in Provence, France, owe their homes
and environment to a little known peasant shepherd.
Elezard Bouffier lived alone, in 1910, in a barren region
where there were very few trees. While tending his flock in
the autumn, the shepherd would pick up each acorn that he
saw. In the early spring, while watching the sheep, he
would prod the earth with his staff and drop in a nut. He
did this each year between 1910 and 1947. At his death, the
barren countryside was covered by trees and teeming with
wild life. It is now the pleasant site of a new housing
development.

Anon.

556

He does most in God's great world who does his best in his
own little world.

Thomas Jefferson

557

I long to accomplish a great and noble task, but it is my
chief duty to accomplish small tasks as if they were great
and noble. Green, the historian, tells us that the world is
moved along, not only by the mighty shoves of its heroes,
but also by the aggregate of the tiny pushes of each honest
worker.

Helen Keller

558

I come in the little things,
Saith the Lord;
Yea! on the glancing wings
Of eager birds, the softly pattering feet
Of furred and gentle beasts, I come to meet
Your hard and wayward heart. In brown bright eyes
That peep from out of the brake, I stand confest.
On every nest
Where feathery Patience is content to brood,
And leaves her pleasure for this high emprise
Of motherhood –
There doth my Godhead rest.

Evelyn Underhill

559

Exactness in little duties is a wonderful source of cheerfulness.

F.W. Faber

560

An old legend tells us that Jesus and his disciples were
going one summer's day from Jerusalem to Jericho. Peter
was at Jesus' side. On the road lay a horseshoe, which the
Master desired Peter to pick up. But the disciple let it lie.

Jesus, however, stooped and picked it up. In the village he exchanged it for a measure of cherries. When they came to a hill and the way lay between heated rocks, Peter was tormented with thirst and fell behind. Then the Master dropped a ripe cherry every few steps, teaching him that things despised often come to unexpected uses.

Edgar W. Work

561

On being asked why God had made Miss Davis so little, and Mrs Smith so large, Robert Burns, the great Scottish poet, wrote on a windowpane in an inn at Moffat, the following:

> Ask why God made the gem so small,
>   An' why so huge the granite?
> Because God meant mankind should set
> That higher value on it!

Anon.

562

A man who had hitch-hiked from coast to coast of the USA, and who had walked many miles in the process, was asked what he found the hardest to endure. To the surprise of his questioner, it was not the steep mountains or the dazzling sun or the scorching desert heat that had troubled him most, but – in the words of the traveller – 'it was the sand in my shoe'.

Anon.

563

In one of his essays Tolstoy says of Brulof, a celebrated Russian painter, how one day he corrected his pupil's study. The pupil having glanced at the altered drawing

explained, 'Why, you only touched it a tiny bit!' But Brulof
replied, 'Art begins where the tiny bit begins.' 'That
saying', Tolstoy goes on, 'is strikingly true, not of art alone,
but of all life.'

Anon.

Lord's Prayer

564

Papa bilong mipela,
Yu i stap long heven.
Nem bilong yu i mas i stap holi,
Kingdom bilong yu i mas i kam long ol ples.
Maus bilong yu ol i bihainim long heven
Olsem tasol mipela olgeta i mas bihainim long
graun tu.
Kaikai bilong mipela bilong de nau yu givem
mipela.
I usim sin bilong mipela.
Mipela tu i lusim sin ol i mekim long mipela.
You no bringim mipela long samting bilong
traim mipela.
Tekewe mipela long olgeta samting nogut.
Kingdom na strong na bikem i bilong you tasol.

oltaim oltaim, Tru.

This is the Lord's prayer in Pidgin English. Pidgin is used
widely in New Guinea, where there are over seven hundred
languages spoken by different New Guinea tribes. Pidgin
helps a New Guinean to talk with other New Guineans
from other tribes.

565
Every day we plead in the Lord's Prayer, 'Thy will be

done,' yet when his will is done we grumble and are not
pleased with it.

Meister Eckhart

566
Daily Bread

And there was manna in the wilderness.
Hunger and weakness were the only things
Remembered and the land of all desire
Was merely a vague promise, long forgotten.
At odds with life, at variance with themselves,
Lost, but for one more conscious than the rest,
They prayed for food and lavish for the asking
Was that bread eaten at the Master's table.

Nourish the seed of the truth in me, that I
May find fulfilment of my destiny.
Sustain in me the flower of understanding,
That in this sterile and ungentle place,
This wilderness, the urgent word of God
May live, and not be lost to me for ever.

David Scott Blackhall

567

I have a creed, none better and none shorter.
It is told in two words – the
first of the Paternoster. And when I say
these words I mean them.

Oliver Wendell Holmes

568
Deliver us from evil

Evil is real and cannot be destroyed
By making a blind bargain with my soul

To call it good. Temptation is the dream
Which fabicates the specious compromise.
There is no solemn battle with temptation,
It is against myself I must contend,
For no man sanctions evil till he finds
A way to justify it to himself.

That I may make this point of consciousness
More live and lovelier than the will of life,
May find my meaning in a new direction
And come untroubled to the house of God,
The strength and wisdom which are yours alone
To give, Father, do not withhold from me.

For Thine is the kingdom, and the power,
and the glory, for ever. Amen.

David Scott Blackhall

Love

569

This theme of love is the most important in the world. All
the world's tragedies, tragedies of individuals and of
groups, are tragedies of love. One could always ask, 'What
are they seeking?' Wars of course are just the clash of loves.
One country loves this and finds that another country is
loving the same thing, perhaps loving the right thing in the
wrong way. What domestic tragedies there are, all centred
around love! Love is at the heart of all great struggles.

Vincent McNabb

570

Some 800 years after her death, the solicitude of an
Englishwoman for the poor continues to have its effects.
    To this day, as a result of her remarkable bequest, a

supply of six pounds of flour is given to each adult and three pounds to each child in two small Hampshire villages.

Her husband, the story goes, who had little compassion for the poor, was impatient when she asked, shortly before her death in the twelfth century, that he give something to the poor every year in her memory.

Setting fire to a branch, he told her he would donate the produce from as much land as she could crawl around while the branch still burned.

Despite her weakened condition, she is said to have crawled around twenty-three acres before the flame died out. Touched by her love for others, her husband kept his word.

Anon.

571

Give me such love for God and men, as will blot out all hatred and bitterness.

Dietrich Bonhoeffer

572

Late have I loved you, O beauty so ancient and so new; late have I loved you! For behold you were within me, and I outside; and I sought you outside and in my ugliness fell upon those lovely things that you have made. You were with me and I was not with you. I was kept from you by those things yet had they not been in you, they would not have been at all. You called and cried to me and broke upon my deafness; and you sent forth your beam and shone upon me, and chased away my blindness; you breathed fragrance upon me, and I drew in my breath and do not pant for you; I tasted you and I now hunger and thirst for you; you touched me, and I now burned for your peace.

Augustine of Hippo

573

It is wrong to think of love without pain, As soon as the soul begins to love God a painful process begins. God brings a scourge and goes on scourging. At least He has not forgotten us when we are being scourged; and when we look at the matter properly, as we speak of pain, we will not be able to say God doesn't love us. He is driving out from the soul all its ill humours, to get it back to spiritual health. Very few healing treatments are free from pain. If we try to dull the pain, we dull consciousness.

Vincent McNabb

574

You had pierced our hearts with the arrow of Your love, and our minds were pierced with the arrows of Your words.

Augustine of Hippo

575

God lies in wait for us with nothing so much as love.

Now love is like a fishhook.

A fisher cannot catch a fish unless the fish first picks up the hook. If the fish swallows the hook, no matter how it may squirm and turn the fisher is certain of the fish. Love is the same way. Whoever it captured by love takes up his hook in such a fashion that foot and hand, mouth and eyes, heart and all that is in that person must always belong to God. Therefore, look only for this fishhook, and you will be happily caught. The more you are caught, the more you will be liberated.

Meister Eckhart

576

Someday,
after mastering
the winds, the waves,

the tides and gravity,
we shall harness for God
the energies of love,

and then,
for the second time
in the history of the world,
man will discover fire.

Teilhard de Chardin

577

'Love', wrote a survivor of the Ravensbruck concentration camp, 'is larger than the walls which shut it in' (Corrie ten Boom). This was certainly true of the growing Christian movement in the Acts of the Apostles – literally!

Richard Bewes

578

We are put on earth a little space that we may learn to bear the beams of love.

William Blake

579

Without charity, we may have patience, but we will not have the virtue of patience. We may have temperance, but not the virtue of temperance; fortitude, but not the virtue of fortitude. We wouldn't have the virtue in its totality. The one thing that makes a virtue of all good habits is charity, doing things through the love of God. It seems such a small thing, but if the seed of charity is really there, all the other virtues proceed to branch forth.

Vincent McNabb

580

The renowned theologian, Dr Karl Barth, was spending an evening within the intimate circle of friends. Curious to know more about the great theologian's thinking, one of those present asked him: 'What is the most profound thought that ever entered your mind?'

After a brief moment of reflection Dr Barth replied very simply: 'The most profound thought I have ever known is the simple truth: Jesus loves me, this I know, for the Bible tells me so.'

Anon.

581

Love has a hem to its garment
    That touches the very dust;
It can reach the stains of the streets and lanes,
    And because it can, it must.

Anon.

582

Jesus asked a small child 'How much do you love me?'
    The child smiled back and replied 'Lots and lots.'
    Then the child asked Jesus 'How much do you love me?'
    Jesus stretched his arms out wide and tenderly said 'I love you this much.'
Then, they nailed him to the Cross.

'Thought for the Day'

583

Love seeketh not itself to please,
    nor for itself have any care,
but for another gives it ease,
    and builds a heaven in hell's despair.

William Blake

584

A father complained to the Besht that his son had forsaken
God.

'What, Rabbi, shall I do?'

'Love him more than ever,' was the Besht's reply.

Jewish saying

Love Your Neighbour

585

Aristides, a non-Christian, defended the Christians before
the Emperor Hadrian, in the second century AD, in the
following words:

Christians love one another. They never fail to help
widows; they save orphans from those who would hurt
them. If a man has something, he gives freely to the man
who has nothing. If they see a stranger, Christians take him
home and are happy, as though he were a real brother.
They don't consider themselves brothers in the usual sense,
but brothers instead through the Spirit, in God. And if they
hear that one of them is in jail or persecuted for professing
the name of their Redeemer, they all give him what he
needs ... This is really a new kind of person. There is
something divine in them.

Aristides

586

The Rabbi Hillel was a renowned scribe in Jerusalem about
the time of Christ's birth; he seems to have died about AD
10, aged eighty. He was called 'the Great' or 'the Elder',
and his interpretations of the Law were less severe than
others. He is said to have been the grandfather of Gamaliel
(Acts 22.3) who taught Paul. Our Lord must have heard

often of Hillel, and could possibly have spoken with him during the three days before the finding in the Temple.

Here is one of the tales our Lord might have heard. A certain gentile came to Shammai (Shammai was the leader of the more strict school of interpretation) and said that he would like to become a proselyte, but could not stay long in Jerusalem. 'Can you teach me the whole Torah while I am standing on one foot?' Shammai sent him away angrily. So the gentile went to Hillel with the same question. Hillel admitted him as a convert, and said, 'Whatever is hateful to thee, do not do to thy fellow-man. This is the whole Law: all the rest is interpretation. Now go and study.'

F.H. Drinkwater

587

Believe nothing against another but on good authority; nor report what may hurt another, unless it be a greater hurt to conceal it.

William Penn

588

Tolstoy's story of *The Two Pilgrims* tells of two Russians who set out on a pilgrimage to Jerusalem intent on being present at the solemn Easter festivities. One had his mind so set on the journey's end and object that he would stop for nothing and take thought for nothing but the journey. The other, passing through, found people to be helped at every turn and actually spent so much time and money along the way that he never reached the Holy City. But something came to him from God which the other missed: and something came through him from God into the lives of men which the other failed to find in the great Easter celebration.

William P. Merrill

589

Imagine thyself always to be the servant of all, and look upon all as if they were Christ our Lord in person; and so shalt thou do Him honour and reverence.

Teresa of Avila

590

A Persian poet has put it all in a single stanza:

No one could tell me what my soul might be;
I searched for God, and God eluded me;
I sought my brother out, and found all three,
My soul, my God, and all humanity.

Frank D. Adams

591

A small boy from a poor family wrote to God for help. His letter, addressed simply 'To God', asked if he could send £50 to buy food and clothing badly needed for his family. He said his father was out of work and his mother was ill and they had no money.

A Post Office official intercepted the letter and read it. He decided to give it to the local Rotary Club. The Club investigated and found the family was indeed destitute. However, as they only had £40 in their benevolent fund they gave that.

Some weeks later the Post Office official noticed another letter addressed 'To God'. He opened it and read: 'Dear God, thanks for the money you sent but next time could you deal direct? Those Rotary blokes took a commission out of it!'

Anon.

Loyalty

592

The year was 1940 and Joseph Meister, gatekeeper at the Pasteur Institute in Paris, was ordered by the German invaders to open Louis Pasteur's burial crypt. Rather than obey, he committed suicide.

There was good cause for his loyalty to Pasteur's memory. Fifty-five years earlier, he had been savagely bitten on his hands, legs and thighs by a mad dog. His case was hopeless – he would die a horrific and terrifying death, though it might be a month before the first signs of hydrophobia appeared. There was only one person who might save him – and he was not a doctor.

Louis Pasteur had been experimenting with his theory of inoculation against rabies, through giving repeated doses of vaccine taken from a rabid dog. So far he had experimented only on other animals – but always with success. Yet he dared not risk his vaccine on a human being. Friends and relatives appealed to him to help Meister. He had been so severely bitten that he was certain to contract the disease. There was nothing to lose.

After much mental anguish, Pasteur agreed to inoculate Joseph. Sixty hours after the accident, he had the first, weak dose of vaccine. Twelve more followed – each stronger than the last. At the end of them all, the patient showed no signs of the disease and returned home, full of health and gratitude to Pasteur.

His case made history. Only fifteen months later, 2,490 people had received the life saving anti-rabies vaccine.

Anon.

Luxury

593

Croesus, King of Lydia, born in 590 BC, had immense wealth and lived luxuriously. He filled his house with all manner of costly treasures. He thought he was the happiest of mortals. Solon, one of the seven wise men of Greece, paid him a visit and was received into a magnificent chamber. Solon showed no surprise or admiration. The king, angry at his indifference, asked Solon, 'Why do you not think me the most truly happy?' Solon replied, 'No man can be esteemed truly happy but he whose happiness God continues to the end of his life.'

Anon.

594

We act as though comfort and luxury were the chief requirements of life, when all that we need to make us really happy is something to be enthusiastic about.

Charles Kingsley

595

News Item: £100,000 is being bid for something special. The car number plate VIP 1 has come on to the market and the bidding is expected to begin at £100,000!

Anon.

596

Luxuries are what other people buy.

David White

597

A poor mother when asked why she was spending precious money to exchange her black and white television set for a

colour receiver, replied, 'I don't want my children growing
up not knowing what colour is!'

Anon.

598

It is easier to renounce worldly possessions than it is to
renounce the love of them.

Walter Hilton

599

Luxury is the first, second and third cause of ruin of
reputation. It is the vampire which soothes us into a fatal
slumber while it sucks the lifeblood of our veins.

Hamilton Malve

Mankind

600

Out of the raw materials, e.g., eyes, ears, nerve cells, fibres,
muscles, glands, etc., the self arises. The self passes through
many experiences; habits are acquired and built in by the
autonomic nervous system. All these things go to make
your personality.

But 'no man is an island entire of itself.' Thus, these
'little bits of personality' are woven together into larger
units – love for home, country. Some tendencies also
develop, e.g., selfishness or unselfishness; meanness or
generosity; honesty or dishonesty.

All go to make a person, a self, that can think long
thoughts; a being that can reflect on the past, live well in
the present and dream of the future. He has a capacity to
think of life in terms of God. It is not strange, therefore, to
speak of man being a walking miracle, a being 'made in the
image of God'.

John Leaver

601

Lord, what is man, whose thought, at times,
Up to Thy sevenfold brightness climbs,
  While still his grosser instinct clings
  To earth, like other creeping things!

John Greenleaf Whittier

602

Mankind has taken up just a fraction of Earth's time. It is almost impossible to imagine the vast expanse of time since the Earth was born out of gas and cosmic dust 5,000 million years ago.

Imagine the planet's history condensed into a single century. On the time scale produced by this leap of imagination, the oldest-known rocks began to form at the dawn of year 15, and life in its most primitive form of bacteria and algae appeared in the year 26. Until the year 80 life evolved slowly as the continents drifted about, and it was not until eight years ago that the first amphibians struggled ashore.

Dinosaurs were dominant three years ago, but by the following year they had become extinct.

Three weeks ago, the first man emerged in Africa, using tools and walking upright. The last Ice Age ended two hours ago, the Industrial Revolution started two minutes ago . . . and four seconds ago man set foot on the moon.

Anon.

603

God wants to come to his world, but he wants to come to it through man. This is the mystery of our existence, the Superhuman chance of mankind.

Martin Buber

604

What a chimera, then, is man!
what a novelty, what a monster,
what a chaos,
what a subject of contradiction,
what a prodigy!
A judge of all things,
feeble worm of the earth,
depository of the truth,
cloaca of uncertainty and error,
the glory and the shame
of the universe!

Blaise Pascal

Materialism

605

If you want to destroy a nation, give it too much – make it greedy, miserable and sick.

John Steinbeck

606

Jesus, on whom peace, has said:
The world is a bridge,
Pass over it,
But build not your dwelling there.

Inscription on the Great Mosque in Fateh-pur-Sikri, Delhi

607

Is this material progress? A recent report reveals that there are 7,000 pieces of metal, of all shapes and sizes from a complete satellite to a lost screwdriver, floating in space and continually circulating planet Earth!

Anon.

608

Theirs an endless road, a hopeless maze, who seek for goods before they seek for God.

Bernard of Clairvaux

609

A miser in France used to keep all his gold and precious things in a cellar under the floor of his house. One day he went down through a secret trap-door at the top of the cellar to gloat over his treasure. Then the trap-door banged down so that he could not get out. No one in the house knew about the cellar and the miser could not be found. People searched all over the place without finding him. After a long time, they gave up and the house was sold. The new people who bought the house wanted some new building work done and the cellar was found. When it was opened, the miser was found sitting at a table with all his gold glittering around him. The dead man had even eaten a candle before dying of hunger.

M. Nassan

610

The Sunday School teacher was talking to her class of ten-year-olds when she suddenly asked: 'Now, why do you think the Children of Israel made a golden calf?'

The children were silent until one little boy put up his hand and said: 'Please, Miss, perhaps it was because they didn't have enough gold to make a cow.'

Anon.

Marriage

611

In the ideal marriage husband and wife are not loyal to each other because it is their duty, but because it is their joy.

E. Merrill Root

612

Before President Ford married Elizabeth Bloomer, in 1948, they drew up a private marriage contract together.

'We sat down before the wedding, and in a very businesslike way, defined our objectives,' says Mrs Ford.

'We decided the number of children we would have, and ardently agreed to the mutual promise that one would never try to "change" the other.

'We decided, too, that a successful marriage is never really a fifty-fifty proposition and settled for a seventy-five twenty-five arrangement. Sometimes the seventy-five would emanate from my side. Sometimes it would have to be Jerry's gesture. We have carefully worked out the art of generous compromise.'

Marian Christy

613

Marriage is one long conversation, chequered by disputes.

R.L. Stevenson

614

'Adam and Eve must have scolded each other roundly during their 900 years together. Eve would have said, "You ate the apple!" And Adam would have replied, "But why did you give it to me?" There is no doubt that during their long life, they encountered numberless evils as they sighed over their Fall. It must have been an extraordinary regime! And so Genesis is a remarkable book of wisdom and reason.'

This was the kind of table talk you might have heard if Martin Luther had asked you to a meal in 1536. Having plumped for the marriage of the clergy, his mind constantly ran on the inconveniences of the married state. He had his strict side, too, and put up a notice to warn the University students of Hallé against prostitutes, and said that if he had his way, such women should be broken on the wheel and flayed for ruining young men. The students should pray God to provide them with pious wives, he said, adding grimly: 'You will have trouble enough as it is.'

Douglas Woodruff

615
A successful marriage is an edifice that must be rebuilt every day.

André Maurois

616
When the late Mr and Mrs Henry Ford celebrated their golden wedding anniversary, a reporter asked them, 'To what do you attribute your fifty years of successful married life?'

'The formula', said Ford, 'is the same formula I have always used in making cars – just stick to one model.'

Anon.

617
A husband should never address an angry word to his wife in the presence of a third party.

The more one criticizes, the less one loves.

Honoré de Balzac

618
A group of cinema engineers classified the following as the ten most dramatic sounds in the movies: a baby's first cry; the blast of a siren; the thunder of breakers on rocks: the roar of a forest fire; a fog-horn; the slow drip of water; the galloping of horses; the sound of a distant train whistle; the howl of a dog; the wedding march.

And one of these sounds causes more emotional response
and upheaval than any other, has the power to bring forth
almost every human emotion: sadness, envy, regret, sorrow,
tears, as well as supreme joy. It is the sound of the wedding
march.

James Florn

619
All marriages are happy. It's the living together afterwards
that causes all the trouble.

'Farmers' Almanac'

620
Dietrich Bonhoeffer, sitting in a Nazi prison cell, once
wrote a wedding sermon for a niece who was about to be
married. In it he said, 'Marriage is more than your love for
each other. It has a higher dignity and power, for it is God's
holy ordinance, through which he wills to perpetuate the
human race till the end of time. In your love you see only
your two selves in the world, but in marriage you are a link
in the chain of generations, which God causes to come and
to pass away to his glory, and calls into his kingdom. In
your love you see only the heaven of your happiness, but in
marriage you are placed at a post of responsibility towards
the world and mankind. Your love is your own private
possession, but marriage is more than something personal
it is a status, an office.'

Anon.

621
The essence of a good marriage is respect for each other's
personality combined with that deep intimacy, physical,

mental and spiritual, which makes a serious love between man and woman the most fructifying of all human experiences.

Bertrand Russell

622

On their fiftieth wedding anniversary, a couple summed up the reason for their long and happy marriage. The husband said, 'I have tried never to be selfish. After all, there is no "I" in the word "marriage".'

The wife said, 'For my part, I have never corrected my husband's spelling.'

Robert Brault

623

Falsely your Church seven sacraments does frame: Penance and Matrimony are the same!

Richard Duke

624

'When you're a married man, Samivel, you'll understand a good many things as you don't understand now; but vether its worth while goin' through so much to learn so little, as the charity-boy said when he got to the end of the alphabet, is a matter o' taste. I rayther think it isn't.'

Charles Dickens, 'Pickwick Papers'

625

Wife, reading husband's fortune card from weighing-machine: 'You are a leader with a magnetic personality and a strong character. You are intelligent, witty and attractive to the opposite sex.' She paused. 'It has your weight wrong too.'

F.A.J. Bernhardt

Mercy

626

A notable instance of mercy shown to enemies occurred in Swiss history, when, in 1318, the town of Solothurn was being besieged by the Emperor Leopold. The river Rare, near which the town stands, was much swollen at the time, and a bridge that the beleaguered forces had thrown across was carried away by the flood, and their men were being drowned in large numbers.

Then the Solothurners, forgetting all injuries, rushed out with boats to save their enemies. Leopold was so touched by this magnanimity that he at once raised the siege, and presented the town with a beautiful banner.

Anon.

627

There's a wideness in God's mercy
Like the wideness of the sea,
There's a kindness in his justice,
Which is more than liberty.

Frederick W. Faber

628

Among the attributes of God, although they are all equal, mercy shines with even more brilliance than justice.

Cervantes

629

A mother sought from Napoleon the pardon of her son. The Emperor said it was the man's second offence, and justice demanded his death.

'I don't ask for justice,' said the mother, 'I plead for mercy.'

'But', said the Emperor, 'he does not deserve mercy.'

'Sir,' cried the mother, 'it could not be mercy if he deserved it, and mercy is all I ask.'

'Well, then,' said the Emperor, 'I will have mercy.' And her son was saved.

Anon.

630

Teach me to feel another's woe, to hide the fault I see; that mercy I to others show, that mercy show to me.

Alexander Pope

631

A boy was sent by his teacher to the principal of the school for doing something wrong. After hearing the facts the principal took out a blank book and wrote down the boy's name, observing as he did so: 'You have not been sent to me before. Now, I don't know you: you may be a good boy, for all I know. Good boys sometimes make mistakes. Now I'll just make a note in pencil that you were sent to me today, and I will also note why you were sent. But you see I am making this memorandum in pencil, and I am not bearing on very hard. And if you are not sent to me again this year, I shall erase this from my book and no one will ever know anything about it.' It was a lesson in mercy the boy never forgot.

F.H. Drinkwater

Ministry

632

He who goes up with fear comes down with honour.

Ancient inscription on a pulpit

633

'My friends,' said a village churchwarden, addressing a meeting of parishioners, 'our dear vicar, as you know, will shortly be leaving us to take up work in another parish, and I therefore propose we take up a collection to give him a little momentum.'

Anon.

634

No man preaches his sermon well to others if he doth not first preach it to his own heart.

John Owen

635

The clergy can be the greatest barrier to spiritual growth in the world.

Leon Suenens

636

Everyone who can preach the truth and does not preach it, incurs the judgment of God.

Justin Martyr

637

A little boy who was hoping to become a preacher, was horribly dismayed when his mother told him he would have to be always good. 'What!' said he. 'Shall I have to be *always* good?' 'Yes,' said his mother, 'always good!' 'But, mother, shall I have to be always *very* good?' 'Yes, you will have to be always very good.' 'Then,' said the boy, after he had thought a bit: 'I think I shall be a *local* preacher.'

Anon.

Miracles

638

I cannot understand people having historical difficulties about miracles. For, once you grant that miracles *can* happen, all the historical evidence at our disposal bids us believe that sometimes they do.

R. A. Knox

639

Miracles are the swaddling-clothes of infant churches.

English proverb

640

Miracles are important, and are only important because they provide evidence of the fact that the universe is not a closed system, and that effects in the natural world can be produced by the reactions of non-human will.

Arnold Lunn

641

Jesus was himself the one convincing and permanent miracle.

Ian MacLaren

642

Some of the Christians referred to are in prison for the crime of 'miraculous healings'. According to the Communist authorities, such things are impossible!

However, I myself was sick in prison with lung, spinal and intestinal tuberculosis and recurring jaundice. The 'medicines' I received were beatings, neglect and lack of food. Doctors in Oslo who later examined me and took X-

rays could not believe at first that I had survived the
Rumanian prison conditions, with four vertebrae infected
with tuberculosis, lungs like sieves, and without food and
drugs. The healing virtue of Christ had proved to be the
same as in the times of the Gospel. Today He delivers many
of the fighters of the Underground Church from their
infirmities through the prayers of the faithful.

We read in the *Journal* of George Fox, the founder of the
Quakers, that when he was released from the prison in
Newcastle he could heal. So can many who have passed
through Communist jails.

The Communists may mock such healings as fakes –
again they put the dunce's caps on our heads! But I know
that I was mortally sick and I know that I am now very
much alive! Thousands can tell the same story.

Richard Wurmbrand

643

When Moses threw the wand into the Red Sea, the sea,
quite contrary to the expected miracle, did not divide itself
to leave a dry passage for the Jews. Not until the first man
had jumped into the sea did the promised miracle happen
and the waves recede.

Jewish legend

644

A miracle in the Biblical sense is an event which happens in
a manner contrary to the regularly observed processes of
nature . . . It may happen according to higher laws as yet
but dimly discerned by scientists, and therefore must not be
thought of as an irrational irruption of divine power into
the orderly realm of nature.

Alan Richardson

645

Little Wayne Norgate prayed for a miracle as he was swept
out to sea in a rubber dinghy.

With his father unable to swim to his rescue because of
the strong current Wayne, eight, sat sobbing as the flimsy
craft was buffeted by the waves. 'I just prayed to God for
help,' he said. 'Then I felt something under the water
nudging the boat. When I looked down I saw a seal.'

The seal edged Wayne towards the safety of the shallow
water near the beach where he was picked up by lifeboat.

Wayne's grandmother Ina McFarlane, forty-eight, said
last night: 'God helped Wayne. If the seal hadn't been there
he would be dead. It was a miracle.'

Drama struck when Wayne, from Nottingham, clambered
into the dinghy while on holiday with his family at
Mablethorpe, Lincs.

Father Denis, thirty, heard his son's cries for help as the
current carried him a mile out to sea.

Mr Norgate and lifeguards swam out but couldn't reach
him. Wayne's mother Ina, twenty-eight, said: 'Then one of
the lifeguards using binoculars saw the seal nudging the
dinghy. It stopped it going out further.'

Anne Carr

646

Owing to the excitement caused by several alleged miracles
in the St Medard Cemetery in Paris in 1732, Louis XV had
this sign placed upon the locked gates: 'By order of the
King, God is hereby forbidden to work miracles in this
place.' With similar arrogance the 'I' on the throne of our
unsurrendered hearts forbids God to work his miracles
within us.

John Schmidt

Mission

647

In 1771, an English-speaking soldier-preacher who was being sent to the colonies in response to young Francis Asbury's urgent pleading for more preachers, received a stirring letter:

Dear George; The time has arrived for you to embark for America. You must go down to Bristol where you will meet with T. Rankin, Captain Webb, and his wife. I let you loose, George, on the great continent of America. Publish your message in the open face of the sun and do all the good you can.
I am, dear George, yours affectionately,

John Wesley

648

My son, if God has called you to be a missionary, your Father would be grieved to see you shrivel down into a king.

Charles H. Spurgeon

649

I gave up my position of professor in the University of Strasbourg, my literary work, and my organ playing in order to go as a doctor to Equatorial Africa. How did that come about? . . . I resolved, when already thirty years old, to study medicine and to put my ideas to the test . . . I had read about the physical miseries of the natives in the virgin forests; I had heard about them from missionaries, and the more I thought about it the stranger it seemed to me that we Europeans trouble ourselves so little about the great humanitarian task which offers itself to us in far-off lands. The parables of Dives and Lazarus seemed to me to have been spoken directly to us! And just as Dives sinned against the poor man at his gate because for want of thought he never put himself in his place, and let his heart and conscience tell him what he ought to do, so we sin against the poor man at our gate.

Albert Schweitzer

650

The church exists by mission, as fire exists by burning.

Emil Brunner

651

Azariah was tall and very dark, quick in movement and speech, with the knack of stirring up enthusiasm by his swift passionate words. A phrase that was constantly on his lips was 'Every Christian a witness'. It was absolutely necessary, he said, that every convert should at once bear witness. He drove this home at Madras in his own vivid way. 'It was', he said, 'by the witness of the common man that the Gospel spread in the early church, from slave to slave, from soldier to soldier, from artisan to artisan; and as I have gone around among the churches, I have had the baptised members place their hands on their heads and repeat after me, "I am a baptised Christian. Woe is me if I preach not the Gospel."'

A.M. Chirgwin

652

Before Christ sent the Church into the world, he sent the Spirit into the Church. The same order must be observed today.

John R.W. Stott

653

A Moravian missionary named George Smith went to Africa. He had been there only a short time and had only one convert, a poor woman, when he was driven from the country. He died shortly after, on his knees, praying for Africa. He was considered a failure.

But a company of men stumbled on the place where he had prayed and found a copy of the Scriptures he had left. Presently they met the one poor woman who was his convert. A hundred years later his mission counted more than 13,000 living converts who had sprung from the ministry of George Smith.

A.J. Gordon

654

Dr Mason of Burma once wanted a teacher to visit and labour among a warlike tribe and asked his converted boatman if he would go. He told him that as a teacher he would receive only four rupees per month whereas as boatman he was then receiving fifteen rupees.

After praying over the matter, the boatman returned to the doctor and the following conversation occurred:

'Well, Shapon,' said the doctor, 'what have you decided? Will you go for four rupees a month?'

'No teacher,' replied Shapon, 'I will not go for four rupees a month but I will go for Christ.'

Anon.

655

A young Canadian mission worker said that he was always looking for guidance from the Lord and he had come to South America because when he was considering his vocation he had suddenly seen a chocolate bar with a Brazil nut. 'What would you have done if it had been a Mars bar?' asked his sceptical friend.

Anon.

Money

656

A London newspaper offered a prize for the best definition of money. This was the winning answer: Money is an instrument that can buy you everything but happiness and pay your fare to every place but heaven.

Anon.

657

You can see what God thinks of money, when you see the people he gives it to.

Abraham Lincoln

658

A man who shows me his wealth is like the beggar who shows me his poverty; they are both looking for alms – the rich man for the alms of my envy, the poor man for the alms of my guilt.

Ben Hecht

659

My little granddaughter eagerly searched under the pillow one morning after having a tooth extracted. She burst into tears after discovering that the tooth had not been replaced by a coin during the night. Trying to comfort her, I said, 'Darling, you don't still believe in those old fairy stories do you?' 'Maybe not,' she replied, 'but I still believe in money.'

Anon.

660

A six-year-old went into a bank and asked to see the manager. A courteous clerk showed her into his private office. She explained that her girls' club was raising money for a new clubroom and asked if he would please contribute. The banker laid a pound note and a penny on the desk and said, 'Take your choice, Miss.'

She picked up the penny and said, 'My mother always taught me to take the smallest piece.' Picking up the pound note also, she added, 'But so I won't lose this penny, I'll wrap it in this nice piece of paper.'

Anon.

Nature

661

Nature herself has imprinted on the minds of all the idea of God.

Marcus Tullius Cicero

662

Francis of Assisi found a flowering meadow, there he preached: and he called upon it to praise the Lord, even as if it had been a rational being. In the same manner did he treat the sown fields and the vineyards, the stones and the forests, all the fair meads, the running streams, the green gardens, the earth, the fire, the air and the wind. And he counselled them all with upright purity of heart to love God; and in a strangely hidden way he penetrated into the heart of each creature with his sharp-sightedness; as though he were penetrating into the glorious freedom of the Son of God.

Thomas of Celano

663

Nature has some perfections, to show that she is the image of God; and some defects, to show that she is only His image.

Blaise Pascal

664

One of the most beautiful and joyous songs in the world is the 'Canticle of the Sun', in which Francis of Assisi praised God for all His good gifts. The circumstances under which he composed it are interesting.

Although only forty-four years of age, Francis' health had broken down. He had serious trouble with his eyes, and was in danger of going blind. He had worn himself out with his work and manner of life, and now was so weak that he could hardly walk, and had to ride his last journey as he came back to Assisi to die. Arrived at S. Damian, his friend Clare made for him a shelter of reeds in the monastery gardens where he could lie quiet and alone. It was here, as he lay suffering, that he composed his beautiful song.

'A single sunbeam', he used to say, 'is enough to drive away many shadows'; and although he could not use his eyes, he passed many an hour singing. He invented a kind of violin to which he sang the old French songs of his boyhood and the great hymns of the Church, and finally this song of his own.

Maud Higham

665

God Almighty first planted a garden; and, indeed, it is the purest of human pleasures.

Francis Bacon

666

The Emperor Hadrian once said to Rabbi Joshua, 'I want to see your God.' The Rabbi replied, 'That is impossible.' The Emperor said, 'You must show Him to me.' The Rabbi made the Emperor go outside with him. It was summer. He said to the Emperor, 'Look at the sun.' 'I cannot,' answered the Emperor. Then the Rabbi replied, 'If you cannot even

look at the sun, which is but one of the servants of the Holy
One, blessed be He, how shall you look at the Holy One
Himself?'

The Talmud

667

A. J. Gossip used to love to tell a story about Mungo Park,
the great explorer. He had been journeying for days in the
wilds of China, in the most desolate surroundings. Then
quite suddenly he saw on the ground at his feet a little blue
flower. And, as he saw it, he said gently, 'God has been
here!'

Anon.

668

A child's view:

I like the country because it is so peaceful. Out there the
quiet just goes sliding along.

God sews up the buds of flowers very tight and after a
while He lets the sun and rain open the stitches. When
waves come in on the beach they look like big, open mouths
ready to gobble up things. Sometimes they look like white,
lacy arms hugging the whole world.

Anon.

669

Gerry Carr, member of US Skylab 4 crew, on viewing
Earth from space:

'I would look at the Earth's horizon and see the Earth's
atmosphere. It is very beautiful. It is blue and white, gold
and orange. But it is so thin and fragile. That atmosphere is
all that keeps Earth habitable, but it's no thicker than the
skin on an orange – no, thinner than that, like the skin on

an apple. There's no way to explain how clearly you can see
the fragility of the Earth. You have to have been there.'

Molly Ivins

670
Half our misery and weakness
derives from the fact
that we have broken with the soil
and that we have allowed the roots
that bound us to the earth to rot.
We have become detached from the earth,
we have abandoned her.
And a man who abandons nature
has begun to abandon himself.

Pierre Van Passen

671
In AD 1309, an Aztec Indian inhabitant of what is now
Mexico City was found guilty of burning charcoal in the
city and polluting the air. He was ordered to be hanged for
the offence.

Today, Mexico City has a carbon monoxide level greater
than metropolitan New York, a sulphur dioxide level
greater than that of London, and ten times the industrial
contaminants of the industrialised Rhine River valley.

John McLaughlin

672
Sean McDonagh quotes part of the famous letter by the
Indian chief Seattle in reply to the US President who, in
1850, requested the Indians to sell their lands and move to
another reservation:

How can you buy or sell the sky, the warmth of the land?

The idea is strange to us. If we do not own the freshness of
the air and the sparkle of the water, how can you buy them?
Every part of this Earth is sacred to my people. Every
shining pine needle, every sandy shore, every mist in the
dark woods, every clearing and humming insect is holy in
the memory and experience of my people. The sap which
courses through the trees carries the memories of the red
man. The white man's dead forget the country of their birth
when they go to work among the stars. Our dead never
forget this beautiful Earth, for it is the mother of the Red
man. We are part of the Earth and it is part of us. The
perfumed flowers are our sisters; the deer, the horse, the
great eagle, these are our brothers. The rocky crests, the
juices in the meadows, the body heat of the pony, and man
– all belong to the same family.

Sean McDonagh

673

In a Spanish park posted on a tree are these words: I am a
tree. You who would pass by me and would raise your hand
against me, remember that I am the heat of your hearth on
cold nights; the friendly shade screening you from summer
heat; the source of refreshing draughts; the beam of your
house; the board of your table; the bed on which you lie; the
timber of your boat; the handle of your hoe; the wood of
your cradle; and the shell of your coffin. Harm me not.

Anon.

Obedience

674

Occasionally I meet someone who seems to have a secret,
some special knowledge that sets that person apart. Such a
person was Ruby Free. I met her when she was conducting
a Holy Land tour. 'She must have a secret,' I said to myself

enviously. 'How else can she accomplish so much, so easily?' She was a good listener, a troubleshooter, an organiser, a mother-hen to all seventy-two of us, plus her own two children; yet she was never tired, never out of sorts.

Then, back home, I visited Ruby. And I think I discovered her secret. There it was, a two-word motto over her sink: 'YES LORD.'

Rosa Cornelia Veal

675

That thou art happy,
owe to God;
That thou continuest such,
owe to thyself.
That is, to thy obedience.

John Milton

676

Centuries ago, in one of the Egyptian monasteries, a man came and asked to be admitted. The abbot told him that the chief rule was obedience, and the man promised to be patient on all occasions, even under excessive provocation. It chanced that the abbot was holding a dried-up willow-wand in his hand; he forthwith fixed the dead stick into the earth and told the newcomer that he was to water it until, against all the rules of nature, it should once again become green. Obediently the new monk walked two miles every day to the River Nile to bring back a vessel of water on his shoulders and water the dry stick. A year passed by, and he was still faithful to his task, though very weary. Another year, and still he toiled on. Well into the third year he was still trudging to the river and back, still watering the stick, when suddenly one day it burst into life.

This story is related in the *Dialogues of Sulpicius Severus*,

on the authority of an acquaintance named Postumianus
who had travelled in the East. 'I myself', said the latter,
'have beheld the green bush – the former dead stick – which
flourishes to this day in the atrium of the monastery. Its
waving green foliage is a living witness to the mighty
virtues of obedience and faith.'

F.H. Drinkwater

677

Every revelation of God is a demand, and the way to
knowledge of God is by obedience.

William Temple

678

God sets the soul long, weary, impossible tasks, yet is
satisfied by the first sincere proof that obedience is
intended, and takes the burden away forthwith.

Coventry Patmore

679

No man securely commands but he who has learned to
obey.

Thomas à Kempis

680

Mother announced that in future a prize would be given
every Saturday to the member of the family who had been
the most obedient.

'Oh, but, Mummy,' chorused the children, 'that wouldn't
be fair. Daddy would win every time!'

Anon.

681

Obedience is the fruit of faith; patience the bloom on the fruit.

Christina Rossetti

682

Three-year-old Bobby insisted on standing up in his high chair although mother had admonished him to remain seated, then emphasised her admonishment twice by reseating him. After the third time, little Bobby remained seated but looked at his mother searchingly and said, 'Mummy, I'm still standing up inside.'

Anon.

One God

683

God is present everywhere, he hears and sees all, he penetrates even hidden and secret places. For so it is written, 'I am a God at hand, and not a God far off. If a man hides himself in secret places, will I therefore not see him? Do I not fill heaven and earth?' And again; 'The eyes of the Lord are in every place: keeping watch on the evil and the good.'

Cyprian

684

When Robert Louis Stevenson was seeking for spiritual light and had found it, he wrote to his father, 'No man can achieve success in life until he writes in the journal of his life the words, Enter God.'

Anon.

685

Four Hebrew letters, YHVH (which appear 6,823 times in the Old Testament) form the Hebrew name for God. 'Adonai' is a substitute for the sacred letters. The title 'Adonai' is never pronounced by pious Jews except during solemn prayer and with the head covered.

Anon.

686

Two men please God – who serves Him with all his heart because he knows Him; who seeks Him with all his heart because he knows Him not.

Panin

687

Once upon a time the fishes of a certain river took counsel together and said: 'They tell us that our life and being is for the water, but we have never seen water, and know not what it is.'

Then some among them wiser than the rest said: 'We have heard that there dwelleth in the sea a very learned fish who knoweth all things; let us ask him to explain to us what is water.'

So several of their number set out, and came to where this sage fish resided. On hearing their request he answered them:

> 'Oh ye who seek to solve the knot!
> Ye live in God, yet know him not.
> Ye sit upon the river's brink,
> Yet crave in vain a drop to drink.
> Ye dwell beside a countless store,
> Yet perish hungry at the door.'

This little parable has lived a thousand years in Persian literature.

Anon.

688

Voltaire, as everyone knows, had little use for religion. He was one day walking with a friend when they passed a church. Voltaire raised his hat as they passed. 'I thought', said the friend, 'that you did not believe in God.' 'Oh,' said Voltaire, 'we nod, but we do not speak.'

William Barclay

689

The atheist staring from his attic window is often nearer to God than the believer caught up in his own false image of God.

Martin Buber

690

'I listen with reverence to the birdsong cascading at dawn from the oasis, for it seems to me there is no better evidence for the existence of God than in the bird that sings, though it knows not why, from a spring of untrammelled joy that wells up in its heart.' These lines are attributed to an Arab chieftain. He had all the simple proof he needed: proof which no theological disputation could ever present half so convincingly. That Arab chieftain had the sensitive ear, the receptive heart, and a mind able to interpret.

T.B.C.

691

The heart has its reasons, which reason knows not, as we feel in a thousand instances.

It is the heart which is conscious of God, not the reason. This then is faith: God sensible to the heart, not to the reason.

Blaise Pascal

692

Johnny, aged five, was told by his mother that he must finish his breakfast porridge. He said he didn't want to. His mother replied, 'You must finish it. If you don't, God will be very angry.'

She went into the kitchen to wash up, leaving Johnny looking with a sullen determination at the porridge. Outside it was raining, and suddenly there was a heavy roll of thunder.

Johnny's mother came back into the room and found him eating his porridge as quickly as he could, and meanwhile muttering to himself, 'All that fuss over a small plate of porridge!'

Anon.

Pain

693
Alter Christus

(Poem written in a Mental Home)

Lord, for the pain I cursed You for last night
I do most gladly offer thanks today . . .
For, not with pride but deep humility
In me, and by me, and through me, I find – You!
In my stripped loneliness, Your own imprisonment –
My bruises mark Your scourging: and the same
Rude jests ring in my ears that rang in Yours –
And round my aching head I seem to feel
Even today, the racking crown of thorns . . .
I too was bound – and, though I never died,
I was like You – my *spirit* crucified.

Eithne Tabor

694

God washes the eyes by tears until they can behold the invisible land where tears shall come no more.

Henry Ward Beecher

695

Most of the people who beat their breasts and proclaimed to the world that God was dead were thousands of miles from Dachau. We know that many hundreds of these victims of Nazi psychopathia went to the gas chambers with a serenity that astounded even their cynical executioners. Following the example of the second-century Palestine Sage and Martyr, Rabbi Akiba, they walked calmly to their deaths with the *Shema* on their lips, that same watchword that Jewish martyrs had uttered throughout the ages as the final affirmation of faith in the one God of mankind and of their abiding love for him.

David Manning White

696

Man should remember in his pain that God speaks the truth and promises by Himself, the Truth. If God were to be false to his word, his Truth, He would be false to his divinity, and then He would not be God. It is his promise that our pain shall be changed to joy.

Meister Eckhart

Patience

697

The Chinese tell of one of their countrymen, a student who, disheartened by the difficulties in his way, threw down his book in despair. Seeing a woman rubbing a crowbar on a

stone, he enquired the reason, and was told that she wanted
a needle, and thought she would rub down a crowbar till
she got it small enough. Provoked by this example of
patience to 'try again' he resumed his studies and became a
famous scholar.

Anon.

698

Faith takes up the cross, love binds it to the soul, patience
bears it to the end.

H. Bonar

699

There is a story of a man who prayed earnestly one
morning for grace to overcome his besetting sin of
impatience. A little later he missed a train by half a minute
and spent an hour stamping up and down the station
platform in furious vexation. Five minutes before the next
train came he suddenly realised that here had been the
answer to his prayer. He had been given an hour to practise
the virtue of patience; he had missed the opportunity and
wasted the hour.

Bernard Hodgson

700

Those things than a man cannot amend in himself or in
others, he ought to suffer patiently, until God orders things
otherwise.

Thomas à Kempis

701

Once some robbers came into the monastery and said to
one of the elders: 'We have come to take away everything

that is in your cell.' And he said: 'My sons, take all you
want.' So they took everything they could find in the cell
and started off. But they left behind a little bag that was
hidden in the cell. The elder picked it up and followed after
them crying out: 'My sons, take this, you forgot it in the
cell!' Amazed at the patience of the elder, they brought
everything back into his cell and did penance, saying: 'This
one really is a man of God!'

Tales of the Desert Fathers

702
A lot of the road to heaven has to be taken at thirty miles an
hour.

Evelyn Underhill

703
That's the advantage of having lived sixty-five years. You
don't feel the need to be impatient any longer.

Thornton Wilder

704
When Stanley went out in 1871 and found Livingstone, he
spent months in his company, but Livingstone never spoke
to Stanley about spiritual things. Throughout those months,
Stanley watched the old man. Livingstone's habits were
beyond his comprehension, and so was his patience. He
could not understand Livingstone's sympathy for the
Africans. For the sake of Christ and His Gospel, the
missionary doctor was patient, untiring, eager, spending
himself and being spent for his Master. Stanley wrote,
'When I saw that unwearied patience, that unflagging zeal,
those enlightened sons of Africa, I became a Christian at
his side, though he never spoke to me about it.'

Anon.

705

Found scratched on a wall at the Tower of London by prisoners: 'It is not adversity that kills, but the impatience with which we bear with adversity.'

Anon.

706

Some years ago, a fourteen-year strike came to an end in Dun Laoghaire, Ireland.

The strike at Downey's Public House had started in 1939 when publican Pat Downey fired a barman. As Downey refused to rehire the dismissed man, pickets began their marathon wait. Each year, Downey observed the anniversary of the strike by dressing his pub in flags and offering drinks to the pickets.

When Downey died in May of 1953, striker Val Murphy put aside his sandwich-board and walked into the pub to offer his sympathy to the widow.

Anon.

707

A little Scottish schoolgirl was asked, 'What is patience?' Her reply: 'Wait a wee while, and dinna weary.'

Bob Edwards

Peace

708

The peace concluded on 24th June, 1502, between England and Scotland was called 'Perpetual Peace'. In the agreement Margaret, daughter of Henry VII, was betrothed to James IV of Scotland. However, the Scots invaded England

in 1513! The name has been given to other treaties, as that
between Austria and Switzerland in 1471 and between
France and Switzerland in 1516.

Anon.

709

The following was found inscribed on the wall of a shelled
house in a devastated French village during the First World
War.

> War provokes pillage,
> Pillage brings ruin,
> Ruin brings patience,
> Patience implies peace;
> Thus does war produce peace.
>
> Peace provokes abundance,
> Abundance brings arrogance,
> Arrogance brings war;
> Thus does peace produce war.

Anon.

710

During 1986, the Year of Peace, 1.7 million dollars a
minute were spent on arms!

Anon.

711

> Waste of Muscle, waste of Brain,
> Waste of Patience, waste of Pain,
> Waste of Manhood, waste of Health,
> Waste of Beauty, waste of Wealth,
> Waste of Blood, and waste of Tears,
> Waste of Youth's most precious years,

Waste of ways the Saints have trod,
Waste of Glory, waste of God – War!

G.A. Studdert-Kennedy

712

We need to feel more
to understand others.
We need to love more
to be loved back.
We need to cry more
to cleanse ourselves.
We need to laugh more
to enjoy ourselves.
We need to see more
other than our own little fantasies.
We need to hear more
and listen to the needs of others.
We need to give more
and take less.
We need to share more
and own less.
We need to look more
and to realise that we are not so
different from one another.
We need to create a world where
everyone can peacefully live
the life they choose.

Susan Schutz

713

One day a little boy asked his parents. 'How do wars break
out? How are they declared?' So the father, who was very
learned in economic matters, started talking about wheat,
oil and all the things that divide the world. But the mother
thought the little boy was far too small to understand such

things, and she said, 'Let me explain it.' The mother began to explain and the father grew angry, and a great argument developed. The little boy was very frightened indeed, and held up his hands and cried, 'Stop, stop! Now I know how wars begin.'

Irene Laure

Peace – Personal

714

It is the will of God for us that in the world's most crowded street, in the din of life, when the rush and hurry are at their most intense . . . in joy or sorrow, in love or in bereavement, in all that makes up our outer and inner life, we should have a place of retirement, a permanent retreat, ever at hand for renewal and peace. It is God's will for us that we should possess an Interior Castle, against which the storms of life may beat without being able to disturb the serene quiet within; a spiritual life so firm and so secure that nothing can overthrow it.

Evelyn Underhill

715

Peace is not made at the council tables, or by treaties, but in the hearts of men.

Herbert Hoover

716

Peace is not won
By man's eternal strife,
Peace is the power of God
In human life.
It dwells with joy and love,

Is manifest in grace;
The star above His crib.
The light that is His face.

Anon.

717

When Christ came into the world, peace was sung; and
when he went out of the world, peace was bequested.

Francis Bacon

718

Five great enemies to peace inhabit with us, namely,
avarice, ambition, envy, anger and pride. If these enemies
were to be banished, we should infallibly enjoy perpetual
peace.

Petrarch

719

To a disciple who was forever complaining about others,
the Spiritual Master said, 'If it is peace you want, seek to
change yourself, not other people. It is easier to protect
your feet with slippers than to carpet the whole of the
Earth.'

Anthony De Mello

720

The world rests upon three things: upon truth, upon justice
and upon peace. All those three are really one, for when
justice is done the truth becomes an actuality, peace a
reality.

The Talmud

721

A great many people are trying to make peace, but that has already been done. God has not left it for us to do; all we have to do is to enter into it.

Dwight L. Moody

722

The devil often tries to wreck our peace and make the service of God irksome. Loving God is not irksome at all. God doesn't create difficulties by His love. It is the things that resist His love that cause the difficulties. Love itself is a source of joy. It may occasion resistance. Our dear Lord said, 'I came not to bring peace, but the sword.' He didn't come with the sword at all. He is the Prince of Peace. But as soon as He came, all kinds of swords were unsheathed against Him. He takes the blame on Himself. Some people do not understand the meaning of His words. They think Our Lord came with a sword. He came without a sword, but the people took their swords out at once and said, 'We will kill Him.'

His love doesn't mean trouble. Faith doesn't mean trouble. It brings peace from certitude. When you are quite certain of the love of your friend, that is a source of great peace.

Vincent McNabb

Perseverance

723

M. Louis Blériot, the famous airman who was first to cross the Channel in an aeroplane of his own designing, only achieved his object through marvellous perseverance. Ten machines were built and wrecked, but still he did not give up; it was with his eleventh aeroplane that he finally, on

25th July 1909, flew the Channel in thirty-seven minutes. And even then he was badly lame with a scalded foot, which would have prevented most men from attempting the adventure.

F.H. Drinkwater

724

After Sir Walter Raleigh's introduction to the favour of Queen Elizabeth I, he wrote with a diamond on a window pane:

Fain would I climb, but that I fear to fall.

The Queen, seeing the words, wrote underneath with a diamond:

If thy heart fail thee, do not climb at all.

Anon.

725

Accidents happen so easily, and once they have happened nothing can undo them, no matter how we may regret that they have befallen.

A small boy, born on 4th January, 1809, was the victim of such an accident when he was only three years old. His father, harness-maker in a village near Paris, had been boring holes in leather with an awl but had put down his tool for a moment. It was Louis' chance to try it for himself but instead of making a hole in the leather, he succeeded in making a hole in his eye. For days he was in pain. The infection spread to the other eye and that was the last young Louis ever saw. For the rest of his life he was blind. For many that might have been the end of a useful life.

But as soon as he was old enough, he was sent to a school for the blind in Paris, where he was taught to read by touching large raised letters with his fingers. Louis was so successful that he soon found himself teaching others to read by the same method.

But it was not easy. Some people just could not do it. Louis Braille determined to invent another method by which blind people could read. He worked and persevered for many a long hour to try to perfect an alphabet for the blind. When he was twenty years old he succeeded.

The Braille alphabet consists of groups of raised dots, which can be recognised by touching them with the finger-tip.

Braille requires much more space than ordinary print and is expensive but it has proved a blessing to thousands of blind people who are enabled to read without using their eyes.

Anon.

726

On the voyage which resulted in the discovery of America, Columbus refused to listen to the threats of his sailors. As day after day no land appeared the sailors threatened to mutiny and demanded that they turn back. Columbus would not listen and each day entered two words in the ship's log, 'Sailed on.'

Anon.

727

King Robert the Bruce of Scotland, pursued after defeat in battle, hid in a lonely cave. He tried to plan the future, but was tempted to despair. He had lost heart and had decided to give up when his eye was caught by a spider. The insect was carefully and painfully making its way up a slender thread to its web in the corner above. The king watched as it made several unsuccessful attempts, and thought, as it fell back to the bottom again and again, how it typified his own efforts. Then at last the spider made it! The king took courage and persevered and the example of the spider brought its reward.

Anon.

728

A suitor in Wales, who was rebuffed for forty-two years, eventually won his fair lady. After writing 2,184 love letters, the persistent but rather shy man, receiving neither written nor spoken answer, summoned enough courage to present himself in person. He knocked on the lady's door and asked for her hand. To his delight and surprise she accepted! The couple married at seventy-four years of age.

Anon.

729

An old black preacher was asked to define Christian perseverance. He answered: 'It means, firstly, to take hold; secondly, to hold on; thirdly and lastly, to never leave go.'

Anon.

Pets

730

More than a few legends attest the affection which existed between the prophet Mahomet and his cat Muezza. The most familiar one was brought from the Orient by a traveller in the year 1702, and relates that one day, while the prophet sat lost in deepest thought, Muezza lay on the sleeve of his robe, purring contentedly. But so long did Mahomet remain absorbed that Muezza fell asleep; and when he had to rise to go to his devotions he cut off his sleeve rather than disturb the slumber of his little friend.

Clarence Madden

731

A child's view:

Cats have very sad faces. They look at you a long time and think about you. They are peaceful to have around.

732

Busy at the sink, Julia Flynn looked up in alarm as something rapped against the kitchen window of her home perched on the cliffs in a remote part of America's Massachusetts coastline. Then she smiled with relief. It was only one of the seagulls which she and her sister Rachel had been feeding every day for the past year. It was the one gull which the spinster sisters were convinced they could always identify. Because of that they had dubbed it Nancy and made a fuss of it by making sure it got a little more food than the others. The gulls, however, had already been fed and Julia assumed that Nancy had hit on a ruse to get an extra meal on its own. It had never done that or rapped on the window before.

Yet there it was on the sill, beady eyes staring at Julia. Every few seconds it would flutter into the air, fly a few yards towards the cliff and then fly back. Julia chuckled at its antics and decided to go outside, without any food, just to see what it was up to. Once she was outside the gull kept flying ahead and then flying back. 'Just like a dog trying to get someone to follow it,' said Julia.

She followed Nancy for nearly half a mile along the deserted cliff top. Suddenly she heard a cry for help and looking cautiously over the cliff edge, Julia saw her sister helplessly wedged between two large rocks twenty feet below.

While on her customary afternoon walk, Rachel had tripped and tumbled over the cliff edge. Gashed, bruised and in a state of shock she had been trapped there for more than an hour, calling out for help. But nobody had passed that way and, if Julia had not arrived, it is likely that

Rachel would have lain there all night and suffered severe exposure, or perhaps died from the night frost. Julia hurried home, called the police, and an hour later Rachel was hauled to safety.

Fred Wehner

Pity

733

There are problems which only the heart's knowledge, piercing to the heart of things where God's pity abides, can solve; and to solve them is to be grateful to God, for the solution is the pity.

Gerald Vann

734

Pity melts the mind to love.

John Dryden

735

It is for God to say, 'To know all is to pardon all.' It is for God to say that He saw us all the way; that 'He knoweth our frame, He remembereth that we are dust.' It is for Him to have pity on us; it is never for us to cultivate pity of ourselves.

John A. Hutton

The Poor

736

When I was in Japan I met one of the greatest robot inventors and engineers in the world. There is nothing he

cannot think of. I thought, God must be happy that there
are co-creators like this among human beings. But I
thought of my people in Recife, Brazil, too, who obviously
are not thinking of how to get out of work – very often they
cannot get enough work to feed their families. So I had a
prayer in my heart that God would let this Japanese robot-
creator meet my people, and that would give him the idea
that the fantastic progress that he has in his head and
hands should serve first of all to make the poor less poor,
and not the rich more rich,

Helder Camara

737
The earth is a Moon Satellite

Apollo 2 cost more than Apollo 1
Apollo 1 cost plenty.

Apollo 3 cost more than Apollo 2
Apollo 2 cost more than Apollo 1
Apollo 1 cost plenty.

Apollo 4 cost more than Apollo 3
Apollo 3 cost more than Apollo 2
Apollo 2 cost more than Apollo 1
Apollo 1 cost plenty.

Apollo 8 cost a fortune but nobody minded
because the astronauts were Protestants
and from the moon they read the Bible
to the delight and edification of all Christians
and on their return Pope Paul gave them his blessing.

Apollo 9 cost more than all of them together
and that includes Apollo 1 which cost plenty.

The great-grandparents of the Acahualinca people
were less hungry than the grandparents.

The great-grandparents died of hunger.

The grandparents of the Acahualinca people
were less hungry than the parents.

The grandparents died of hunger.

The parents of the Acahualinca people
were less hungry than the people are today.

The parents died of hunger.

The people who live today in Acahualinca
are less hungry than their children.

The children of the Acahualinca people
are not born because of hunger

and they hunger to be born
so they can die of hunger.

And that is what the Acahualinca people do
they die of hunger.

Blessed are the poor
for they shall possess the moon.

Leonel Rugama (Nicaragua)

738

Lawrence was a Deacon of the Church at Rome who was
put to death during a persecution of Christians in the third
century.

When it was ascertained that Lawrence was the keeper of
the treasures of the Church, he was arrested and ordered to
give them up. He asked for a day's delay, at the end of
which time he promised to produce all that was most
precious. All night he hurried about Rome, in and out of its
poorest streets and alleys, and, on the morrow, he appeared
before the Court with a crowd of the poor, the maimed, the
halt, the blind, and the sick. 'These', said he, 'are what the
Church holds most dear, and counts as her greatest
treasures. The gold, which you so eagerly desire, is a vile

metal, and serves to incite men to all manner of crimes, The light of Heaven, which these poor objects enjoy, is the true gold!'

A.C. Bouquet

Power

739

Place yourself in the middle of the stream of power and wisdom which flows into you as life, place yourself in the full centre of that flood, then you are without effort impelled to truth, to light, and a perfect contentment.

Ralph Waldo Emerson

740

We are the wire, God is the current. Our only power is to let the current pass through us.

Carlo Carretto

741

We do not believe that the human enterprise will have a tragic conclusion; but the ground of our hope lies not in human capacity but in divine power and mercy, in the character of the ultimate reality, which carries the human experience.

Reinhold Niebuhr

742

The electrician was puzzled. 'Hi!' he called to his assistant, 'put your hand on one of those wires.' The assistant did as he was told. 'Feel anything?' 'No.' 'Good!' said the electrician, 'I wasn't sure which was which. Don't touch the other or you'll drop dead.'

Anon.

Praise

743

God be praised, that to believing souls gives light in darkness, comfort in despair.

William Shakespeare

744

Tune me, O Lord, into one harmony with Thee, one full responsive vibrant cord; unto thy praise, all love and melody, tune me, O Lord.

Christina Rossetti

745

A great conductor was rehearsing an oratorio with a large orchestra. All manner of instruments were there, each contributing its part to the great harmonies – violins and 'cellos; harps and flutes; trumpets and drums; cornets and cymbals, The music rose and fell, as the performers watched the conductor's baton, his ear alert to note every tone that gave its particular value to the interpretation of the great theme.

Suddenly the baton rapped: the music stopped: the conductor's voice was heard in the silence.

'Where', cried he, 'is the piccolo?'

Listening, he had noticed something was missing: the music was not perfect because the player of one of the most insignificant of the instruments had forgotten his part.

Even amid the chorus of praise sent up by the angels and archangels, the music of heaven is not complete if the least of us human choristers is not in his place.

Maud Higham

746

It is a sure sign of mediocrity to be niggardly with praise.

Marquis de Vauvenargues

747

Men sometimes feel injured by praise, because it assigns a limit to their merit. Few people are humble enough to be content to be estimated at their true worth.

Anon.

Prayer

748

We should never break off an act of charity to others in order to pray. If our prayer is inconvenient to somebody else we ought to be serving, it is not in the right place. If it is a burden to someone else to whom we have a duty, it will have no cutting edge, it will be of little value. That is often a distinct difficulty among some Christians. They make it appear that the church fosters a kind of piety which depends on somebody else working so that we may pray. We learn that Our Lord was busy right up to the time when He went up into a mountain to pray. It is no good starting our prayers until we have fulfilled all our duties,

Vincent McNabb

749

In the Catacombs, and in very early Christian art, there is an attitude adopted by the person praying which has entirely disappeared but which has a suggestion of its own. The supplicants, who are represented looking up to heaven, are shown with their hands stretched out. In all probability this attitude was suppressed on the plea that it was

unbecoming, and yet does it not express the true inward-
ness of faith and loving trustfulness in God's promises?

Anon.

750

Really to pray is to stand to attention in the presence of the
King and to be prepared to take orders from him.

Donald Coggan

751

Martin Luther, the Reformer, said, 'If I fail to spend two
hours in prayer each morning, the devil gets the victory
through the day. I have so much business, I cannot get on
without spending three hours daily in prayer.' He had a
motto: 'He that has prayed well has studied well.'

Dr Lancelot Andrews, the saintly Bishop of Winchester in the
reigns of James I and Charles I, spent the greater part of
five hours every day in prayer and devotion, His book of
Devotions was his legacy to the Church.

Thomas Ken, Prebendary of Winchester Cathedral (where
his name is cut in the cloister over the dates 1656–7),
afterwards Bishop of Bath and Wells, rose habitually at two
or three in the morning for prayer, attending Matins in the
school chapel at five, or later in the Cathedral.

Nicholas Ferrar, of Little Gidding, in Huntingdonshire, lived
with his family and relations a life of ordered prayer and
devotion between the years 1593 and 1637. Twice a week he
kept a prayer watch in the oratory from nine p.m. till one
a.m. On the other days he rose at one, and continued in
prayer and meditation till the morning,

John Wesley, the great revivalist preacher, spent two hours
daily in prayer. He lived a most strenuous, adventurous
life, and once he said, 'Today I have such a busy day before
me that I cannot get through it with less than two hours
prayer.'

Maud Higham

752

Like the Israelites we are prone to idolatry, and in the lives of those who pray the idols tend to be of a refined and sophisticated character. Prayer itself can be an idol, and so can a spiritual self-image.

Maria Boulding

753

I have lived to thank God that all my prayers have not been answered.

Jean Ingelow

754

We are told that at the top of every music manuscript of the great Johann Sebastian Bach appear the two Latin words: *'Iesu, iuva!'* – 'Jesus, help!' The world's mightiest master of music did not dare place his fingers on the organ or compose a single melody without first calling on his Lord for help.

Anon.

755

Two went to pray! or rather say
One went to brag, th'other to pray:

One stands up close and treads on high,
where th' other dares not send his eye:

One nearer to God's altar trod,
The other to the altar's God,

Richard Crashaw

756

Merely scrubbing floors is not prayer, but it can be made

into a very beautiful prayer. If the prayer of the humble pierces the clouds, it is a pretty quick road from the scrubbing brush to heaven,

Vincent McNabb

757

A small boy was seen kneeling reverently as if in prayer, but the words he was heard to be saying were the letters of the alphabet! The sympathetic grown-up who had watched this, on questioning the little chap, found out that he knew God liked his children to pray to him but he didn't know any prayers, so was telling him the alphabet, which he had just learnt.

Anon.

758

Johnny liked church pretty well except for the intercessory prayers, which he thought were far too long, So when his dad asked the priest to say grace one day at a meal, Johnny was worried. But, to his surprise, the prayer was brief and to the point. Pleased, Johnny said: 'You don't pray long when you're hungry, do you?'

Anon.

759

A child's view:

When I say my prayers I ask God to bless all the old men with walking sticks and all the old ladies with no purses.

Anon.

760

Ten-year-old Robert had not done his homework the night before. And so he struggled through his written test in geography, doing a lot more guessing than he should have.

All evening, as his mind went back to the written test and some of the answers he had given, he was deeply troubled. What if too many of his answers had been wrong? What if he should not get a pass mark? That night after he had said his prayers, he suddenly blurted the nervous postscript: 'And please, God, make Paris the capital of Sweden!'

Anon.

Preaching

761

If you go to Bedford you can visit the prison in which one of the most famous books in the world, *The Pilgrim's Progress,* was written. It tells the story of Christian, who sets off for the celestial city, helped by such people as Faithful and Hopeful and having his way barred by many such as Apollyon, a foul fiend, hobgoblins and evil spirits, and Giant Despair who lived in Doubting Castle.

The book was first published on 18th February, 1678. Its author, John Bunyan, was a man who knew what it was like to be thwarted in his work for God. He was a very powerful lay preacher and spent two spells in prison because he refused to leave off preaching in days when only clergymen were supposed to preach.

Anon.

762

Whoever preaches with love preaches effectively.

Francis of Sales

763

The decline of the Ministry of the Word in Protestant England can perhaps be traced in hour glasses. In the seventeenth century they lived up to their name, and it was really at the end of an hour that the preacher, if in good form, would turn them over and say 'another glass'. If he stopped before the sand, he was thought an idle, shirking dog.

But early in the last century, habits changed, and Queen Victoria, restoring the Chapel Royal in 1867, had an hour-glass fitted which gave the preachers eighteen minutes. Her son, Edward, improved on this royal hint, and made it known that to go beyond ten minutes was to displease him.

Of Isaac Barrow, in Charles II's reign, it is related that 'he was three-and-a-half hours delivering a sermon on charity before the Lord Mayor and aldermen and on one occasion when preaching in Westminster Abbey the servants of the Church caused the organ to be struck up against him and he was fairly blown out of the pulpit.'

Douglas Woodruff

764

The expertise of the pulpit can only be learned slowly and it may well be, with a strange mixture of pain and joy.

Donald Coggan

765

The great eighteenth-century actor David Garrick was once asked by a church leader how he produced such wonderful effects on his listeners, when reciting fiction. 'Because', said Garrick, 'I recite fiction as if it were truth, and you preach truth as if it were fiction.'

Richard Bewes

766

The Devil will let a preacher prepare a sermon if it will keep him from preparing himself.

Vance Havner

767

An ancient historian points out this difference between Cicero, the polished speaker, and Demosthenes, the burning orator. After a great speech in Rome, every tongue was loud in the praise of Cicero. But the people who listened to Demosthenes forgot the orator. They went home with hurried stride, lowering brow, clenched fist, muttering in a voice like distant thunder, 'Let us go and fight Philip.'

Anon.

768

It is very important to live your faith by confessing it, and one of the best ways to confess it is to preach it.

Thomas Merton

769

A white clergyman was once reportedly preaching in India by interpretation. His opening sentence ran: 'The beatific familiarity of this chapter, traditionally appointed for Quinquagesima, must not cause us to neglect its profundity.' The Indian interpreter put it a little differently: 'So far the speaker has not said anything worth remembering. When he does I will let you know.'

Richard Bewes

770

A preacher whose sermon had gone down very badly asked a friend afterwards, 'How would you have delivered that sermon?' 'Under an assumed name,' he replied.

Anon.

Prejudice

771

If you do not like me because I am ignorant, I can be sent to school and educated. If you do not like me because I am dirty, I can be taught to wash and be clean. If you do not like me because of my unsocial habits, I can be taught how to live in society. But if you do not like me because of the colour of my skin, I can only refer you to the God who made me.

A negro minister in 1958

772

Passion and prejudice govern the world; only under the name of reason.

John Wesley

773

There is a legend in the Talmud of a traveller coming at twilight to a camping place. As he looked off yonder he saw a strange object. Through the gathering dusk it seemed to take the shape of a terrible monster, and he resolved to go closer to see, if possible, what it was. Drawing nearer, he saw that it was a man. Much of his fear then vanished. Thereupon he ventured still nearer and found that not only was the object a man like himself but that it was his own brother.

George Willets

774

She spoke of heaven
And an angelic host;
She spoke of God

And the Holy Ghost;
She spoke of Christ's teachings
Of man's brotherhood;
Yet when she had to sit beside a Negro once –
She stood.

Elizabeth Hart

775

A great many people think they are thinking when they are merely rearranging their prejudices.

William James

776

First they came for the Jews
and I did not speak out –
because I was not a Jew.

Then they came for the Communists
and I did not speak out –
because I was not a Communist.

Then they came for the trade unionists
and I did not speak out –
because I was not a trade unionist.

Then they came for me –
and there was no one left
to speak out for me.

Pastor Niemoeller
(victim of the Nazis)

777

Robert was born at Aldershot; his mother was Japanese and father English. When Robert started school, he was tormented by the other children. One Christmas, his parents bought him a watch, but this was taken from him

by some other older children and thrown against the school
wall. The school crossing warden asked Robert one day
why he was walking over a mile to school and crossing a
busy main road instead of using the school bus. His parents
had wanted him to use the bus but Robert had refused. He
told the traffic warden he was frightened of the other
children because they called him a 'wog', a 'chink' and a
'bloody jap'! He walked to school for three weeks until one
day, when crossing the road, he was knocked down by a car
and killed.

Anon.

Presence of God

778

God is especially present in the hearts of his people, by his
Holy Spirit, and indeed the hearts of holy men are temples
in the truth of things, and in type and shadow they are
heaven itself. For God reigns in the hearts of his servants;
there is his kingdom. The power of grace hath subdued all
his enemies; there is his power. They serve Him night and
day, and give Him thanks and praise; that is his glory. This
is the religion and worship of God in the temple. The
temple itself is the heart of man, Christ is the High Priest,
who from thence sends up the incense of prayers, and joins
them to his own intercession and presents all together to his
Father; and the Holy Ghost by his dwelling there hath also
consecrated it into a temple, and God dwells in our hearts
by faith, and Christ by his Spirit, and the Spirit by his
purities; so that we are also cabinets of the mysterious
Trinity, and what is this short of heaven itself, but as
infancy is short of manhood and letters of words? The same
state of life it is, but yet true, representing the beauties of
the soul, and the grace of God, and the images of his eternal
glory, by the reality of a special presence.

Jeremy Taylor

779

See that you seek God where He is to be sought, in the temple and dwelling place of the divine glory, which is your heart and your soul.

Johannes Denck

780

You are behind me
I do not have to turn around.

You are in front of me
I am walking towards you.

You are beside me more than any abyss
and any mountain.

You are in me
I do not have to look elsewhere.

With You in me
I can find You everywhere.

J. Scheffler

781

Poor creature though I be, I am the hand and foot of Christ. I move my hand and my hand is wholly Christ's hand, for deity is become inseparably one with me. I move my foot, and it is aglow with God.

Symeon the New Theologian

782

God sleeps in a stone, dreams in a flower, moves in an animal and wakes in man.

Irenaeus

Prophets

783

The prophet is to be no mere announcer, he is rather God's agent who by the 'word' accomplishes what he foretells, whether good or bad.

Fleming James

784

God's anger is not a tempest in a void full of mystery and dread. The world is dark, and human agony is excruciating, but the prophet casts a light by which the heart is led into the thinking of the Lord's mind. God does not delight in unleashing anger.

Abraham Heschel

785

If you want to get across an IDEA, wrap it up in a PERSON.

Ralph Bunche

786

The prophet is primarily the man, not to whom God has communicated certain divine thoughts, but whose mind is illuminated by the divine spirit to intercept aright the divine acts; and the act is primary.

William Temple

Prosperity

787

A sick man asked Sengai to write something for the

continued prosperity of his family, to be treasured from generation to generation. Sengai wrote: 'Father dies, son dies, grandson dies.' The sick, rich man was indignant. 'Is that what you write for the happiness of my family.'

Sengai replied, 'If your son would die before you, that would be very sad. If your grandson would die before you and your son, you would be broken-hearted. If your family dies in the order I have written down, isn't that prosperity and happiness?'

Sengai

Reconciliation

788
Poor Gainsborough, the artist, lay dying. He thought of the small rivalries and misunderstandings which had kept him and Reynolds apart, and he sent begging Reynolds to visit him. Reynolds went, and many a tear has been shed over the reconciliation of these two splendid men. Gainsborough bravely talked of getting better, and had some of his pictures brought to his bedside to show his friend. But his words began to fail, and his last utterance to Reynolds was: 'We are all going to Heaven, and Van Dyck is of the company.'

'My Magazine'

789
Reconciliation sounds a large theological term, but it simply means coming to ourselves and arising and going to our Father.

John Oman

790

At the period of history when Britain maintained a
presence in the north-west frontier of India, two English
officers, Colonel Stoddart and Captain Conolly, were sent
to Bukhara on Government business. They never returned
but news at length came that both had been murdered,
after terrible treatment, by the Amir.

Nineteen years passed, and then one day in St Petersburg
in Russia, an old English Prayer Book was found by a
visitor in the house of a Russian officer. Its fly-leaf and the
margins were covered with pencilled notes. It had been
picked up on a stall in Bukhara, but the Russian officer to
whom it belonged could not read it. His visitor, however,
could. It had belonged to Captain Conolly, and the
pencilled notes told how from December till June he and
Colonel Stoddart had spent months of suffering half-clad in
the bitter cold of an Afghan winter, wounded, ill-treated,
and with no change of clothes. At last they were led to an
open square outside the prison, where, before a crowd of
natives, Stoddart was executed. Then Captain Conolly was
offered his life if he would become a Muslim, but he replied,
'I will not be a Muslim. I am ready to die.' And he too was
beheaded.

Now, the Russian officer's visitor knew Conolly's family,
and sent the Prayer Book to England to the Captain's
sister, and his sister endowed a bed in the frontier hospital
for Afghan tribesmen.

When the hospital patients heard this story they would
say, with amazement, 'The sister of that man pays that men
of the nation who killed him may be cured? Has she
forgotten about his death?' 'No,' is the reply. 'It is that he
may not be forgotten that she does it. That is the way of
Christian reconciliation.'

Anon.

791

A madman came into a shop carrying a hammer; he swung

it at the china and smashed it all to pieces. People stopped, rushed across from elsewhere, and gazed in astonishment. Some hours later a little old man came into the shop with a box under his arm; he took off his coat, put on his glasses and very, very patiently, among all those broken pieces, began mending the pots. No one, you can be perfectly sure, stopped to watch him!

Aristide Briand

Relationships

792

A blind man and a lame man happened to come at the same time to a piece of very bad road. The former begged the latter to guide him through his difficulties. 'How can I do that,' said the lame man, 'as I am scarcely able to drag myself along? But if you were to carry me I can warn you about anything in the way; my eyes will be your eyes and your feet will be mine.' 'With all my heart,' replied the blind man, 'let us serve one another.' So taking his lame companion on his back, they travelled in this way with safety and pleasure.

Aesop

793

A faithful friend is an image of God.

French proverb

794

There is only one thing that can survive personal death, and that is love. It follows therefore that man's great work while on earth is the forging of relationships – that life is a constant relationship – as Martin Buber puts it: 'All real living is meeting.'

It is the quiet, unobtrusive opening of ourselves to all

manner of men in humble service, above all the service of
simply giving them our attention, that brings its own
reward on the other side of life. It is not great intellectual
knowledge, political power, material wealth or physical
strength that can forge an enduring relationship.

Anon.

795

Life is mostly froth and bubble,
Two things stand like stone:
Kindness in another's trouble,
Courage in your own.

Adam L. Gordon

796

As I went up and he came down, my little six-year boy,
Upon the stairs we met and kissed, I and my tender Joy.
O fond and true, as lovers do, we kissed and clasped and
    parted;
And I went up and he went down, refreshed and happy-
    hearted.

What need was there for any words, his face against my
    face?
And in the silence heart to heart spoke for a little space
Of tender things and thoughts on wings and secrets none
    discovers;
And I went up and he went down, a pair of happy lovers.

His clinging arms about my neck, what need was there for
    words?
O little heart that beat so fast like any fluttering bird's!
'I love,' his silence said, 'I love,' my silence answered duly;
And I went up and he went down comforted wonderfully.

Katherine Tynan

797

The proud owner of the world's largest collection of termites, 230,000 of them, says that these insects have a 'secret formula' that helps them survive. The 'formula' is that they co-operate with one another. Zoologist Alfred Emerson says that 'one of the main ways that termites survive is through co-operation, not competition.'

Anon.

798

Christianity is not a religion, it is a relationship.

Dr Thieme

799

Kevin, a ten-year-old from the country, came to spend the Easter holidays with his aunt, who lived in the London suburb of Wimbledon. Curious to explore not only her large garden but also an overgrown path at the back, he heard odd noises coming from a shed in a neighbour's garden. When he asked his aunt about the noise she told him that she thought her unmarried lady neighbour kept chickens. Kevin had been brought up on a chicken farm and he knew immediately that what he had heard was not 'chicken-noise'.

He went back through a hole in the fence to investigate. The neighbouring garden was very overgrown but with a clear path running from the house to the old shed, The shed door was padlocked and the window was blacked out but there was a large sort of letter-box slit in the door. First checking that no one was watching, Kevin peeped through the 'letter-box'. It was covered on the inside by a piece of hanging material but a powerful stench caught Kevin's nose. Just as he was about to turn away the cover was lifted and a pair of wild staring eyes appeared at the slit. Kevin gave a startled scream and bolted out of the garden back to his aunt's, He ran straight into her. He was so upset that he blurted out just what he had seen. His aunt called the police.

The dignified maiden lady was very indignant at first when the police asked to inspect her garden shed, When they insisted, her resistance collapsed and she gave them a key. On opening the door a sight met the eyes of the two constables that they are never likely to forget. Cowering in a darkened corner from the bright light, and the strange intruders, was a naked figure of what seemed to be a strange animal. It was on all fours, and had long black hair. There was fear in the wild eyes and 'it' made strange little noises. The police officers, taken aback by the sight and the stench, closed the door again and radioed for assistance.

The nine-year-old boy was taken into very special care, He had been in the shed for seven years, since the age of two, when the woman, fearing the discovery of her secret illegitimate child, had incarcerated him in the shed. Besides the filth, long hair and nails, his back was bent in such a way that he would never be able to learn to walk upright. Terrified at the presence of other people, he could not communicate but merely express emotions by grunts. He had never known any caring relationships and there was no hope of a return to full human existence.

Paul Frost

Religion

800

Religion is that faith that God is the ultimate Personal Creator and Sustainer of all values, and that human beings realise the utmost value when they join Him, conscientiously and joyously, in the creation of value.

Peter A. Bertocci

801

A believer and a sceptic went for a walk. The sceptic said, 'Look at the trouble and misery in the world after thousands of years of religion. What good is religion?' His companion noticed a child, filthy with grime, playing in the gutter. He said, 'We've had soap for generation after generation yet look how dirty that child is. Of what value is soap?' The sceptic protested, 'But soap can't do any good unless it is used!' 'Exactly,' replied the believer.

Anon.

802

Religion is the vision of something which stands beyond, behind and within the passing flux of immediate things. The worship of God is not a rule of safety – it is an adventure of the spirit, a flight after the unattainable.

Alfred N. Whitehead

Repentance

803

When Dostoyevsky, the Russian novelist, knew that he had but a little time to live he made his children come into his room, and begged their mother to read the parable of the Prodigal Son. He listened with his eyes closed, absorbed in his thoughts. 'My children,' he said in his feeble voice, 'never forget what you have just heard. Have absolute faith in God, and never despair of his pardon. I love you dearly, but my love is nothing compared with the love of God for all those he has created. Even if you should be so unhappy as to commit a crime in the course of your life, never despair of God. You are his children; humble yourselves before Him as before your father, implore his pardon, and He will rejoice over your repentance, as the father rejoiced over that of the Prodigal Son.

D. Williamson

804

Repentance is not a free and fair highway to God. God prefers that you approach Him thoughtful, not penitent, though you are the chief of sinners. It is only by forgetting yourself that you draw near to Him.

Henry David Thoreau

805

A soldier asked a holy monk if God accepted repentance. He said, 'Tell me, if your cloak is torn, do you throw it away?' The soldier replied, 'No, I mend it and use it again.' The old man said to him, 'If you are so careful about your cloak, will not God be equally careful about his creature?'

Anon.

Respect for Life

806

Maurice Baring used to tell the following story:

One doctor said to another doctor: 'About the termination of a pregnancy, I want your opinion. The father was a syphilitic. The mother was tuberculous. Of the four children born, the first was blind, the second died, the third was deaf and dumb, the fourth also tuberculous. What would you have done?

'I would have ended the pregnancy.'

'Then you would have murdered Beethoven.'

807

I think we honour God more if we gratefully accept the life he gives us with all its blessings, having it and drinking it to the full and also grieving deeply and sincerely when we have impaired or wasted any of the good things of life than if we are insensitive to life's blessings and may therefore also be insensitive to pain.

Dietrich Bonhoeffer

Resurrection

808
An old cathedral stood on the site of the present St Paul's in London. It perished in the great fire of 1666. After the fire, the brilliant young architect, Christopher Wren, designed a new cathedral which took thirty-five years to erect. The first stone that Wren picked up from the ruins of the old building bore a Latin inscription whose meaning is 'I shall rise again.'

Anon.

809
It is also stated that after his execution and entombment He disappeared entirely. Some people actually assert that He had risen; others retort that his friends stole Him away. I for one cannot decide where the truth lies.

Josephus

810
There was no mistaking the conviction with which the early message of the Resurrection came across. There were no 'Ifs' and 'Buts', no trace of 'It is reasonable to suppose', or 'In all probability'. There were no furrowed brows about the 'problem' of the Resurrection. *They knew it had happened* – and only seven or eight weeks previously! Quite frankly, if Jesus Christ had not risen from the dead, clearly and unmistakeably, as the permanent conqueror of death for all

mankind, we would never have heard of him. The demoralised movement, comprising eleven scared men, would have fizzled out on the launching pad.

Richard Bewes

811

The basic meaning of the Resurrection is the liberation of Jesus Christ. John Masefield in his play tells in imagination how Procla, the wife of Pilate, sent for Longinus, the centurion in charge of the crucifixion, and asked him what happened. 'He was a fine young man,' said Longinus, 'but when we were finished with him, he was a poor broken thing on a cross.' 'So you think', said Procla, 'that he is finished and ended?' 'No, madam, I do not,' said Longinus. 'He is set free throughout the world where neither Jew nor Greek can stop his truth.'

William Barclay

812

Without sacrifice there is no resurrection. Nothing grows and blooms save by giving. All you try to save in yourself wastes and perishes.

André Gide

813

The resurrection that awaits us beyond physical death will be but the glorious consummation of the risen life which already we have in Christ.

D.T. Niles

814

Over the magnificent mausoleum that holds the mortal remains of Queen Victoria and those of her royal husband are inscribed the words: 'Here at last I will rest with thee, and with thee in Christ I shall also rise again.'

Anon.

815

One ancient symbol of Christian belief in the resurrection is the phoenix. This bird symbolised hope and the continuity of life after death. According to legend, only one phoenix could live at a time. The Greek poet Hesiod, writing in the eighth century BC, said it lived nine times the lifespan of the long-living raven. When the bird felt death approaching, it built itself a pyre of wild cinnamon and died in the flames. But from the ashes there then arose a new phoenix, which tenderly encased its parent's remains in an egg of myrrh and flew with them to the Egyptian city of Heliopolis, where it laid them on the Altar of the Sun. These ashes were said to have the power of bringing a dead man back to life.

Scholars now think that the germ of the legend came from the Orient, and was adopted by the sun-worshipping priests of Heliopolis as an allegory of the sun's daily setting and rebirth. In Christian art the resurrected phoenix became a popular symbol of Christ risen from the grave.

Paul Frost

Revelation

816

God hides nothing. His very work from the beginning is revelation – a casting aside of veil after veil, a showing unto men of truth after truth. On and on from fact divine he advances, until at length in his son Jesus he unveils his very face.

George MacDonald

817

We do not believe that God has added, or ever will add, anything to his revelation in his Son. But we can now see many things in that revelation which could not be seen by those who first received it. Each generation of Christians, and each people to which the Christian Gospel is preached, makes its own contribution to the understanding of the riches of Jesus Christ.

C.B. Moss

818

Every revelation of truth felt with interior savour and spiritual joy is a secret whispering of God in the ear of a pure soul.

Walter Hilton

819

In Cracow, a rabbi dreamt three times that an angel told him to go to Livovna. 'In front of the palace there, near the bridge,' the angel said, 'you will learn where a treasure is hidden.' The rabbi went to Livovna. When he arrived at the palace, he found a sentinel near the bridge, so he told him the dream. The sentinel replied; 'I, too, have had a dream, The angel told me to go to a rabbi's house in Cracow, where a treasure is buried in front of the fireplace.' Hearing this, the rabbi returned home and dug in front of the fireplace. There he found the treasure. All revelation will show that God is to be found nowhere else but within.

Paul Frost

820

The Lord Jesus Christ loves to reveal Himself to those who dare to take the bleak side of the hill with Him.

Anon.

Sacrifice

821

Man's strongest instinct is to self-preservation; grace's highest call is to self-sacrifice.

Paul Frost

822

The most perfect and complete form of sacrifice, that was most costly to the giver, was called the *holah* from the verb 'to go up'. With this, translated in Greek as 'holocaust' meaning 'totally burnt', every part of the sacrificial animal, apart from the skin as fee for the priest, was burnt up on the altar. The earliest example is Abraham's sacrifice of the ram in place of Isaac (Gen. 22.13).

The person offering the animal, the one who cut its throat, had to be in a state of ritual purity. He was depriving himself of a valuable part of his livelihood in order to give fitting homage to God. As the prophets frequently and vociferously pointed out, unless this reflected sincerely felt belief it would be no use to anyone, for God does not need any created thing (Isa. 57.15; 66.2; Amos 5.21–5). However, when performed as a true expression, it finds acceptance by God.

Debbie Jones

823

It is only through the mystery of self-sacrifice that a man may find himself anew.

Carl Gustav Jung

824

An eleven-year-old girl gave her own life to save three younger children from death under the wheels of an onrushing railroad train in New Jersey. The young girl was walking along the tracks with her brother, six, and a sister and cousin, both five, when the train suddenly rounded a curve and bore down on them.

She pushed her brother off the tracks and shouted warnings to the other children, enabling them to escape in time. But the speeding train struck and killed her before she could get away. Self-preservation is a powerful instinct in every human being, but man has a deeper and nobler impulse. It is the divine inclination to sacrifice even life itself in the service of others.

Anon.

Salvation

825

The terms for 'salvation' in many languages are derived from roots like salvus, saos, whole, heil, which all designate health, the opposite of disintegration and disruption. Salvation is healing in the ultimate sense; it is final cosmic and individual healing.

Paul Tillich

826

From the ingrained fashion
Of this earthly nature
That mars thy creature;
From grief that is but passion,
From mirth that is but feigning,
From tears that bring no healing,
From wild and weak complaining,
Thine old strength revealing,
Save, oh!, save.

Matthew Arnold

827

One of the unsung heroes of the Townsend Ferry Disaster demonstrated last night how he formed a human bridge over which more than twenty terrified passengers scrambled to safety.

Mr Andrew Parker, thirty-three, lay spread-eagled across two metal bars for more than half an hour as horror-stricken men, women and children clambered over him to avoid the drop into a water-filled chasm. Mr Parker, an ex-policeman and now a bank clerk, was bruised and shocked in the ordeal and was reluctant to talk of his bravery. But he showed how the bridge had been formed by laying his hands on a wall, stretching to his full 6ft 2in. frame and spreading his legs apart to let passengers stride and crawl across his body

For twenty-four hours afterwards, Mr Parker, from Herne Hill, South London, believed he had lost his wife Eleanor and twelve-year-old daughter Janice. He spoke of his 'indescribable joy' when he was reunited with them in hospital.

Mrs Parker said the family were with friends in the cafeteria when trays of food slid across the table. Then suddenly, they were thrown across the ship. She said, 'We heard a crashing of cutlery and suddenly everything went black. We were quite calm because we were all together and we didn't know at that stage just what had happened.'

Mrs Parker went on: 'Then we could hear the water rushing in and could feel the ship sinking. Even then I don't think we felt scared. We just thought everything would turn out all right.' But her daughter Janice was becoming hysterical and shouting that she felt certain she would die. 'My daughter was underneath and we were all lying together in a heap, with my husband telling everyone to keep calm.'

The family discovered their only path to safety was over a large chasm which had opened up and quickly filled with water. The gap between the dangerous spot they were in and the haven on the other side was too great for most of the children and women to jump.

Mrs Parker said: 'Andrew has a very large frame and he started shouting at me to step on his back and jump to the other side. But the rails were wobbly and I was worried that we would go down together and both die. He wouldn't let me say no. I felt as though I had to do it because there were so many people waiting. If it failed the rest would be left behind for good.'

She gripped her husband tightly and climbed slowly over his arms, back and legs and leapt to the other side. Next over the bridge was her daughter quickly followed by friends and then other passengers.

Then the task began of hauling Mr Parker to safety. With the help of several of the other rescued passengers he was pulled up and they all headed for a porthole.

Daily Mail

828

What is salvation? It is the putting of a man right with God. Not by anything that he does. He cannot merit it, nor can he earn it. It is something which God gives him. It is offered freely and unconditionally, and it is offered to everyone, regardless of race or colour. It is there to be claimed. Where is it to be found? In and through the Person of Jesus Christ. All that is needed is for a person to enter into that relationship with him that we call trust.

Gerald Ellison

829

The Ganges was calm. Peace was upon the waters as the young girl walked the banks of the river. Her thoughts were the thoughts of youth. Who would she marry? How many children would she have? Would she be rich and have servants? Ahead of her she noticed an old woman. She was dressed in a beautiful sari and her face was radiant. Next to her the Ganges appeared a troubled river.

As the young woman approached her, the old woman suddenly bent over some branches that had washed into shore. Her hand moved among the branches; then she quickly pulled it out. When the young woman was close enough, she saw what was happening. A spider had impaled itself on a thorn and the woman was trying to free it. But every time she attempted to lift the spider off, he bit her. She would remove her hand, suck the poisonous blood from her finger and try again.

The young woman watched her for a while and spoke. 'Old woman, what foolishness is this? Leave the spider to its fate. Every time you try to help it, it repays you with a bite.'

The old woman smiled. 'The spider's nature is to bite. Mine is to save. Will I lose myself on the banks of this sacred river?'

The younger woman said nothing but her face showed that she was puzzled. In her heart the old woman hoped that her smile was not lost on the young one.

John Shea

830

A Scotsman was once asked how many it took to convert him. 'Two, he replied. 'Two! How was that? Didn't God do it all?' 'The Almighty and myself converted me,' he said. 'I did all I could against it, and the Almighty did all he could for it, and he won!'

Anon.

831

A spark of genius helped save a man who was entombed in snow for seventy-six hours. As he struggled for survival in his car – buried two feet under the snow – travelling salesman Mr Billy Sutherland, sixty-four, remembered he had a huge stock of women's tights with him. He pulled several pairs on over his trousers, then calmly settled down to await rescue. They helped to keep him warm.

A search party out in the Scottish blizzards finally tracked down his car last night using a highly sensitive metal detector. He had bored an air-hole through the snow to help him breathe. Mr Sutherland was able to speak to his rescuers, who carried him two miles to an ambulance to take him to hospital in Golspie near Sutherland.

At Golspie, he jumped out of the ambulance and ran into the hospital waving. In hospital last night, he said: 'I just kept calm and prayed help would come. The only food I had was snow but at least that kept me going.

'I couldn't believe it when the rescuers began tapping on the roof of my car. I was just getting ready to sleep for the fourth night.'

Daily Mail

Satan

832

The character of Satan is pride and sensual indulgence, finding in self the sole motive of action.

Samuel Taylor Coleridge

833

There's something that pulls us upwards
  And there's something that pulls us down;
And the consequence is we wobbles
  Twixt muck and a golden crown.

Anon.

834

There is an old tale about Satan walking in the Street of
Life, sulking in the shadows with his hunting dogs, the little
imps of human weakness. A man, Albert, came walking
down the Street; Satan said to a little imp, scowling with a
bitter face: 'Go, get him for me!' Quickly the imp crossed
the street, silently and lightly hopped on to the man's
shoulder. In his ear he whispered, 'You are discouraged.'
'No,' said the man, 'I am not discouraged.' 'You are
discouraged!' insisted the imp. This time the man replied,
'I don't think I am.' Louder and more decidedly, the little
imp repeated, 'I tell you, you are discouraged.' Albert
dropped his head and murmured: 'Well, I suppose I am.'
The little imp darted back to Satan and said proudly, 'I've
got him; he's discouraged.' Another man, Carlson, passed.
Again, old Satan said: 'Get him for me!' The proud little
demon of discouragement repeated his tactics. The first
time he said, 'You are discouraged,' the man replied,
emphatically, 'No.' The second time Carlson replied, 'I tell
you I am not discouraged!' The third time he said, 'You lie!
I am not discouraged,' and he walked down the street, his
head erect, going straight towards the light. The imp of
discouragement returned to his master, crestfallen, 'I
couldn't get him,' he reported. 'Three times I told him he
was discouraged. The third time, he called me a liar, and
that discouraged me!'

P. Fontaine

835

I am a great enemy to flies; when I have a good book, they
flock upon it and parade up and down it, and soil it. 'Tis
just the same with the devil. When our hearts are purest, he
comes and soils them.

Martin Luther

836

The devil wrestles with God, and the field of battle is the human heart.

Fyodor Dostoevsky

Seeking God

837

It is in silence that God is known, and through mysteries that He declares Himself.

R.H. Benson

838

Six hundred and thirteen commandments were given to Moses . . . Then David came and reduced them to eleven. Then came Isaiah, and reduced them to six. Then came Micah, and reduced them to three. Then Isaiah came again, and reduced them to two, as it is said, 'Keep ye judgement and do righteousness.' Then came Amos, and reduced them to one, as it is said, 'Seek you me and live.'

Rabbi Samlai

839

Those who roam to other lands in pilgrimage to find the God that dwells within them are like a shepherd who searches his own flock for the sheep he has under his arm.

Telugu proverb

840

Carl Jung was counselling a man who had been receiving therapy for six months and was getting no better. Finally

Dr Jung said: 'Friend I cannot do any more for you. What you need is God.'

'How do I find God, Dr Jung?' the man asked.

'I do not know,' said Jung, 'but I suspect if you find a group of people that believe in Him passionately and just spend time with them you will find God.'

'Methodist Recorder'

841

O thou Great Chief, light a candle in my heart that I may see what is therein and sweep the rubbish from thy dwelling place.

African child's prayer

Seeking Perfection

842

The noble love of Jesus impels a man to do great things, and stirs him up to be always longing for what is more perfect.

Thomas à Kempis

843

The great sculptor, Michaelangelo, was at work on one of his statues when a friend called on him, and said, 'I can't see any difference in the statue since I came here a week ago. Have you not been doing any work all the week?' 'Yes,' said the sculptor, 'I have retouched this part, softened this feature, strengthened this muscle, and put more life into that limb.' 'But those are only trifles,' said the friend. 'True,' said Michaelangelo, 'but trifles make perfection, and perfection is no trifle.'

Anon.

844

Perfection does not lie in seeing the world, but in not tasting or relishing it.

Francis of Sales

845

In my unforgettable college days, a boy who played next to me in the college orchestra never made a mistake. Not once was he called down by the professor. But one day this lad ceased to be a member of the orchestra, and the professor told us why that boy never made a mistake. He did not play loud enough for anyone to hear him. It is human to err. Any man who is playing his God-given part in life may make a mistake, may do some wrong, he may be a victim of circumstances. The important thing is not the mistake he makes, but his reaction to that mistake and the circumstances surrounding it.

P. Fontaine

846

Do all the good you can,
In all the ways you can,
In all the places you can,
At all the times you can,
To all the people you can,
As long as ever you can.

John Wesley

847

Youth is not a time of life . . . it is a state of mind.
Nobody grows old by merely living a number of years;
people grow old only by deserting their ideals.
Years wrinkle the skin, but to give up enthusiasm wrinkles
the soul.

Worry, doubt, self-distrust, fear and despair . . .
these are the long, long years that bow the head and turn
the growing spirit back to dust.
Whether seventy or sixteen, there is in every being's
heart the love of wonder, the sweet amazement at the stars
and the starlike things and thoughts, the undaunted
challenge of events, the unfailing childlike appetite for what
    next,
and the joy of the game of life.
You are as young as your faith, as old as your doubt;
as young as your self-confidence, as old as your fear;
as young as your hope, as old as your despair.

Anon.

848

You will never be sorry
For doing your level best,
For your faith in humanity,
For being kind to the poor,
For asking pardon when in error,
For being generous with an enemy,
For sympathising with the oppressed.

Anon.

849

A group of boys were trying to see who could make the
straightest track across the snowy field. Only one of them
succeeded in making a path which was almost perfectly
straight. When asked how he managed to do it, he said, 'It
was easy, I just kept my eyes fixed on the lightning rod on
top of the barn at the end of the field – while the rest of you
kept looking at your feet.'

Anon.

850

Florence Nightingale who bandaged the world's battle wounds, said:

'I solemnly pledge myself before God and in the presence of this assembly to pass my life in purity and to practise my profession faithfully. I will abstain from whatever is deleterious and mischievous, and will not take or knowingly administer any harmful drug.

I will do all in my power to elevate the standard of my profession, and will hold in confidence all personal matters committed to my keeping and all family affairs coming to my knowledge in the practice of my profession. With loyalty will I endeavour to aid the physician in his work, and devote myself to the welfare of those committed to my care.'

Self-knowledge

851

As the light grows, we see ourselves to be worse than we thought. We are amazed at our former blindness as we see issuing from our heart a whole swarm of shameful feelings, like filthy reptiles crawling from a hidden cave. But we must be neither amazed nor disturbed. We are not worse than we were; on the contrary, we are better.

François Fénelon

852

The picture human beings have of themselves, to a large extent, determines the picture they have of God.

F.F. Van der Water

853

A man has many skins in himself, covering the depths of his heart. Man knows so many things; he does not know himself. Why, thirty or forty skins or hides, just like an ox's or a bear's, so thick and hard, cover the soul. Go into your own ground and learn to know yourself there.

Meister Eckhart

854

The highest and most profitable reading is the true knowledge and consideration of ourselves.

Thomas à Kempis

855

No man has learned to live
until he can rise above the narrow confines
of his individualistic concerns
to the broader concerns of all humanity.
Length without breadth
is like a self-contained tributary
having no outward flow to the ocean.
Stagnant, still, and stale,
it lacks both life and freshness.
In order to live creatively
and meaningfully,
our self-concern must be wedded to other concern.

Martin Luther King

856

The Managing Director of one of the largest commercial interests in the world was sitting in his New York office talking to a client. Suddenly a secretary came into the room obviously harassed, bearing in his hands a sheaf of impressive documents. He talked excitedly at great length seeking to impress upon his chief the desperate nature of his problem. 'Jones,' said the Managing Director, 'please don't forget rule three.' The secretary looked startled, then smiling, he folded his papers and left the room. Overcome by curiosity the client asked the Managing Director to tell him about rule three. 'Rule three', said the Managing Director, 'is "Don't take yourself too seriously".' 'And what are the rules one and two?' asked the client. 'There are no other rules in this business,' the Manager Director replied, 'only rule three.'

John Heenan

Self-love

857

There is a parable in India of the Selfish Fool, to whom a rice field was bequeathed. The first season the irrigation water covered his field and made it fruitful, and then flowed on to his neighbour's fields, bringing fertility everywhere. But the next season the Selfish Fool said within his heart, 'This water is wealth, it is liquid harvest. I was a fool to let this treasure escape to my neighbour's land.' He robbed his neighbour – and he spoiled his own crop. For the irrigation water brought blessing while it flowed, but when it became stagnant it bred a marsh.

'Sunday School Times'

858

Balzac, the French novelist, was so conceited, that he raised his hat every time he spoke of himself.

Robert S. Broughton

859

'I am writing a great book,' remarked the Pen. 'It will make me famous.'

'Indeed!' exclaimed the Ink-bottle. 'I was rather of the opinion that I was writing that book. How much would you write without my ink?'

'Well, of all the conceited fools!' sneered the Paper. 'It is not your book at all, but mine. I am the book. It is written on my pages. Take it from me if you can!'

'You are all wrong,' said the Dictionary. 'What is a book but words? And where does the writer get the words except from me? You have all seen how often he comes to me for them. The book is manifestly mine.'

Thereupon the author, who had overheard the conversation, chuckled aloud. 'I suppose,' he mused, 'no one ever did something worthwhile but a dozen assistants, completely his inferior, took credit for it themselves.'

A.R. Wells

860

He who hates not in himself his self-love, and that instinct which leads him to make himself a God, is indeed blind.

Blaise Pascal

861

An inflated frog, the usual type of the boaster, wanted to accompany a brood of wild geese on their migration from the cold north to the sunny southern climes. As he heard the geese planning their trip in his northern pool, the frog proposed the idea of accompanying them. But they said: 'How can you ever fly? We are provided with wings and you can only croak and swim.' 'Oh, but', said he, 'I have brains, and if you will carry out my directions you will be surprised at the ingenuity of my plan.' The geese consented, and immediately the frog directed them to a strong reed in

the swamp, which they pulled up and brought to him.
'Now,' he said, 'you just take hold of this reed in your
mouths, one at each end, and I will hold on with my mouth
in the middle, and you will carry me without difficulty.'
And so they started. But as they flew over the village the
people were attracted by the strange sight of the aerial
caravan, and, with open mouths and eyes, they began
expressing their wonder and admiration at the strange
contrivance, and asking, 'Whoever could have thought of
such a bright idea?' This was too much for the frog. He was
in danger of losing the credit for this splendid scheme, and
so, without stopping to think, he shouted, 'I did it!' But of
course the moment he opened his mouth he lost his hold
and down he dropped among the villagers.

'Sunday School Times'

Self-sacrifice

862

Elizabeth Pilenko came from a wealthy land-owning family
in the south of Russia. She became a keen socialist
revolutionary and during the years 1914–17 her life was
taken up with revolutionary activities. After the October
Revolution she worked with extraordinary skill and audacity
in rescuing victims from the Terror. In 1923 she came to
Paris. She found her way back to religious faith. She
presented herself to the authorities of the Russian Church
in Paris and announced that she wished to become a
religious, 'beginning at once, today', and to found a
monastery. She had her way, but she was not the
traditional Russian Orthodox religious. She was accused by
some of neglecting the long services and the traditional
contemplation. 'I must go my way,' she said, 'I am for the
suffering people.' When the German occupation took place

Mother Maria summoned her chaplain and told him that she felt that her particular duty was to render all possible assistance to persecuted Jews. She knew that this would mean imprisonment and probably death, and she gave him the option of leaving. He refused. For a month the convent was a haven for Jews. Women and children were hidden within its walls. Money poured in to enable them to escape from France and hundreds got away. At the end of a month the Gestapo came. Mother Maria was arrested and sent to the concentration camp at Ravensbruck. Her chaplain was sent to Buchenwald, where he died of starvation and overwork.

She was known even to the guards as 'that wonderful Russian nun' and it is doubtful whether they had any intention of killing her. She had been there two and a half years when a new block of buildings was erected in the camp and the prisoners were told that there were to be hot baths. A day came when a few dozen prisoners from the women's quarter were lined up outside the buildings. One girl became hysterical. Mother Maria, who had not been selected, came up to her, 'Don't be frightened,' she said, 'Look, I shall take your turn,' and in line with the rest, she passed through the gas chamber doors. It was Good Friday, 1945.

'Christian Newsletter'

863

In this world it is not what we *take* up, but what we *give* up, that makes us rich.

Henry Ward Beecher

864

Henri Nouwen tells of a Lutheran bishop who was imprisoned in a German concentration camp during World War II and beaten by an SS officer in order to extract a

confession from him about his political action. The beatings
continued to increase in intensity, but the bishop maintained his silence. Finally, the infuriated officer shrieked,
'Don't you know that I can kill you?' The bishop looked in
the eyes of his torturer and said, 'Yes, I know – do what you
want – but I have already died.'

Instantly as though paralyzed, the officer could no longer
raise his arm. It was as if power over the bishop had been
taken from him. All his cruelties had been based on the
assumption that the bishop's physical life was his most
precious possession and therefore he would be willing to
make any concession to save it. But with the grounds for
violence gone, torture was futile.

Henri Nouwen

865
They that deny themselves for Christ shall enjoy themselves
in Christ.

John Mason

866
Librarian Derek Thomas sacrificed his life to save his
girlfriend after she was badly injured in a mountain fall.

For almost two miles twenty-eight-year-old Mr Thomas
carried and dragged his semi-conscious companion, Susan
Hamilton, across the slopes of Helvellyn in the Lake
District.

Zero temperature and torrential rain slowly sapped his
strength. After hours of effort he was forced to leave twenty-
four-year-old Susan by a hikers' footpath and struggle on
alone.

Slightly built Mr Thomas stumbled only another thirty
yards before he collapsed at the side of a stream – and died.
But his effort ensured that Susan lived. The next morning

walkers heard her cries for help. She had back and leg injuries.

Dr James Ogilvie, of the Patterdale mountain rescue team, said yesterday: 'This was an incredibly heroic act by a young man who, from what we can piece together, gave his own life to save the girl.'

Daily Mail

Sharing

867

A merchant in quest of precious stones was one day riding through the bazaar of Damascus. A quivering beam of the sun upon a shelf caught his attention. There, shining with a light that never was on land or sea, was the jewel of his heart, the pearl of his dreams that henceforth would mean more than all the world for him. Dismounting from his camel he got permission to hold the pearl in the palm of his hand. Yes, it was worth the cost!

Excitedly he jumped on his camel and raced back to his palace. 'My wife,' he said exultantly as he entered the door, 'I have found at last what all my life I wanted most. But you and I will have to leave all this. To get the pearl it will take everything I have.'

'My husband,' answered the wife, 'I am not afraid to give up comfort or security. This palace is a trifling thing.'

Back to Damascus hurried the merchant. In return for the pearl he gave all his wealth. He and his wife spent the rest of their days in a shack. Their food was roots and bread. But the merchant was satisfied. Every day at noon he would hold up the pearl for the sun to shine upon; and there, in the palm of his hand, it would glow with the grace of unspeakable things. In time the glory of it seemed to fade. The merchant and his wife were puzzled. At last they nodded their heads in understanding, and the merchant said to his wife, 'This pearl will be of worth to us only as we share it with the world.'

Allan A. Hunter

868
It is easier to renounce worldly possessions than it is to renounce the love of them.

Walter Hilton

869
A Christian's virtue is the only possession that cannot be conquered or destroyed.

Eusebius of Caesarea

870
I heard recently of a Christian speaker in Hyde Park who declared rhetorically, expecting the answer 'Yes': 'If you had two houses, you would give one to the poor, wouldn't you?' 'Yes,' said the man to whom the question was directed, 'indeed I would.' 'And if you had two motor cars,' went on the orator, 'you would keep one and give the other away?' 'Yes, of course,' said the man. 'And if you had two shirts, you would give one away?' 'Hey, wait a minute,' said the man, 'I've got two shirts!'

Douglas Woodruff

871
One child said to another, 'If one of us would get off this tricycle, I could ride it much better.'

Anon.

872

Teacher asked Peter how he would divide ten potatoes equally among people. Peter promptly replied, 'I'd mash them.'

Anon.

873

'Er – about that umbrella I lent you last week,'

'Sorry, old chap, but I lent it to Brown. Were you wanting it?'

'Well not for myself – but the chap I borrowed it from says that the owner's getting a bit anxious about it.'

Anon.

Sick – Care of

874

Hilary Pole was a young woman who was totally physically handicapped, while being extremely active, mentally and intellectually. She was only able to move her left big toe one-sixteenth of an inch.

To make it possible for Hilary to communicate with her family and the world around her, Reg Maling, a medical scientist, who had invented the Possum, developed in 1967 a special mechanism to make use of Hilary's minute movement.

The Possum is a machine which makes it possible to dial a telephone number, open a front door, switch on a light or fire without lifting a finger, by using special electronic equipment. A sequence of lights on a display board is operated by blowing on a stem pipe, or in Hilary's case, tapping lightly with her big toe. The release of pressure activates the gadget. A code of sucks and blows enables disabled people to operate an electric typewriter at up to forty words a minute.

Hilary made good use of her Possum winning the MBE in 1973 for her work for the handicapped! She died on 18th June, 1975, aged thirty-seven.

Paul Frost

875
The best prayers have often more groans than words.

John Bunyan

876
Jesus came to save persons not just souls. He came to help the suffering in whatever way they were suffering. Sickness of the body was part of the kingdom of Satan he had come to destroy.

Francis MacNutt

877
Before all things and above all things, care must be taken of the sick, so that they may be served in very deed as Christ himself . . . But let the sick on their part consider that they are being served for the honour of God, and not provoke their brethren who are serving them by their unreasonable demands. Yet they should be patiently borne with, because from such as these is gained a more abundant reward.

Benedict

878
O beloved sick, how doubly dear you are to me. You personify Christ. And what a privilege is mine to be allowed to tend you.

Mother Teresa

879

Disease makes man more physical; it leaves them nothing
but body.

Thomas Mann

880

On a parcel sent from Norway to England was affixed a
label with the words 'Glass with anxiety' in large letters, to
indicate the fragile nature of the contents and obtain for the
parcel cautious handling. The sender, with a limited
knowledge of English, evidently thought that 'anxiety' was
a synonym for 'care'. Perhaps we should speak of pastoral
anxiety for the sick!

Anon.

881

I have always loved to think of devoted suffering as the
highest, purest, perhaps the only quite pure form of action.

Baron von Hügel

882

A minister was summoned in haste by a woman taken ill
suddenly. He answered the call though somewhat puzzled,
for he knew that she was not of his parish, and was
moreover, known to be a devoted worker in another parish.
While he was waiting to be shown to the sickroom he fell to
talking to the little girl of the house. 'It is very gratifying to
know that your mother thought of me in her illness,' he
said. 'Is your own minister away?' 'Oh, no,' answered the
child in a matter of fact tone, 'he's home. Only we thought
it might be something contagious – and we didn't want to
take any risks!'

Anon.

883

Lady: I want a nice book for an invalid.
Bookseller: Yes madam. Something religious?
Lady: Er-no-no-er-he's convalescent!

'The Churchman'

884

A woman was telling her married daughter that the cold
weather was bad for her rheumatism. Her little granddaughter was present and overheard the conversation. She
didn't say anything then, but that night when she went to
bed she knew what she was going to do. After she had said
her usual prayers she concluded by saying: 'And please
God, make it hot for Gran!'

Anon.

Silence — Solitude

885

Love silence, even in the mind; for thoughts are to that, as
words are to the body, troublesome: much speaking, as
much thinking, spends. True silence is the rest of the mind;
and it is to the spirit, what sleep is to the body, nourishment
and refreshment.

William Penn

886

The market is as good a place for silence as the monastery,
for silence is the absence of the ego.

'The Wellsprings'

887

One day last summer, after I'd been working on some

songs, I left the harp before the open window. Suddenly I heard the sound of distant and very lovely music. It lasted only a few seconds and left me very puzzled. When it happened again I noticed that the sound came from the instrument and was caused by the gentle breeze from the open window playing on the harp strings.

At times of prayer we can be like that harp, by allowing sufficient calm to gather round us so that the Holy Spirit, the Breath of God, may play his music on us. But remember, it was a very gentle breeze and the music could be heard only because of the surrounding stillness.

Mary O'Hara

888
If we have not quiet in our minds, outward comfort will do no more for us than a golden slipper on a gouty foot.

John Bunyan

889
For many young people today silence is unknown, disturbing, unacceptable. Without noise and music they can't concentrate, they can't work. Here is a poem by a community of young people who still believe in the value of silence.

Silence is Meekness
When you don't return an offence,
when you don't claim your rights,
when you leave to God the defence of your honour,
silence is meekness.

Silence is Mercy
When you don't disclose your brother's faults,
when you forgive without enquiring into the past,
when you don't condemn, but plead in your heart,
silence is mercy.

Silence is Patience
When you suffer without complaint,
when you don't seek consolation from people,
when you don't intervene, but wait for the seed
to germinate slowly,
silence is patience.

Silence is Humility
When you keep quiet to let your brother stand out,
when you surround God's gifts with discretion,
when you tolerate your action being misinterpreted,
when you leave to others the glory of success,
silence is humility.

Silence is Faith
When you keep silent because He is the One who acts,
when you leave world sounds and voices aside
to be in his presence,
when you don't look for understanding
because it's enough to be known by Him,
silence is faith.

Silence is Adoration
When you embrace the cross without asking 'Why',
silence is adoration.
Jesus was silent. (Matt. 26.63)

Anon.

890

All the troubles of life come upon us because we refuse to sit
quietly for a while each day in our rooms.

Blaise Pascal

Sin

891

Sin is essentially a departure from God.

Martin Luther

892

It is not enough to say that one must be set free from sin . . .
It is possible to be possessed by the idea of sin . . .
It is not only real sin which enslaves man, but also
possession by the idea of sin which corrodes the whole life.

Nikolai Berdyaev

893

Men are not punished for their sins, but by them.

Elbert Hubbard

894

An Arab fable tells of a miller who was startled by seeing a
camel's nose thrust in at the window of a room where he
was sleeping. 'It is very cold outside,' said the camel, 'I
only want to get my nose in.' The nose was allowed in, then
the neck, finally the whole body. Soon the miller began to
be inconvenienced by such an ungainly companion in a
room not large enough for both.

'If you are inconvenienced,' said the camel, 'you may
leave; as for myself I shall stay where I am.' 'Give but an
inch,' says Lancelot Andrewes, 'and the devil will take an
ell; if he can get in but an arm, he will make shift to shove in
his whole body. As we see, if the point of a nail have once
made entry, the rest will soon be in.'

A.M.C.

895

To sin is nothing else than not to render to God his due.

Anselm

896

In the ruins of Pompeii there was found a petrified woman

who, instead of trying to flee from the city, had spent her
time in gathering up her jewels. In one of the houses was
found the skeleton of a man who, for the sake of sixty coins,
a small plate and a saucepan of silver, had remained in his
house till the street was half-filled with volcanic matter,
then was trying to escape from the window.

Anon.

897

For the religious man to do wrong is to defy his King; for
the Christian, it is to wound his Friend.

William Temple

898

One summer afternoon on the River Mississippi, a steamer,
crowded with passengers, many of them miners from
California, suddenly struck a submerged wreck. In a
moment her deck was a wild confusion. The boats were
able to take off only one quarter of the passengers. The rest,
divesting themselves of their garments, succeeded in
swimming to shore. Immediately after the last had quitted
the vessel a man appeared on deck. Seizing a spar, he leapt
into the river but instantly sank like a stone. When his body
was recovered, it was found that, while the other passengers
were escaping, he had been rifling the miners' trunks and
round his waist he had fastened bags of gold. In a quarter of
an hour he had amassed more than most men do in a
lifetime, but he lost himself in an instant.

'Thou fool, this night thy soul shall be required of thee.'

Anon.

899

When Leonardo da Vinci was painting his masterpiece *The
Last Supper*, he looked for a model for his Christ. At last he

located a chorister in one of the churches of Rome who was lovely in life and features, a young man named Pietro Bandinelli.

Years passed, and the painting was still unfinished. All the disciples had been portrayed save one – Judas Iscariot. Now he started to look for a man whose face was hardened and distorted by sin – and at last he found a beggar on the streets of Rome with a face so villainous that he shuddered when he looked at him. He hired the man to sit for him as he painted the face of Judas on his canvas. When he was about to dismiss the man, he said, 'I have not yet found out your name.' 'I am Pietro Bandinelli,' he replied, 'I also sat for you as your model of Christ.' The sinful life of years so disfigured the once fair face of the young man that it now looked as though it were the most villainous face in all Rome!

'Indian Christian'

900

Sin; rub out the first and last letters, and you have I – or carnal self – the root of sin.

Anon.

901

There is an Indian fable of a swan, that, pitying a poor pig in its muddy environment, began to describe the beautiful country further up the river, with green banks and rising slopes, and invited the pig to join the happy company of white swans that lived there. The pig was willing enough to go, but asked the question, 'Is there any mire up in that fine country?' 'Oh, no!' replied the swan, 'it is clean and free from mud and mire.' 'Then', said the pig, 'I'm sorry I cannot accompany you. I must stay here in the mire.'

Anon.

902

The line separating good and evil passes not through states,
nor between classes, nor between political parties either –
but right through every human heart. Even in the best of
hearts, there remains a small corner of evil.

Alexander Solzhenitsyn

903

Sin has four characteristics; self-sufficiency instead of faith,
self-will instead of submission, self-seeking instead of
benevolence, self-righteousness instead of humility.

Paul Hovey

904

Lucy says to Charlie Brown: 'You know what the whole
trouble with you is, Charlie Brown?'

'No; and I don't want to know! Leave me alone!'

'The whole trouble with you is you won't listen to what
the whole trouble with you is!'

Robert Short, 'The Gospel According to Peanuts'

905

Mrs Brown was shocked to learn that her son had told a lie.
Taking the youngster aside for a heart-to-heart talk, she
graphically explained the consequences of falsehood: 'A tall
black man with red fiery eyes and two sharp horns grabs
little boys who tell lies and carries them off at night. He
takes them to Mars where they have to work in a dark
canyon for fifty years! Now,' she concluded, satisfied, 'you
won't tell a lie again, will you, dear?'

'No, Mum,' replied her son gravely. 'You tell better
ones.'

F.G. Kernan

Sincerity

906

The word for sincerity in the Greek original of the New
Testament means 'edged in the sunlight'; and the English
word is derived from the Latin *sine cera*, which means
'without wax'. In the days when art flourished in ancient
Greece, it was the common practice to repair with
'invisible' wax any vase or statue that had, as a result of
carelessness or misadventure, been damaged.

A rich man or a person of high rank might employ a
sculptor to chisel his bust in marble. Sometimes, if the
chisel slipped, the end of the nose would be chipped off.
Rather than go to all the trouble of making a new bust, the
sculptor would so mend the features with wax that the flaw
could not be detected unless scrutinised closely. He would
then palm off on the customer his defective workmanship.
If the client happened to be a knowing person, he would
carry the finished statuette out of the studio into the open
and examine it 'carefully in the sunlight; otherwise, in
course of time, he would have the chagrin of seeing the nose
drop off his statuette in the heat of his house. The statue
was not 'sincere', not 'without wax', and could not bear
careful scrutiny in the sunlight.

Paul Frost

Starting Afresh

907

Two men lost their way in Ireland and asked an Irishman
to tell them the way to Dublin. He said, 'If it was to Dublin
I was going, it would not be from here I would be starting.'
That is often our answer to the difficulties of life! We
continually try to start not from where we are, but from
where we are not, and when we fail we do not realize that it

is because we do not take the situation exactly as it is now and start from there, but think to ourselves, 'If I were going to heaven, it is not these parents I would have chosen. If I were going to be good, attractive and lovable, it is not with this family, in this home, in this job, with this disagreeable set of people I would have started.' But we can only start from where we are.

A. Maude Royden

908
Nothing is more expensive than a start.

Friedrich Nietzsche

909
There was an old sailor my grandfather knew,
who had so many things that he wanted to do,
That just when he thought it was time to begin,
He couldn't – because of the state he was in!

Anon.

Success

910
There is a legend of an Indian chief who was wont to try the strength of his youths by making them run in a single effort as far up the side of a mountain as each could reach by his own strength. On an appointed day, four left at daybreak. The first returned with a branch of spruce, indicating the height to which he had attained. The second bore a twig of pine. The third brought an alpine shrub. But it was by the light of the moon that the fourth made his way back. Then he came, worn and exhausted, and his feet were torn by the rocks.

'What did you bring and how high did you ascend?' asked the chief.

'Sire,' he replied, 'where I went there was neither spruce nor pine to shelter me from the sun, nor flower to cheer my path, but only rocks and snow and barren land. My feet are torn, and I am exhausted, and I have come late, but' – and as a wonderful light came into his eyes, the young brave added – 'I saw the sea.'

Edward W. Bok

911
The figure of the Crucified invalidates all thought which takes success for its standard.

Dietrich Bonhoeffer

Suffering

912
It is infinitely easier to suffer in obedience to a human command than to accept suffering as free, responsible men. It is infinitely easier to suffer with others than to suffer alone. It is infinitely easier to suffer as public heroes than to suffer apart and in ignominy. It is infinitely easier to suffer physical death than to endure spiritual suffering. Christ suffered as a free man alone, apart and in ignominy, in body and in spirit, and since that day many Christians have suffered with him.

Dietrich Bonhoeffer

913
God washes the eyes by tears until they can behold the invisible land where tears shall come no more.

Henry Ward Beecher

Suffering Servant

914

In Jocelyn Gibb's *Light on C.S. Lewis*, Nevill Coghill tells a story C.S. Lewis once told him.

Lewis married late in life. In his marriage he found the very perfection of love, but so soon the wife he loved so much died of cancer. Once when Lewis was with Coghill he looked across the quadrangle at his wife. 'I never expected', he said, 'to have in my sixties the happiness that passed me by in my twenties.'

'It was then,' writes Nevill Coghill, 'that he told me of having been allowed to accept her pain.' 'You mean', said Coghill, 'that the pain left her, and that you felt it for her in your body?' 'Yes,' said C.S. Lewis, 'in my legs. It was crippling. But it relieved hers.'

915

Let nothing disturb thee,
Nothing affright thee;
All things are passing;
God never changeth;
Patient endurance
Attaineth to all things;
Who God possesseth
In nothing is wanting;
Alone God sufficeth.

Teresa of Avila

916

'Lament not thy path of woe, O loved man –
it is not unbearable. I hold thee dear,
and will set My guard in power about thee.
My might is above all on this mid-earth,
victory speeds Me . . .

See now the path where thy blood poured down,
the road dark-stained by thy bone-breaking
and thy body bruises, no more may their blows
harm thee, who hast borne their hard hate.'
The beloved champion looked backward then,
hearkening to the words of the Glory-King;
he saw groves standing, fair, green-blowing,
bright with blossoms where his blood had fallen.

From the anonymous poem 'Andreas', early 9th century

917

An extract from the diary of Henri Perrin, a young Jesuit
priest, who trained as a mechanic and volunteered to work
alongside the French conscript workers in the German
factories. After six months he was imprisoned for his
religious activities.

For a week I had been giving my whole mind to the Passion
of Christ. At Jerusalem, as I knelt on the flagstones of
Lithostrotos, where Jesus spent the first hours of Good
Friday, I had been profoundly moved. How much more so
now, at the thought of the hours He spent in prison . . .
During my long hours of silence, I saw Him in his cell, in
the midst of the other prisoners. For He 'did time', too, and
so many others after Him, from Peter to Joan of Arc, from
Paul to Louis. This would henceforward be a bond creating
a special and unforgettable love. However, I passed long
hours in His company – sometimes in his prison, that
cellar of Caiphas' house. I often wondered what He can
have said to the other prisoners – for indeed He must have
talked to them. He who was as able to console the wretched
as to silence the Pharisees.

Henri Perrin

918

From the Will of Count Schwerin von Schwanenfeld who

was executed September 8, 1944, for his part in the plot
against Hitler . . . 'Further it is my desire that in that part
of the gravel bed in my forest of Sartowitz where the victims
of the massacres of the late autumn of 1939 are laid to rest,
a very high oaken cross be erected as soon as the conditions
of the time permit, with the following inscription:

Here lie from 1,400 to 1,500 Christians and Jews.
May God have mercy on their souls and on their
  murderers.'

Kathe Kuhn

919

In the musical *Sound of Music* Sister Maria, when confronted
by a momentous decision which was to change the entire
course of her life, spoke the well-known line of assurance:
'When God closes a door, somewhere he opens a window.'
Millions of Christians who have faced many 'closed doors'
(heartaches, trials and disappointments) in their lives will
rise up to say a hearty 'Amen' to her confident expression of
faith.

In fact many of the world's great have achieved their
most heroic accomplishments in the face of 'closed dors'.
John Milton wrote *Paradise Lost* and *Paradise Regained* after
having been afflicted with total blindness. Beethoven wrote
some of his greatest music, including his Ninth Symphony,
after he was completely deaf.

Anon.

Sunday

920

A world without a Sabbath would be like a man without a
smile, like a summer without flowers and like a homestead
without a garden. It is the joyous day of the whole week.

Henry Ward Beecher

921

Even in the slave-camps of Russia under Stalin, Sunday was not always forgotten.

Slavomir Rawicz, in *The Long Walk*, describes his experiences in forced-labour Camp 303, in northern Siberia, from which he escaped with a few others, reaching India after many months of terrible endurance across the Gobi desert and the Himalayas.

At Camp 303, soup and bread were the regular diet, but 'there was an occasional treat on Sunday when we were given dried fish . . . We worked hard for six days and had an easy day on the seventh.'

'Sunday was the day when the Commandant addressed the prisoners.'

F.H. Drinkwater

922

Better a man ne'er be born,
Than he trims his nails on a Sunday morn.

Warwickshire traditional

923

One Sunday, our young minister announced that he would dispense with the formality of standing at the door to shake hands with the faithful at the end of the service. Instead, he now goes out and shakes hands with the parents waiting to pick up their children from Sunday School.

C.W.F.

924

A little girl, trying to learn the Ten Commandments, was told by her mother to write them out. When she brought forth the result for inspection she had written, 'Remember the Sabbath day to keep it wholly.' The mother said, 'Why,

don't you know how to spell better than that? The word
should be "holy" not "wholly".' The Grandmother who
was sitting by, said, 'Maybe the child has not made such a
mistake. At least her idea of holy is nearer the truth. A day
of rest should not be a shopping day or a decorating day.'

Anon.

925

During the Second World War, for basic training, the men
were divided according to their religious denominations
and expected to attend service at the Anglican, Roman
Catholic or Jewish places of worship, as the case might be.
One of the men in an attempt to evade attendance
proclaimed himself an atheist.

'Don't you believe in God?' asked the officer.

'No,' said he.

'Nor in keeping the Sabbath Day holy?'

'No, one day is as good as another to me.'

Then', said the officer, 'you are just the man we have
been looking for. You will stay and clean out the latrines!'

Anon.

Talents

926

You will ask where my ideas come from. I cannot say for
certain. They come uncalled, sometimes independently,
sometimes in association with other things. It seems to me
that I could wrest them from Nature herself with my own
hands, as I go walking in the woods. They come to me in
the silence of the night or in the early morning, stirred into
being by moods which the poet would translate into words,
but which I put into sounds; and these go through my head

ringing and singing and storming until at last I have them before me as notes.

Ludwig van Beethoven

927

Nature has concealed at the bottom of our minds talents and abilities of which we are not aware.

La Rochefoucauld

928

One day, Michelangelo saw a block of marble which the owner said was of no value. 'It's valuable to me,' said Michelangelo. 'There is an angel imprisoned in it and I must set it free.'

Anon.

929

The real tragedy of life is not in being limited to one talent, but in the failure to use the one talent.

Edgar W. Work

930

Talent is God-given; be thankful. Conceit is self-given; be careful.

Thomas La Mance

931

There is a great deal of unmapped country within us.

George Eliot

932

To raise money for the church tower, the Vicar of
Grundisburgh, England, gave 100 of his villagers a £1 coin
each and they returned six months later with thirteen times
that amount – considerably more than the most enterprising servants in the parables, who only doubled their money.
'It was a great success,' the vicar said last week after a
special harvest festival service in the thirteenth-century
church of St Mary's in Grundisburgh, Suffolk. Villagers
found many novel ways to reap where their vicar had sown.
Taking £1 a piece, they invested their talents in everything
from rabbit-breeding and shoe-shining to lemonade-
making. One of the most enterprising was Mrs Helen
Taylor, the local hairdresser, She bought £1 worth of
material to make pots at the local college and, by re-
investing the profits to buy more material, eventually raised
£93.50. Mrs Ann Johnson spent her £1 on ingredients for
two cakes. And with the £6 profit on those, held a cream tea
party in her garden – making £43. Unlike the master in
Matthew, Chapter 25, the vicar had no need to reproach
any of his flock for burying their talent. 'One of our ladies
put her £1 in a fruit machine,' he said. 'I suppose I ought
not to approve, but she did double the money!'

Anon.

933

Teacher: When George Washington was your age, he was
head of his class.

Pupil: Yes, sir. And when he was your age, he was
President of the United States!

Anon.

Talk

934

The best conversation is that in which the heart has a greater share than the head.

Jean de la Bruyère

935

From a slip of the foot you may soon recover,
But a slip of the tongue you may never get over.

Benjamin Franklin

936

If people would only stop talking when they stop knowing, half the evils of life would come to an end.

Edward Everett Hale

937

A small boy, on his way to church for the first time, was being briefed by his elder sister. 'They won't allow you to talk,' she warned him.

'Who won't?' asked the boy.

'The Hushers.'

'The Sign'

938

For three years Amy Clegg's parrot had not said a single word, and eventually she became convinced it was simply a stupid parrot unable to learn to speak English. Then one day as she was feeding it a piece of lettuce as a special treat, the parrot suddenly squeaked: 'There's a maggot on it; there's a maggot on it!' Amy Clegg was astonished. 'You

can talk!' she exclaimed. 'But why haven't you spoken all
the three years that I've been keeping you?' 'Oh,' replied
the parrot, 'the food has been excellent up to now.'

Anon.

Temptation

939
The absence of temptation is the absence of virtue.

Goethe

940
In the old legend the sirens sang so sweetly that all who
sailed near their home in the sea were fascinated and drawn
to their shore only to be destroyed. Some tried to get safely
past the enchanted spot by putting wax in their ears, so that
they should not hear the luring, bewitching strains. But
Orpheus, when he came, found a better way. He made
music on his own ship which surpassed in sweetness that of
the sirens and thus their strains had no power over his men.

The best way to break the charm of this world's alluring
voices is not to try to shut out the music by stopping our
ears, but to have our hearts filled with the sweeter music of
the joy of Christ. Then temptation will not have power over
us.

R.H.

941
Every moment of resistance to temptation is a victory.

Frederick W. Faber

942
Go to dark Gethsemane,
  Ye that feel the tempter's power.
Your Redeemer's conflict see,
  Watch with him one bitter hour.

James Montgomery

943
There is hardly any power in the mechanical world greater
than that of the wedge. Once you get the thin edge in, it is
only a question of time and force how far the remainder
shall be driven. The hardest stone, the toughest wood, are
not able to resist its power for separation. Beware the thin
edge of sin.

Anon.

944
One eighty-two-year-old Father Christmas put too much
enthusiasm into his job last Christmas and found himself
out of work. The pensioner was paid to sit in his red coat
and white beard in a Nottingham store and speak kindly to
the shy children.

When they would whisper their wishes in his ear,
however, he began to melt. 'I couldn't bear to see them go
away disappointed,' he said later. 'There were a lot of toys
on the shelves nearby that no one seemed to be buying. So I
started handing them to some of the children as an extra
present.' While store officials sympathised with the senti-
ment, they insisted on the hard facts of commercial life. The
old man was politely sacked.

Anon.

945
A shop-keeper, seeing a boy hanging about outside where

there was a tempting display of various fruits, went out to him and said, 'What are you trying to do, young man; steal my apples?'

'No, sir,' said the boy, 'I'm trying not to!'

Anon.

Ten Commandments

946

Love of God is the root, love of our neighour the fruit, of the Tree of Life. Neither can exist without the other; but the one is cause and the other effect, and the order of the Two Great Commandments must not be inverted.

William Temple

947

Six hundred and thirteen commandments were given to Moses: 365 negative, corresponding to the days of the year, and 248 positive, corresponding to the number of joints in the human body.

Talmud

948

In Oscoda, Michigan, Rev. John Silen gives the Ten Commandments the Chippewa Indians had long ago.
   They are:

1. Never steal, except from an enemy.
2. Respect the aged and hearken to them.
3. Be kind to the sick and deformed.
4. Obey your parents.
5. Be modest.
6. Be charitable.

 7. Be of good courage, suffer in silence.
 8. Avenge personal and family wrongs.
 9. Be hospitable.
10. Pray to the Great Spirit.

Many people criticise some of these Chippewa commandments and at the same time look upon God's Ten Commandments as ghostly whispers of a dead age.

949

A minister taking his morning walk came across a stone-breaker. After giving him a cheery 'Good morning', he remarked that he had a deal of work to get through. 'Aye,' said the man, 'them stones are like the Ten Commandments.' 'Why so?' replied the minister. 'You can go on breaking 'em,' came the reply, 'but you can never get rid of 'em.'

Anon.

950

An Englishman and a Jew were talking about the ways of their respective races. 'You people', said the Jew, 'have been taking things from us for thousands of years. The Ten Commandments for instance.' 'Well, yes,' said the other, 'we took them from you all right, but you can't say that we've kept them!'

Anon.

951

An aged Scot told his minister that he was about to make a pilgrimage to the Holy Land. 'And when I'm there,' said the pilgrim, complacently, 'I'll read the Ten Commandments aloud frae the tap o' Mount Sinai.'

The Minister looked at him with an eye of pity, and said, 'Sandy, tak' my advice; bide at hame and keep them.'

D. Williamson

Thanksgiving

952

The legend goes that two angels were once sent down from
heaven, each with a basket. They went from place to place,
to poor houses and rich houses, visiting the children saying
their prayers, the people in the churches, old and young.
Then at length they came flying back with their loads. The
basket borne by one angel was laden, but that of the other
was very light, hardly worthwhile, one would have thought,
to go so far and collect so little. 'What have you in your
basket?' asked one angel of the other. 'I was sent to collect
the prayers of all the people who said, "I want," and
"Please give me," answered the angel who carried the
heavy load.

'And what have you in yours?' 'Oh,' replied the other
angel sadly, 'I have been sent to collect the "Thank yous"
of all the people to whom the great God had sent a blessing;
but see how few have remembered to give!'

Anon.

953

Every furrow in the book of Psalms is sown with the seed of
thanksgiving.

Jeremy Taylor

954

A man went into a flower shop and selected a few flowers,
saying: 'They are my wife's favourites.' The young lady
expressed sympathy at the illness of his wife. 'Ill!' exclaimed
the husband. 'My wife is as well as you are.' The assistant
apologised, saying: 'I beg your pardon for my mistake; but,
to tell you the truth, husbands don't usually buy flowers for

their wives unless the wives are ill or dead.' Gratitude, like love, ought to express itself more frequently.

Anon.

955

Gratitude is born in hearts that take time to count up past mercies.

Charles E. Jefferson

956

If one should give me a dish of sand and tell me there were particles of iron in it, I might look for them with my eyes, and search for them with my clumsy fingers, and be unable to detect them; but let me take a magnet and sweep through it, and how would it draw to itself the almost invisible particles by the mere power of attraction! The unthankful heart, like my finger in the sand, discovers no mercies; but let the thankful heart sweep through the day, and as the magnet finds the iron, so it will find in every hour some heavenly blessings; only the iron in God's sand is gold

Henry Ward Beecher

957

A little girl was going to a party and her mother told her to be a good girl and to remember, when she was leaving, to thank her hostess. When she arrived home the mother asked if she had thanked her hostess and the little girl replied: 'No, the girl in front of me did and the lady said, "Don't mention it" – so I didn't.'

Anon.

Thoughts

958
Such as are thy habitual thoughts, such also will be the character of thy mind; for the soul is dyed by the thoughts.

Marcus Aurelius

959
Have you ever noticed how an icicle is formed? If you have, you noticed how it froze one drop at a time until it was a foot or more long. If the water was clear, the icicle remained clear, and sparkled almost as brightly as diamonds in the sun; but if the water was slightly muddy, the icicle looked foul and its beauty was spoiled. Just so our characters are forming – one little thought or feeling at a time. If each thought be pure and bright, the soul will be lovely and sparkle with happiness; but if impure and wrong, there will be deformity and wretchedness.

'The Evangelist'

960
The soul is dyed the colour of its leisure thoughts.

William Inge

Time

961
Make a careful use of your fragments of time. It is wonderful how much can be got through by these means. A great deal of study, or writing, or other work, can be done by a resolute will in odd quarters of hours, and very often we can get no more. Nothing is more commonly said than that if you want something done, you will have a much

better chance of getting it done by a busy man than by an idle one, and this simply because the former has learnt the secret of economising his time.

Walsham How

962

In a garden next to Gloucester Cathedral there is a sundial which bears this inscription:

> Give God thy heart, thy service and thy gold;
> The day wears on and time is waxing old.'

Anon.

963

Lord Nelson used to say that he owed everything he had done in life to the fact that he was always there a quarter of an hour before the time, rather than a quarter of an hour late.

Anon.

964

There's a quotation from Alexander Pope which has always been a sort of maxim of mine. It says this: 'Be not the first by whom the new is tried, nor yet the last by whom the old is laid aside.' What I like about those words is their warning not to miss the present time of our lives. The constant pursuit of everything new is an escape into the future, and that's one way to miss the present. Never letting go of anything old is simply the opposite way of doing the same thing.

Paul W. Pritchartt

965

A hunter in India with a sling had come to the end of his
stones and wanted one to sling at a bird in a tree. He saw
some fine stones lying near, and took up a handful to hurl
one by one with his sling. Without very much success,
however, for the bird flew gaily off, and the stones fell into
the river, only one remaining of the handful he had taken.
He was going to throw it away, but seeing it was pretty, he
saved it as a plaything for his little daughter. On the way
home, he met a diamond merchant, and showed him the
stone. The merchant saw at once that it was a diamond,
and offered a large sum for it. The hunter started lamenting
his bad fortune, and on being asked why he was so
disconsolate, he explained that it was because he had not
realised the value of the stones he had thrown into the river.
Had he but saved them, a fortune might have been his.
They were now lost to him forever. So is every day of life
precious – it can never be recovered.

Anon.

966

Time is
— too slow for those who wait,
— too swift for those who fear,
— too long for those who grieve,
— too short for those who rejoice; but for those who love,
time is eternity.

Henry Van Dyke

967

The fable is told of a weary wanderer in the Middle Ages
who, trudging all day long with all of his earthly possessions
on his back, came to a gleaming white castle silhouetted
against a gold and purple sunset. With night approaching,
he rapped at the door of the castle and soon the door was

opened, presenting a princely figure. The wanderer hesitated a moment, then inquired: 'Is this thy house, Sir? And could I have lodging for the night?' In poetic Medieval English the prince replied:

> This house is mine, and yet not mine!
> Nor can tomorrow's owner say 'Tis mine.'
> And he who follows him they'll bear away.
> Whose *is* this house? Oh, pilgrim say!

Within a few generations the gleaming castle would still be there but where would its present occupants be?

Anon.

Trinity

968

Think of the Father as a spring of life begetting the Son like a river and the Holy Ghost like a sea, for the spring and the river and the sea are all one nature. Think of the Father as a root, of the Son as a branch, and of the Spirit as a fruit, for the substance in these three is one. The Father is a sun with the Son as rays and the Holy Ghost as heat. The holy Trinity transcends by far every similitude and figure. So when you hear of an offspring of the Father, do not think of a corporeal offspring. And when you hear that there is a Word, do not suppose him to be a corporeal word. And when you hear of the Spirit of God, do not think of wind and breath. Rather, hold your persuasion with a simple faith alone. For the concept of the Creator is arrived at by analogy from his creatures.

John of Damascus

969

The fundamental Christian affirmation is that ultimate

reality is trinitarian, that is Koinonia, communion of three persons.

Donald Nicholl

970

So until Ascensiontide Bede worked with his pupils to conclude his translation of John's Gospel into the English tongue: but the Tuesday before Ascensiontide his sickness increased upon him. Nevertheless, he taught and bade his scholars work, saying cheerfully, 'Write with speed now, for I cannot tell how long I may last.'

The day broke (that is, Wednesday), and about the third hour the scribe said, 'There is yet a chapter wanting: it is hard for thee to continue vexing thyself.' 'That is easily done,' said he: 'take thy pen again and write quickly', and joyfully he dictated until the evening at the ninth hour.

'Dear Master,' said the boy, 'there is yet one sentence to be written.' He answered, 'Write it quickly.' Soon after the boy said, 'It is finished now.' 'Thou has well said. It is finished. Raise my head in thy arms and turn my face towards the holy spot where I was wont to pray, for I desire to sit facing it and call upon my Father.'

So they held him up on the pavement, and he chanted, 'Glory be to the Father, and to the Son and to the Holy Spirit.' Then, as he named the Holy Spirit, his spirit took leave, and departed to the heavenly Kingdom.

Cuthbert (7th cent.) 'The Passing of the Venerable Bede'

971

We say that we know God by his energies. We do not affirm that we can approach the essence itself. His energies come down to us, but his essence remains unapproachable.

Basil

972

One of the great classics in Byzantine iconography is the icon of the *Trinity* painted by the Russian monk, Andrei Rublev (*c.*1408). He used an ancient, traditional image, known in the East from the earliest centuries, of the apparition of the three angels to Abraham by the oak of Mambre (Gen. 18) to describe in iconic forms the dogmatic teaching of the one Godhead and the three Persons in the Trinity. Using a circle as the basic form of composition, and intersecting circles and very vivid colours: blue, green, pink, brown and purple, the iconographer depicts the three Persons: Father, Son and Holy Spirit as three angels brought into a oneness of deep peace and joyfulness.

Unlike so many attempts in Western art to depict the Trinity in images of a grey-bearded Father, with a more youthful son holding the globe of the world and the Spirit as a dove hovering over both of them, this Byzantine statement avoids the 'objectivisation' of making the Divine Persons look like human ones. It is a mystical vision, through harmony and relationship of colours and circular lines, of the inner trinitarian life of movement and rest, peace and joy, of a community of three in a oneness that constantly feeds to the Godhead for it is a nameless form which constantly feeds back through its circular movement from one person to the other two.

George A. Maloney

973

So vast, so penetrating and all embracing is this active and possessing love of the Trinity that in its presence the silence of the creature is absolute.

John of Ruysbroeck

974

Christopher Columbus had a tremendous devotion to the Blessed Trinity. He invoked the Trinity at the beginning of every enterprise, and everything he wrote began with the words: 'In the Name of the Most Holy Trinity.'

When he presented to the Council of Salamanca (that assembly of all the learned of science and theology) his theory of the New World to be discovered, he began: 'I come before you in the Name of the Most Holy Trinity, because our sovereigns have commanded me to submit to your wisdom a project which has certainly come to me inspired by the same Holy Spirit.'

On his third voyage in 1598, he vowed to consecrate to the Trinity the first land that he would discover, and hence the island he reached was called Trinidad.

F.H. Drinkwater

Trust in God

975

In all your affairs, rely wholly on God's Providence . . . Imitate little children, who with one hand hold fast to their father, and with the other hand gather strawberries or blackberries along the hedges. So too, as you gather and handle the goods of this world with one hand, you must with the other always hold fast the hand of your heavenly Father, turning yourself towards Him from time to time to see if your actions or occupations be pleasing to Him. Above all things, take heed that you never leave his hand or think to gather more or to gain some advantage. For should He forsake you, you will not be able to go a step further without falling to the ground.

Francis of Sales

976

My God and I will walk the plank together.
My God and I will jump into the sea.

My God and I will meet all kinds of weather.
My God and I will walk triumphantly.

Anon.

977

The motto on the first coin minted by the United States was
not the familiar 'In God we trust'; it was, if you can believe
it, 'Mind your business', dated 1787.

Anon.

978

God is full of compassion and never fails those who are
afflicted and despised if they trust in him alone.

Teresa of Avila

979

In God alone is there faithfulness and faith in the trust that
we may hold to him, to his promise, and to his guidance. To
hold to God is to rely on the fact that God is there for me,
and to live in this certainty.

Karl Barth

980

Compare two world-class athletes. At the 1988 Olympics in
Korea, the two fastest runners in the world, Ben Johnson of
Canada and Florence Griffith-Joyner (nicknamed Flo-Jo)
both broke world records and won gold medals. However,
Ben Johnson was discovered to have taken drugs; he had
cheated and was sent home in disgrace. In contrast Flo-Jo
ran with a relaxed smile on her face and immediately after
the new world record, when interviewed, said, 'I thank God
that he helped me to win.' The lesson to all young people
must be clear; put not your trust in drugs but in God.

Anon.

981

Many men have just enough faith to trust God as far as
they can see Him, and they always sing as far as they can
see providence go right; but true faith can sing when its
possessors cannot see. It can take hold of God when they
cannot discern Him.

Charles Haddon Spurgeon

982

When a train goes through a tunnel and it gets dark, you
don't throw away your ticket and jump off. You sit still and
trust the engineer.

Corrie ten Boom

983

As the marsh-hen secretly builds on the watery sod,
Behold I will build me a nest on the greatness of God:
I will fly in the greatness of God as the marsh-hen flies,
In the freedom that fills all the space 'twixt the marsh and
    the skies:
By so many roots as the marsh-grass sends in the sod,
I will heartily lay me a-hold on the greatness of God.

Sydney Lanier

Truth

984

In the first year of Hitler's power, out in a suburb of Berlin,
I sat across the desk from Martin Niemoeller. Already he
could see the signs of the evils to come. A few years passed
and Martin Niemoeller was sent to the concentration camp.
Immediately his aged father came out of retirement to take
over his son's pastoral duties. Heinrich Niemoeller preached

as his son had, but in more guarded terms. Before he died he told a friend of mine, 'Yes, it is terrible to have a son in a concentration camp, but it would have been more terrible if God had wanted a witness and Martin had been unwilling to witness to the truth.'

Jack Finegan

985

Dare to be true. Nothing can need a lie:
A fault, which needs it most, grows two thereby.

George Herbert

986

When Aristotle, the Greek philosopher, who was tutor to Alexander the Great, was asked what a man could gain by uttering falsehoods, he replied, 'Not to be believed when he shall tell the truth.' On the other hand, it is related that when Petrarch, the Italian poet, a man of strict integrity, was summoned as a witness, and offered in the usual manner to take an oath before a court of justice, the judge closed the book, saying, 'As to you, Petrarch, your word is sufficient.'

Anon.

987

Only God is, only God knows, only God can do anything. This is the truth, and with the help of my faith I discover this more deeply every day.

Carlo Carretto

988

One can tell lies without literal mis-statement. During a lull in the cold war, a Russian diplomat was explaining to an

English one the difference between Russian and British
newspapers.

'Suppose you and I had a race, and you came in first.
Your newspapers would report: "The Soviet and British
ambassadors yesterday had a race. The British Ambassador
won." In *Pravda* the report would be: "A race took place
yesterday between diplomats. The Soviet Ambassador
came in second. The British Ambassador finished only just
in front of the last man." '

F.H. Drinkwater

989

Truth is not only violated by falsehood; it may be equally
outraged by silence.

Henri Frederic Amiel

990

In a village in India, five blind men lived together. One
day, they happened to come near an animal which someone
told them was an elephant. 'What is an elephant like?' they
asked. They were invited to feel its body. 'Why, an elephant
is like a pillar,' said the first. He had only felt its leg. 'No,
no, it is like a barrel,' said another, who had felt only the
belly. A third said, 'It is like a rope,' for he had felt the tail;
and a fourth, 'Like a hose,' – he had felt the trunk. 'It is like
a winnowing-fan,' said the last man, who had felt only the
ear. So they began to argue among themselves. Each said
that his description of the elephant was the true one.

It is the same with Truth, says the Hindu, who loves
telling this story. His ancient books, the Vedas, say, 'The
Truth is One; people call it by various names.' All of us,
like the blind men, find a part of the truth and think we
have grasped it all. But truth itself must always be One and
the same.

Swami Yogeshnanda

991

The only way to speak the truth is to speak it lovingly.

Henry David Thoreau

992

But there are seven sisters ever serving Truth,
Porters of the Posterns, one called Abstinence,
Humility, Charity, Chastity be the chief maidens there;
Patience and Peace help many a one;
Lady Almsgiving lets in full many.

William Langland, 'Piers Plowman'

993

All truth, wherever it is found, belongs to us as Christians.

Justin Martyr

994

A lecturer in a theological college informed his class that the subject of his next lecture would be the sin of deceit and that, by way of preparation, he wished them all to read the seventeenth chapter of Mark's Gospel. When the time came he asked how many members of his class had complied with his instructions. Every one of them raised a hand. 'Thank you,' said the lecturer. 'It is to people like you that today's lecture is especially addressed. There is no seventeenth chapter of Mark!'

K. Edwards

995

What a shaking thing
The truth can be,
Especially when found
On the family tree.

Anon.

996

If you think fishermen are the biggest liars in the world, ask a jogger how far he runs every morning.

Larry Johnson

997

A young man whose father had been hanged was faced with a life insurance proposal form. After the usual questions enquiring about any hereditary diseases there was one asking for the cause of death of his parents. He put: 'Mother died of pneumonia. Father was taking part in a public function when the platform gave way.'

Cecil Hunt

United in Christ

998

There is in South India a story of a wealthy landowner who had some very quarrelsome sons, always jealous of one another and always arguing among themselves. On his deathbed he called them and divided his property among them. Then he called for some sticks to be brought, nicely tied into a bundle, and asked them one by one, beginning at the eldest, to break the bundle. So long as they were thus closely bound together, they could not break any of the sticks. 'Now,' he said to the eldest, 'untie the bundle, and try to break the sticks singly.' This was not difficult, and soon each of the sticks, broken one by one, lay before them in two pieces.

The father thus taught them that: united they stood; divided they fell.

Anon.

999

Coming together is a beginning, keeping together is progress: working together is success in the Christian assembly: for,

As One Flock we are gathered together (John 10.16).
As One Family, we dwell together (Ps. 133.1).
As One Body, we are joined together (Eph. 4.16).
As One Temple, we are framed together (Eph. 2.21).
As One Household, we are built together (Eph. 2.19–20).
As One Kingdom, we are to strive together (Phil. 1.27).
As One Hierarchy, we are raised up together (Eph. 2.6).

Anon.

1000

Though Christ a thousand times
  In Bethlehem be born,
If he's not born in thee,
  Thy soul is still forlorn.

The cross on Golgotha
  Will never save thy soul,
The cross in thine own heart
  Alone can make thee whole.

Angelus Silesius

1001

In some parts of India there are provided along the road resting-places for those who carry heavy loads on their heads. Such a resting-place is called a *sumatanga*. These rests have a shelf where the traveller can easily drop his burden. Beneath is a shady recessed seat where he can quietly rest. Referring to one of these, a native Christian said, 'Christ is my *sumatanga*.'

Anon.

Universality

1002

The universality of the Church is very well illustrated by the way the European countries (the French always excepted) are quite content that their national patron saints should be foreigners. The English are content with St George of Cappadocia, and do not mind sharing him with Russians and Genoese and Catalans: the Spaniards long ago settled for St James, the Germans for St Boniface from Devon, the Dutch for St Willobrod, also from South England, and the Irish for glorious St Patrick, a Romano-British character from somewhere this side of St George's Channel. As for the Scots, they have accepted an Anglo-Saxon princess, side by side with the Galilean St Andrew.

Douglas Woodruff

Unselfishness

1003

If a man is centred upon himself, the smallest risk is too great for him, because both success and failure can destroy him. If he is centred upon God, then no risk is too great, because success is already guaranteed – the successful union of Creator and creature, beside which everything else is meaningless.

Morris West

1004

It is said of the great artist Michaelangelo that when at work he wore over his forehead, fastened on his cap, a lighted candle, so that no shadow of himself might fall upon the marble or the canvas. We need to take exceeding care that no shadow of ourselves, our personal ambitions, our self-seeking falls upon that which we are doing for Christ.

F.L. McKean

1005

When Father Damien sailed as a missionary for the Hawaian Islands in 1864 he probably knew little and thought nothing of the ever-growing colony of lepers by then segregated in part of the Island of Molokai. A day came when he happened to attend the dedication of a chapel recently erected on the Island of Mani. The Bishop, Monseigneur Maigret, was there, and in his address lamented that, owing to the scarcity of missioners, he was unable to send then a fixed pastor. Some young priests from the Picpus Congregation had just arrived for mission work, and before them Father Damien instantly spoke.

'Monseigneur,' said he, 'here are your new missioners. One of them could take my district; and if you will be kind enough to allow it, I will go to Molokai and labour for the poor lepers, whose wretched state of bodily and spiritual misfortune has often made my heart bleed within me.'

Thus simply was made, by an obscure priest on a far-away island, an offer of which the heroism, when the world came to know of it, made cowards shudder amd brave men wish they had been braver. It was accepted and that same day, without any farewell, Father Damien embarked with the bishop on a boat that was taking some fifty lepers to Molokai.

Anon.

1006

In one of the terrible concentration camps of the Second World War there was a Polish priest, called Father Kolbe. He had been put there because he had published comments about the Nazi regime. One of the prisoners escaped from

the camp, and the camp commandant, to punish the
prisoners, ordered ten of them to be starved to death.
Among the prisoners was a young man who had a wife and
children. When the prisoners' numbers were called out,
Father Kolbe stepped forward and insisted on taking the
young man's place. In the death cell, Father Kolbe helped
the others prepare for death. He was the last to die, and
because he had taken too long, they injected poison into his
arm. After his death, if you had gone into his cell, you
would have seen a picture of Jesus on the cross scratched on
the wall with his nails.

Anon.

1007

They are slaves who fear to speak
For the fallen and the weak;
They are slaves who will not choose
Hatred, scoffing and abuse,
Rather than in silence shrink
From the truth they needs must think;
They are slaves who dare not be
In the right with two or three.

James Russell Lowell

1008

In the mountainous regions of North India, where it is very
cold, travellers are helped to keep warm in this way. They
take a small vessel, put burning coal in it, and cover it up.
They weave strings around it, and, wrapping it with cloth,
carry it under their arms. Three men were travelling thus
towards the sacred place of Amarnath. One of them saw
several others suffering with cold, and, taking the fire out of
his vessel, lit a fire so that everyone could get warm. So
everyone left the place alive. When they had all to walk in
the dark the second man of the party took out the fire in his

vessel and lit a torch with it and helped them all to walk along in safety. The third man of the party mocked them and said: 'You are fools, You have wasted your fire for the sake of others.' 'Show us your fire,' said they to him. When he broke open his vessel there was no fire, but only ashes and coal. With his fire one had given warmth and another had given light.

Anon.

1009

In Pompeii the body of a crippled boy was found with his foot lame. Round his body was a woman's arm, bejewelled. The great stream of fire suddenly issuing from the volcano had driven a terror-stricken crowd for refuge. The woman had evidently taken pity on the cripple. Only the arm outstretched to save was saved itself.

S.D. Gordon

1010

Teacher: Unselfishness means going without something you need voluntarily. Can you give me an example, Jimmy?

Jimmy: Yes, sometimes I go without a bath when I need one!

Anon.

War

1011
War is a fire struck in the Devil's tinder box.

James Howell

1012

At the Somme (July 1 – November 13, 1916) the British
sustained 60,000 casualties on the first day. In October
torrential rains turned the battlefield into a quagmire. By
mid-November the Allies had advanced five miles at a cost
of 450,000 German, 200,000 French and 420,000 British
lives.

21st Clearing Station, Saturday, July 1, 7.30: The heavens and
earth were rolling up, the crazy hour had begun, every gun
we owned fired as hard as ever it could for more than an
hour. From a hill near Veils over us to left and right great
observation balloons hung. 18 in view. Aeroplanes dashed
about, morning mist and gun smoke obscured the view. We
got back for a late breakfast and soon the wounded by
German shells came in, then all day long cars of dying and
wounded, but all cheerful for they told us of a day of
glorious successes. They are literally piled up – beds gone,
lucky to get space on floor of tent, hut or ward, and though
the surgeons work like Trojans many must yet die for lack
of operation. All the CCSs [Casualty Clearing Stations] are
overflowing. Later. We have 1,500 in and still they come,
300–400 officers, it is a sight – chaps with fearful wounds
lying in agony, many so patient, some make a noise, one
goes to a stretcher, lays one's hand on the forehead, it is
cold, strike a match, he is dead – here a Communion, there
an absolution, there a drink, there a madman, there a hot
water bottle and so on – one madman was swearing and
kicking, I gave him a drink, he tried to bite my hand and
squirted the water from his mouth into my face – well, it is
an experience beside which all previous experience pales.
Oh I am tired, excuse writing.

July 2: What a day, I had no corner in the hospital even for
Holy Communion, the Colonel said that no services might
be under cover, fortunately it was fine so rigged up my
packing-case altar on a wood behind the sisters' camp.
Then all day squatting or kneeling by stretchers adminis-

tering Holy Communion, etc. Twice I went to bury, of course we used the trench we had prepared in a field adjoining. I first held a service of consecration, when I turned round the old man labouring in the field was on his knees in the soil.

I buried 37 but have some left over till tomorrow.

From the diary of Rev. John Walker
padre at the Somme

1013

Judge from your own feelings how God, with his infinite sensibility, must feel when he sees men rising up against their fellow men; performing gross deeds of cruelty on every hand; waging wars that cause blood to flow like rivers throughout the globe; when in short, he sees them devastating society by every infernal mischief that their ingenuity can invent.

Henry Ward Beecher

1014

One of the popular poems that came to us after World War I was 'Trees' by Joyce Kilmer, sergeant in the 165th infantry (69th New York) A.E.F. who was killed in action near Ourcy, July 30th, 1918.

> I think that I shall never see
> A poem lovely as a tree.
>
> A tree whose hungry mouth is prest
> Against the earth's sweet flowing breast;
>
> A tree that looks at God all day,
> And lifts her leafy arms to pray;
>
> A tree that may in Summer wear
> A nest of robins in her hair;

Upon whose bosom snow has lain;
Who intimately lives with rain.

Poems are made by fools like me,
But only God can make a tree.

Wholeness

1015

Wholeness concerns how much of Christ has been formed
within.

Rob Warner

1016

There are three qualities you must have if you are going to
succeed finally, however technically proficient you may be.

First, you must have integrity, which I would say in your
own profession [of commerce] is particularly important.

Second, you must have courage, not necessarily physical
courage, because not everyone has that, but moral courage,
standing firm by what one believes to be right.

Third, you must have enthusiasm, the ability to get
something out of life by putting something into it in an
enthusiastic way.

Lord Montgomery

1017

You can easily judge the character of a man by how he
treats those who can do nothing for him.

James Miles

1018

To be honest;
to be kind;

to earn a little
and to spend a little less;
to make, upon the whole,
a family happier for his presence;
to renounce, when that shall be necessary,
and not be embittered;
to keep a few friends,
but these without capitulation;
above all, in the same condition,
to keep friends with himself:
here is a task for all that a man has of
fortitude and delicacy.

Robert Louis Stevenson

1019

We have become too spiritual in a 'holy, holy' sense, whereas we should be biblically holy – that means facing up to the totality of life, in the power of the Cross.

George MacLeod

Will of God

1020

The present moment is the only moment in which any kind of action is possible. If I want to do the will of God, I must recognise that the divine will is always something I must do now – I cannot receive now what God will offer me tomorrow. But I can receive now what he is offering me now. And each moment God is offering me some grace (gift) for my acceptance or some command for my obedience.

Nevill Ward

1021

The eminent John Newton once said: 'If two angels came down from heaven to execute a divine command, and one was appointed to sweep the streets, they would feel no inclination to change employments.' And why not? Because each would have the sure conviction that he was doing what his Lord had asked him to do and that by his service, great or humble, he was glorifying God.

Anon.

1022

'Will you please tell me in a word', said a Christian woman to a minister, 'what your idea of consecration is?' Holding out a blank sheet of paper, the pastor replied, 'It is to sign your name at the bottom of this blank sheet, and let God fill it in as He wills.'

Anon.

1023

All heaven is waiting to help those who will discover the will of God and do it.

Robert Ashcroft

1024

Nothing in the hands of God is evil; not failure, not thwarting, not the frustration of every hope or ambition, not death itself. All in his hands is success, and will bear the more fruit the more we leave it to him, having no ambitions, no preoccupations, no excessive preferences or desires of our own.

Archbishop Goodier

1025

There are no disappointments to those whose wills are buried in the will of God.

Frederick W. Faber

1026

How to find out God's Will
1. Pray.
2. Think.
3. Talk to wise people but do not regard their decision as final.
4. Beware of the bias of your own will but do not be too much afraid of it. God never necessarily thwarts a man's nature and likings, and it is a mistake to think that his will is in the line of the disagreeable.
5. Meanwhile do the next thing, for doing God's will in small things is the best preparation for doing it in great things.
6. When decision and action are necessary, go ahead.
7. Never reconsider the decision when it is finally acted upon.
8. You will probably not find out till afterward, perhaps long afterward, that you have been led at all.

Henry Drummond

1027

If God sends us on stony paths, he provides strong shoes.

Corrie ten Boom

1028

During the American Civil War a lady exclaimed effusively to President Lincoln: 'Oh, Mr President, I feel so sure that God is on our side, don't you?' 'Ma'am,' replied the

President, 'I am more concerned that we should be on God's side.'

K. Edwards

Wisdom

1029
Perfect wisdom hath four parts, viz., wisdom, the principle of doing things aright; justice, the principle of doing things equally in public and private; fortitude, the principle of not flying danger but meeting it; and temperance, the principle of subduing desires and living moderately.

Plato

1030
The art of being wise is the art of knowing what to overlook.

William James

1031
Who knows not, and knows not that he knows not, is foolish; shun him.
Who knows not, and knows that he knows not, is humble; teach him.
Who knows, but knows not that he knows, is asleep; wake him.
Who knows, and knows that he knows, is wise; follow him.

Anon.

1032
A wise old owl sat on an oak
The more he saw the less he spoke;

The less he spoke the more he heard;
Why aren't we like that wise old bird?

Edward Hersey Richards

1033

A great king once came to Solomon, and asked him for a motto. 'It must be one', said he, 'that shall be as much use to me in times of trouble as in times of prosperity.' The wise king gave him his motto, and he had it engraved on a ring which he wore continually. It was this: 'Even this shall pass away.'

Anon.

1034

Wisdom is oftentimes nearer when we stoop than when we soar.

William Wordsworth

1035

And the Lord said unto Noah: 'Where is the ark which I have commanded thee to build?' And Noah said unto the Lord: 'Verily, I have had three carpenters off ill. The gopher wood supplier hath let me down – yes, even though the gopher wood hath been on order for nigh upon twelve months.' And God said unto Noah: 'I want that ark finished even after seven days and nights.' And Noah said: 'It will be so.' And it was not so.

And the Lord said: 'What seemeth to be the trouble this time?' And Noah said unto the Lord: 'Mine subcontractor hath gone bankrupt. The pitch which Thou commandest me to put on the outside and on the inside of the ark hath not arrived. The plumber hath gone on strike. Shem, my son who helpeth me on the ark side of the business, hath formed a pop group with his brothers Ham and Japheth. Lord, I am undone.'

And the Lord grew angry and said: 'And what about the unicorns, and the fowls of the air by seven?' And Noah wrung his hands and wept saying: 'Lord, unicorns are a discontinued line; thou canst not get them for love nor money. And it hath just been told unto me that the fowls of the air are sold only in half dozens. Lord, Lord, Thou knowest how it is.'

And the Lord in His Wisdom said: 'Noah, my son, I know, why else dost thou think I have caused a flood to descend upon the earth?'

E.R.A.

1036

There was a young prince of Persia who, on ascending the throne, summoned his wise men and asked them to prepare a history of the nations for his guidance. They came back in twenty years with twelve camels carrying six thousand volumes; but the King was busy with the cares of State, and sent them back to edit their works. Again in twenty years they came, and again they went back; and so the process was repeated till there arrived at the palace an old wise man with a donkey, with a single volume on its back.

'Hasten! The King is dying,' the officer said. The wise man was taken to the King's bedside, and the King, his gaze falling on the book of history, said, with a sigh: 'Then I shall die without knowing the history of mankind.'

'Sire,' said the wise old man, 'I will sum it up for you in a few words: *They were born, they suffered, they died.*'

Old Legend

1037

Be wise. Take proper care. Get your food regularly; for in order to get the most done, you must go to work in the best way. Learn to distinguish what is vital from what is merely incidental; and above all, resolve by God's help at all costs to keep first things first.

Catherine Bramwell-Booth

1038

Seeing John Wesley coming along the street one day, a man straddled the pavement and said to him: 'I never get out of my way for a fool.' 'But I always do,' replied Wesley, as he stepped aside into the gutter.

Anon.

Woman

1039

Being a woman is a terribly difficult trade, since it consists principally of dealing with men.

Joseph Conrad

1040

Woman was made from the rib of man.
She was not created from his head – to top him,
nor from his feet – to be stepped upon.

She was made from his side – to be equal to him;
from beneath his arm – to be protected by him:
near his heart – to be loved by him.

Anon.

1041

I'm not denying that women are foolish. God Almighty made 'em to match the men.

George Eliot

1042

When Winston Churchill was told that writers were declaring that, by the year 2100, women would be ruling the world, his rejoinder, with a twinkle, was just one word: 'Still?'

Anon.

1043

Oh! the gladness of a woman when she's glad!
Oh! the sadness of a woman when she's sad!
But the gladness of her gladness,
And the sadness of her sadness,
Are nothing to her badness –
When she's bad!

Anon.

1044

There are certain things I believe a man should do at home, like bringing in the wood and coal, mending the car and setting the mousetrap. There's simply no equality when it comes to mice.

Barbara Cartland

1045

Henry VIII is no great favourite with Women's Lib, and I have unearthed another black mark against him. In his regulation about reading the Bible, chained in churches or elsewhere, he encourages it for all men except serving-men, but only for women of the upper class, of education and leisure, to instruct themselves so that they do not misunderstand what they read.

Douglas Woodruff

1046

They say that man is mighty,
　　He governs land and sea,
He wields a mighty sceptre
　　O'er lesser powers that be;
But a mightier power and stronger
　　Man from his throne has hurled,
And the hand that rocks the cradle
　　Is the hand that rules the world.

Anon.

1047

When the good Lord was creating mothers, he was into his sixth day of overtime when an angel appeared and said, 'You're doing a lot of fiddling around on this one.' And the Lord said, 'Have you read the specifications on this order? She has to be completely washable, but not plastic . . . have 180 movable parts – all replaceable . . . run on black coffee and left overs . . . have a lap that disappears when she stands up . . . a kiss that can cure anything from a broken leg to a disappointed love affair . . . and six pairs of hands.'

The angel shook his head slowly and said, 'Six pairs of hands? No way.'

'It's not the hands that are causing me problems,' said the Lord, 'It's the three pairs of eyes that mothers have to have.' 'That's on the standard model?' asked the angel. The Lord nodded. 'One pair that sees through closed doors when she asks "What are you children doing in there?" when she already knows, Another in the back of her head that sees when she shouldn't but what she has to know. And, of course, the ones in front that can look at a child when he gets himself into trouble and say, "I understand and I love you" without so much as uttering a word.'

'Lord,' said the angel, touching his sleeve gently, 'go to bed. Tomorrow is another . . .' 'I can't,' said the Lord. 'I'm so close now. Already I have one who heals herself when she is sick, can feed a family of six on one pound of mince, and can get a nine-year-old to have a bath.'

The angel circled the model of a mother very slowly. 'It's too soft,' he sighed. 'But tough!' said the Lord excitedly. 'You cannot imagine what this mother can do or endure.' 'Can it think?' asked the angel. 'Not only think, but it can reason and compromise,' said the Creator. Finally, the angel bent over and ran his finger across the cheek. 'There's a leak,' he pronounced. 'It's not a leak,' said the Lord. 'It's a tear.' 'What's it for?' 'It's for joy, sadness, disappointment, pain, loneliness and pride.' 'You are a genius,' said the angel. The Lord looked sombre. 'I didn't put it there.'

Anon.

1048

My thirteen-year-old daughter and I were talking about women's liberation one day, and I said firmly, 'I don't want to be liberated.'

My daughter said, 'I don't want to be liberated either – at least not until I know how it feels to be captured.'

Lyn Cannon

Wonders of God

1049

The Seven Wonders of the ancient world were:

1. The Great Pyramid.
2. The Colossus of Rhodes.
3. The Hanging Gardens of Babylon.
4. The Temple of Diana in Ephesus.
5. The Statue of Jupiter in Athens.
6. The Halicarnassus (Mausoleum).
7. The Pharos Lighthouse at Alexandria

God's wonders of creation far exceed any and all of these.

Anon.

1050

A Sunday school teacher was examining her pupils after a series of lessons on God's omnipotence. She asked, 'Is there anything God can't do?' There was silence. Finally, one lad held up his hand. The teacher, disappointed that the lesson's point had been missed, asked resignedly, 'Well, just what is it that God can't do?'

'Well,' replied the boy, 'He can't please everybody.'

Anon.

Word

1051

This Word, this Logos, which Greeks and Hebrews unite in recognising as the controlling power of the whole universe, is no longer unknown or dimly apprehended. The Light which in some measure lightens every man has shone in its full splendour.

William Temple

1052

If you have the Word without the Spirit, you dry up. If you have the Spirit without the Word, you blow up. But if you have both together you grow up.

David Smith

1053

The Word of God is not a sounding but a piercing Word, not pronounceable by the tongue but efficacious in the mind, not sensible to the ear but fascinating to the affection. His face is not an object possessing beauty of form but rather it is the source of all beauty and all form. It is not visible to the bodily eyes, but rejoices the eyes of the heart.

And it is pleasing not because of the harmony of its colour but by reason of the ardour of the love it excites.

Bernard of Clairvaux

1054

The divine and creative Word was not uttered once for all, but it receives perpetual utterance in the radiation of light, in the movements of the stars, in the development of life, in the reason and conscience of man.

William Temple

1055

The Emperor Napoleon I was reviewing some troops in Paris when, in giving an order, he thoughtlessly dropped the bridle upon the horse's neck. The animal instantly set off at a gallop, and the Emperor was obliged to cling to the saddle.

At this moment a common soldier of the line sprang before the horse, seized the bridle, and respectfully handed it to the Emperor. 'Much obliged to you, Captain,' said the chief, by this one word making the soldier an officer. The man caught the Emperor's meaning, believed him, and saluting, quickly responded, 'Of what regiment, sire?' Napoleon, charmed with his faith, replied, 'Of my Guard,' and galloped off. Then the soldier laid down his gun, and instead of returning to his comrades, approached the group of staff officers. On seeing him, one of the Generals asked what he wanted there. 'I am Captain of the Guards,' said the soldier, proudly. 'You, *mon ami* – you are mad to say so!' was the retort. 'He said it,' replied the soldier, pointing to the Emperor, who was still in sight. The General respectfully begged his pardon: the Emperor's word was enough.

If we thus took God at His Word, how different our position would be.

Anon.

Work

1056

Over the Medical School of the old St Bartholomew's Hospital are carved these words: 'Whatever thy hand findeth to do, do it with all thy might.' That was the spirit of Rahere, who founded this great hospital in 1133, and that is the secret of the measure of its successful working during more than 800 years.

Anon.

1057

John Wesley travelled 250,000 miles on horseback, averaging twenty miles a day for forty years; preaching 40,000 sermons; produced 400 books; knew ten languages. At eighty-three he was annoyed that he could not write more than fifteen hours a day without hurting his eyes, and at eighty-six he was ashamed he could not preach more than twice a day. He complained in his diary that there was an increasing tendency to lie in bed until five-thirty in the morning!

'The Arkansas Baptist'

1058

You may have heard the story of a visitor to a quarry who asked the men who were toiling there what they were doing. 'Can't you see I'm breaking stone?' said one gruffly. 'I'm making a living for my wife and family,' said the second. The third man had a greater vision. 'I'm helping to build a cathedral,' he replied with a glowing smile.

Anon.

1059

I think of a story my grandfather Stevenson, a devout

Scotch-Presbyterian, told about the preacher who was driving along a back road in the south when he espied a parishioner wearily clearing up a poor, stony field. 'That is a fine job you and the Lord have done, cleaning up that rocky field,' he shouted, 'Thank you, parson,' the man replied. 'But I wish you could have seen it when the Lord had it all to himself.'

Adlai Stevenson

1060

Some Orthodox Jews will not go to the Synagogue on the Sabbath if it is raining. This is because it would necessitate the opening of an umbrella. In the eyes of an Orthodox Jew, opening an umbrella is symbolic to erecting a tent. To erect a tent is to work – and working on the Sabbath is forbidden.

Anon.

1061

Somebody said that it couldn't be done,
    But he with a chuckle replied,
That maybe it couldn't, but he would be one
    Who wouldn't say so till he'd tried.
So he buckled right in with a bit of a grin
    On his face. If he worried, he hid it;
And he started to sing as he tackled the thing
    That couldn't be done – and he did it!

Anon.

1062

An exasperated mother to her naughty children. 'Well as a punishment, I won't let you play with your train set tomorrow.' 'It doesn't matter,' the nine-year-old retorted, 'we were going on strike anyway.'

Anon.

1063

Blank was a planter, and he was singularly blessed in the possession of a glass eye. Even a man with false teeth is in a pretty strong position with really unsophisticated natives. They simply can't understand how a man can take out his teeth and snap them at people.

Blank was an indolent old devil, and much preferred dozing on a shady veranda to supervising his copra cutters in the broiling sun. So he used to put his eye out on a log so that it would watch them work. The natives worked like Trojans under the baleful eye of the master. But one day the planter awoke to find the work undone and his labourers asleep in the sun. Astonished and indignant, he strode to the log where he had left his eye. It was covered with a jam-tin.

A.JJ. Marshall

1064

A man who needed a job saw an ad. in the local paper for a position open at the zoo. He accepted the job and was to dress up as a monkey and perform in one of the cages. All went well for several days and then, as he was going from limb to limb, he fell.

'Help, help,' he cried.

'Shut up,' said the lion in the next cage, 'or we'll both lose our jobs.'

Anon.

World

1065

To look away from the world, or to stare at it, does not help a man to reach God; but he who sees the world in God stands in God's presence.

Martin Buber

1066

It is a very good world to live in,
To lend, or to spend, or to give in;
But to beg or to borrow, or to get a man's own,
It is the very worst world that ever was known.

Earl of Rochester

1067

Reality is charged with a divine Presence. As the mystics
sense and portray it, everything becomes physically and
literally lovable in God; and reciprocally God becomes
knowable and lovable in all that surrounds us. In the
greatness and depths of its cosmic stuff, in the maddening
numbers of elements and events which compose it, and in
the fullness of the general currents which dominate and set
it in motion like a great wave, the World, filled with God,
no longer appears to our opened eyes as anything but a
milieu and an object of universal communion.

Teilhard de Chardin

1068

The way of the world is to praise dead saints and persecute
living ones.

Nathaniel Howe

1069

Earth's crammed with heaven
and every common bush
afire with God.
And only he who sees
takes off his shoes.
The rest sit around
and pluck blackberries.

Elizabeth Barrett Browning

Worry

1070

'Worry' we are told, is from an Anglo-Saxon word which means 'harm' and is another form of the word 'wolf'. It is something harmful and bites and tears as a wolf which mangles a sheep. There are times, no doubt, when we must feel anxious because of harm suffered or anticipated by ourselves or others, and this may be beneficial because it rouses to necessary activity; but often worry has the opposite effect, it paralyses us and unfits us for duty, and also distracts our thoughts and obscures our vision.

Douglas Woodruff

1071

Bishop Taylor Smith used to write the following in autograph books:

> The worried cow would have lived till now
>   If she had saved her breath;
> But she feared her hay wouldn't last all day,
>   And she mooed herself to death.

1072

John Wesley was walking one day with a worried man who expressed his doubt of God's goodness. 'I don't know what I shall do with all this worry and trouble,' he said. At that moment Wesley noticed a cow looking over a stone wall. 'Do you know,' asked Wesley, 'why that cow is looking over that wall?' 'No,' replied his troubled companion. 'I will tell you,' said Wesley. 'Because she cannot see through it. That is what you must do with your wall of trouble – look over it and above it.'

Anon.

1073

An old story tells of an angel who met a man carrying a heavy sack and enquired what was in it. 'My worries,' said the man. 'Let me see them,' said the angel. When the sack was opened, it was empty. The man was astonished and said he had two great worries. One was of yesterday which he now saw was past; the other of tomorrow which had not yet arrived. The angel told him he needed no sack, and the man gladly threw it away.

Anon.

1074

A husband, mulling over his bills, exclaimed: 'I'd give a thousand pounds to anyone who would do my worrying for me!' 'You're on,' answered his wife, 'where's the thousand?' Replied the husband, 'That's your first worry.'

Anon.

Worship

1075

The word 'worship' is an Anglo-Saxon word and means 'worthship' or 'worthiness'. The word commonly translated 'worship' in the New Testament – though there are several other Greek words – is *'proskuneo'*, to kiss the hand toward. This is thought to be derived from the slave's manner of salutation and homage when he entered the presence of his master, the act being a mark of reverence and respect, and also implying affection. Hence, in ascriptions of worship, we have the expression 'Thou art worthy'.

Anon.

1076

Begin the day with God and 'tis probable 'twill end with him and goodness.

Thomas Wilson

1077

'Sing to the Lord a new song,' the psalm tells us.
'I do sing!' you may reply.
You sing, of course you sing. I can hear you.
But make sure that your life sings the same tune as your
　　mouth.
Sing with your voices.
Sing with your hearts.
Sing with your lips.
Sing with your lives.
Be yourselves what the words are about!
If you live good lives, you yourselves are
the songs of new life.

Augustine of Hippo

1078

God respects me when I work, but he loves me when I sing.

Rabindranath Tagore

1079

As soon as we are with God in faith and in love, we are in prayer.

François Fénelon

1080

Once when Francis was about to eat with Brother Leo, he was greatly delighted to hear a nightingale singing. So he

suggested to his companion that they also should sing
praise to God alternately with the birds. While Leo was
pleading that he was no singer, Francis lifted up his voice
and, phrase by phrase, sang his duet with the nightingale.
Thus they continued from vespers to lauds, until Francis
had to admit himself beaten by the bird, thereupon the
nightingale flew on to his hand, where he praised it to the
skies and fed it. Then he gave it his blessing and it flew
away.

John Moorman

1081

He who does not praise God while here on Earth shall in
eternity be dumb.

John of Ruysbroeck

1082

When the guru sat down to worship each evening the
ashram cat would get in the way and distract the
worshippers. So he ordered that the cat be tied up during
evening worship.

Long after the guru died the cat continued to be tied up
during evening worship. And when the cat eventually died,
another cat was brought to the ashram so that it could be
duly tied up during evening worship.

Centuries later learned treatises were written by the
guru's disciples on the essential role of a cat in all properly
conducted worship.

Anon.

1083

There is a story of some monks in France who were popular
for their loving sympathy and kind deeds; but not one of
them could sing. Try as they would, the music in their

services was a failure, and it became a great grief to them
that only in their hearts could they 'make melody to the
Lord'. One day a travelling monk, a great singer, asked for
hospitality. Great was their joy, for now they could have
him sing at their services, and they hoped to keep him with
them always. But that night an angel came to the abbot in a
dream. 'Why was there no music in your chapel tonight?
We always listen for the beautiful music that rises in your
services.' 'You must be mistaken,' cried the abbot. 'Usually
we have no music worth hearing; but tonight we had a
trained singer with a wonderful voice, and he sang the
service for us. For the first time in all these years our music
was beautiful.' The angel smiled. 'And yet up in heaven we
heard nothing,' he said softly.

'Sunday Companion'

1084

The shopkeeper had just handed me a demonstration pair
of binoculars. I was getting the distant wall nicely into
focus when a passer-by, seeing my Roman collar, quietly
advised, 'Just tell them to move to the front of the church,
Father.'

John Stewart

Youth

1085

Readers of Britain's top-selling pop music paper have voted
Sid Vicious the most 'wonderful human being' of the year.

The former Sex Pistol, awaiting trial in New York on a
charge of murdering his girlfriend Nancy Spungen, came
top in the voting in the poll conducted by the *New Musical
Express*. Former Sex Pistol singer Johnny Rotten was
runner-up.

John Travolta was voted 'creep of the year' with DJ
Tony Blackburn runner-up. David Bowie was named best
male singer and Debbie Harry of Blondie best female
singer. The Clash were voted best group.

Editor Neil Spencer said 'I think the poll shows that our
readers have a droll sense of humour. In general, I doubt if
they have voted for Sid Vicious as the most wonderful
human being out of hero-worship. It's just a little bit of
perversity. Young rock fans will do anything for a laugh.'

James Johnson

1086

Youth in despair is the most frightening thing I have ever
heard of. The worst thing to take from young persons is
their reason for hoping. Have the courage to fight to get it
back for them. And don't just fight: sacrifice, too, if
necessary.

Helder Camara

Violence

1087

In my opinion non-violence is not passivity in any shape or
form. Non-violence as I understand it is the most active
force in the world. Non-violence is the weapon of the
strongest and the bravest. The true man of God has the
strength to use the sword, but will not use it, knowing every
man is the Image of God. Literally speaking non-violence
means non-killing . . . [but] it really means that you may
not offend anybody . . . This is an ideal which we have to
reach and it is an ideal to be reached even at this very
moment, if we are capable of doing so. But it is not a
proposition in geometry, it is not even like solving difficult
problems in higher mathematics – it is infinitely more

difficult . . . You will have to pass many a sleepless night, and go through many a mental torture, before you can even be within measurable distance of this goal. . . . Under this rule there is no room for organised assassination, or for murders openly committed, or for any violence for the sake of your country . . . or even for guarding the honour of precious ones that may be under your charge . . . This doctrine tells us that we may guard the honour of those under our charge by delivering our own lives into the hands of the men who would commit the sacrilege. And that requires far greater courage than delivering blows.

Mahatma Gandhi

Vocation

1088
We must not forget that our vocation is so to practise virtue that men are won to it; it is possible to be morally upright repulsively.

William Temple

1089
I asked God for strength that I might achieve;
I was made weak that I might learn humbly to obey.

I asked for help that I might do greater things;
I was given infirmity that I might do better things.

I asked for riches that I might be happy;
I was given poverty that I might be wise.

I asked for all things that I might enjoy life;
I was given life that I might enjoy all things.

I was given nothing that I asked for;
But everything that I had hoped for.

Despite myself, my prayers were answered;
I am among all men most richly blessed.

Anon.

1090
The vocation of every man and woman is to serve other
people.

Leo Tolstoy

1091
God has created me to do Him some definite service. He
has committed some work to me which He has not committed to another. I have my mission. I may never know it
in this life, but I shall be told it in the next. I am a link in a
chain, a bond of connection between persons. He has not
created me for naught. I shall do good. I shall do his work.
I shall be an angel of peace, a preacher of truth in my own
place while not intending it – if I but keep his commandments.
    Therefore, I will trust Him. Whatever, wherever I am. I
can never be thrown away. If I am in sickness, my sickness
may serve Him; in perplexity, my perplexity may serve
Him; if I am in sorrow, my sorrow may serve Him. He does
nothing in vain. He knows what He is about. He may take
away my friends, He may throw me among strangers. He
may make me feel desolate, make my spirits sink, hide my
future from me – still He knows what he is about.

John Henry Newman

1092
Do not despise your situation. In it you must act, suffer and
conquer. From every point on earth, we are equally near to
heaven and the infinite.

Henri F. Amiel

Zeal

1093

Nothing spoils human nature more than false zeal. The good nature of a heathen is more God-like than the furious zeal of a Christian.

Benjamin Whichcote

1094

One of the stories told of a persecution in China in the old days is about a Chinese Christian lad named Paul Moy. He was dragged before the local mandarin, who tried to induce him to renounce the Christian faith. Other persuasions having failed, the mandarin tried bribery, and promised the boy a purse of silver.

'I thank your Excellency, but a purse of silver is not enough.'

'Very well: I will give you a purse of gold.'

'Excellency, that is still not enough.'

The magistrate had not expected such obstinate bargaining on the part of one so young and was rather annoyed.

'Well, what do you want, then?'

'Most noble, Excellency, if you ask me to renounce the Faith you will have to give me enough to buy a new soul.'

He completed his glorious witness when he was beheaded a few days later.

F.H. Drinkwater

Index of Sources